CYBER VULNERABILITIES

First edition. June 9, 2025.

AF706341

ISBN: 979-8231608836

Written by Artur Victoria.

Introduction

In a world where technology is rapidly advancing, the term "machine" has become increasingly synonymous with computers. In the context of computers, the term "machine" refers to the physical hardware as well as the whole computer system, including hardware and software. The term "machine" includes the CPU, RAM, storage devices, input/output devices, peripherals, operating system, firmware, drivers, and applications that run on it.

The physical parts of a computer system are essential for its operation, enabling the performance of different tasks and processes. The central processing unit (CPU) serves as the brain of the machine, responsible for carrying out instructions and performing calculations. RAM stores data and instructions for the CPU to use temporarily, while storage devices like hard drives and solid-state drives store data and programs for the long term. Devices like the keyboard, mouse, and monitor let you interact with the computer. Printers and scanners add more functions to the computer.

However, the physical components of a computer are only one part of the "machine". The software components, including the operating system, firmware, drivers, and applications, are essential for the computer to function properly. The operating system connects the hardware and the user, while firmware controls the hardware at a low level.

Drivers help hardware communicate with the operating system, while applications let users do different tasks.

Together, the hardware and software components make up the "machine" that has become an integral part of our daily lives.

Computers come in different shapes and sizes, each serving a specific purpose for different users. They provide a convenient and efficient way to complete tasks and communicate with others. Computers are essential in our daily lives, from desktops to laptops, tablets to smart phones, and servers to workstations. They have revolutionized the way we work, learn, and entertain ourselves. Their impact on various industries is undeniable, and the advancements in technology continue to shape the future of computing. As our dependency on computers grows, so does the need for innovation and adaptation in this ever-evolving field.

With advancements in technology, computers have become smaller, faster, and more powerful, making them more accessible to everyone. Whether it's for business, education, or entertainment, there is a computer designed to meet every need.

Computers can do many tasks, from simple word processing to complex calculations, which helps make our lives easier and more productive. Computers are essential tools in our ever-evolving world of technology and will continue to grow in importance in the future.

a) **Desktop computers** are typically larger than other computers, and they are often found in homes and offices. This tower is usually located under the desk or near the monitor and is responsible for storing and accessing data. Desktop computers are powerful and fast, perfect for gaming, graphic design, and video editing.

On the other hand, laptop computers offer a more portable option for users. These compact devices combine all the parts of a desktop computer into one unit, so they are easy to carry and use anywhere. Laptops have become increasingly popular in recent years due to their convenience and versatility. They are great for students, professionals, and anyone who needs to work on the move. However, due to their smaller size, laptops may not have the same level of performance as desktop computers. All-in-one computers offer a unique combination of features from both desktop and laptop computers. These computers contain all the necessary components of a desktop computer, but they are built into the monitor itself. This means that there is no need for a separate tower, making them more compact and space-saving. All-in-one computers are great for those who want the power of a desktop computer without the clutter of multiple devices. They are a good choice for people with limited space, such as students in dorms or people in small offices.

b) Workstations are designed for professional use and are high-performance computers. They are used for various tasks such as CAD/CAM, engineering, graphic design, and scientific applications. These computers are specifically designed to handle complex and resource-intensive tasks. They are also known for their high computing power and fast processing speeds. Most workstations come equipped with high-end components such as multiple processors, large amounts of RAM, and high-quality graphics cards. This allows them to handle tasks that ordinary computers would struggle with. CAD/CAM (Computer-Aided Design/Computer-Aided Manufacturing) is one of the main purposes of workstations. These computers are essential for engineers and designers who need to create complex designs and models.

Workstations are specifically built to handle the intricate calculations and graphics required for CAD/CAM applications. This is because they are equipped with specialized software and hardware that can perform these tasks with ease. Without workstations, it would be nearly impossible for professionals to create the detailed and precise designs needed for their work. In addition to CAD/CAM, workstations are also commonly used for graphic design and scientific applications.

High-performance machines that can process large amounts of data quickly and accurately. Workstations are able to handle these demanding tasks, making them essential tools for professionals in these fields. Workstations are ideal for professionals working on complex and resource-intensive projects due to their powerful processing capabilities and specialized software. They are truly the backbone of industries that rely on advanced computing technology.

c) **Servers** are a vital part of any network. They act as a central hub, providing services and resources to other computers connected to the network. These services can include web hosting, email hosting, file storage, and database management. Without servers, many of the functions that we rely on in our day-to-day lives would not be possible.

- Web hosting is one of the most common functions of servers. It allows individuals and businesses to create and maintain websites that can be accessed by anyone with an internet connection.

- Email hosting, on the other hand, enables users to send and receive emails, making communication easier and more efficient.

- File storage is also an essential function of servers, providing a secure location for users to store and access their files remotely. And lastly, servers are responsible for managing databases, which store and organize large amounts of data for various purposes. In today's digital age, servers are becoming increasingly important as more and more services and resources are being moved online.

They play a central role in keeping our networks running smoothly and efficiently, making our lives easier and more connected. Servers are essential for the internet to exist as we know it and make our daily tasks much easier.

d) **Mainframe computers** are essential for handling the vast amounts of data that are generated in large organizations. These computers can quickly process large amounts of data, making them a popular choice for organizations that need efficient data processing.

This is very useful for important tasks like banking and airline reservations, where accuracy and speed are critical.

In addition to their processing power, mainframe computers are also known for their ability to support numerous users simultaneously.

This is central in large organizations where multiple users need to access the same data at the same time. With mainframes, users can access and manipulate data without affecting the performance of the system, ensuring smooth and seamless operations. One of the main reasons why mainframe computers are preferred in critical applications is their reliability. Powerful machines built to handle large workloads. Redundant components are included to ensure the system remains operational even if hardware fails.

This reliability is essential in industries like banking and airlines, where any downtime can result in significant financial loss. Mainframe computers ensure that important applications run smoothly, so organizations can concentrate on their main activities.

e) Supercomputers are machines that have the ability to perform tasks that normal computers are not capable of doing. These tasks include weather forecasting, scientific research, and simulations that require extremely complex calculations. These machines are often used in government agencies, research institutions, universities, and large corporations. They are designed specifically to handle huge amounts of data at incredibly high speeds.

Supercomputers are considered to be the most powerful computers available, and they are constantly being improved and upgraded. They are able to process data at a rate of millions of calculations per second, making them extremely efficient. This is why they are often used for tasks that require a large amount of data to be processed in a short amount of time. For example, are used in weather forecasting to analyze huge amounts of data and provide accurate predictions. One of the main advantages of supercomputers is their ability to perform simulations. This means they can create virtual models of complex systems and processes to study and analyze real-world scenarios. Supercomputers are very useful in scientific research. They can simulate physical phenomena and study the effects of different variables. Supercomputers are very fast and powerful. They can generate results much faster than regular computers, which make them incredibly useful in many different fields of study.

f) Embedded computers are essential components in many of the devices and machines we rely on every day. They are made for one task in a bigger system, so they work very well. Embedded computers are used in various applications, including household appliances like refrigerators and washing machines, as well as complex industrial machinery and vehicles.

These computers are different from traditional personal computers, as they are not meant to be used for general computing purposes. Instead, they are programmed and configured to perform a specific function within a larger system. This makes them highly reliable and reduces the risk of errors or malfunctions. Embedded computers are smaller and more compact than traditional computers. This makes them great for devices and machines with limited space. Embedded computers are very advantageous because they can make larger systems work better and faster. Task delegation improves system productivity by allowing the main system to focus on other tasks. In a car, computers control functions like the engine, brakes, and air conditioning so the driver can focus on driving. This not only improves the overall performance of the car but also enhances the safety of the driver and passengers.

g) Smartphone's and Tablets are the epitome of the modern technology world. Phones started as devices for making calls on the go and have evolved into pocket-sized mini-computers. While they might look small and insignificant, their computing capabilities are similar to that of personal computers. With the added benefit of portability and usability, these devices have become an integral part of our lives. The touch screen feature is what truly sets these devices apart from PCs. With the simple touch of your finger, you can access all the features of your Smartphone or tablet. This feature has made them extremely user-friendly and has contributed to their popularity.

Not only that, but the mobile operating systems optimized for these devices have made them even more efficient. They let you do multiple things at once, switch easily between different apps, and have access to many features effortlessly. Smartphone's and tablets are more than just devices; they are an extension of us. These devices help us stay connected and informed in our fast-paced world. Smart phones have changed the way we live and works, allowing us to check emails, browse the internet, and stay connected with friends and family. Their small size and powerful processing abilities have made them indispensable in our everyday lives.

h) Gaming Consoles are designed to bring new levels of excitement to the world of gaming. With their specialized designs, they allow players to immerse themselves in the virtual worlds of their favourite games. These consoles are not your typical computer, as they are explicitly built for gaming purposes. The high-speed processors and graphics cards allow for breathtaking graphics and smooth game play, providing a one-of-a-kind gaming experience.

These specialized computers connect to your TV or monitor, allowing you to play your games on a larger screen. This means that you can enjoy your games in a cinematic-like setting, making your gaming experience even more immersive. Gaming consoles have controllers made for gaming, which help players control their characters and interact with the game. These controllers often come with various buttons and joysticks, providing a more realistic and interactive gaming experience. Gaming consoles are popular worldwide and many people own them. They offer a wide range of games, from action-packed shooters to strategic puzzle games, catering to different interests and preferences. Gaming consoles have evolved beyond just playing games.

1 - Cyberspace

Cyberspace is the ultimate realm of endless possibilities, where the physical borders of our world no longer exist. It is a place where you can escape from reality and enter in a virtual world limited only by your imagination.

In this virtual world, computer systems and networks are interconnected, creating endless opportunities. This virtual world is constantly evolving and growing as technology advances. With every new invention, cyberspace expands, creating new paths for users to explore and discover.

Cyberspace is a complex network of connected computer systems and networks that stores, communicates, and provides access to information.

This virtual environment is constantly expanding and evolving, with new technologies and systems being developed and integrated into it. It is a constantly changing landscape, with endless possibilities and potential for growth and development.

The internet is a global network of connected computers that allows data transfer between devices. This has created a new way of communication and sharing information, connecting people and ideas from all over the world.

The dark web is a hidden part of the internet. It is not indexed by search engines and is commonly used for illegal activities. The contrast between the open internet and the dark web shows how diverse and complex cyberspace is.

"Other types of cyberspace include mobile applications, software programs that can be used on smart phones or tablets, and IoT devices, physical objects connected to the internet that can exchange data." These different categories of cyberspace are all essential parts of our daily lives. As technology continues to advance, cyberspace will only become more intricate and integral to our society.

Social media has made it possible for people to connect, communicate, and share information regardless of where they are. This has revolutionized the way we live, work, and interacts with each other.

With every new invention, cyberspace continues to expand and evolve, bringing people closer together and breaking down physical barriers. The internet is a huge virtual world where people can find a lot of information, resources, and opportunities easily. Social media, online shopping, and remote work have made cyberspace an important part of our daily lives, influencing our actions and thoughts. In this digital landscape, people are no longer bound by geographical limitations. TI can connect and communicate with people from all over the world, encouraging a global community and cultural exchange.

The dependence on technology continues to grow, the internet has revolutionized the way to work and do business. With cyberspace, people can connect with customers and clients from around the world in a global marketplace. This has created many opportunities for businesses to grow and enter new markets, which leads to economic growth and job creation.

Moreover, the rise of social media and online platforms has also transformed the way we interact and communicate with others. With geographical limitations no longer a barrier, people can easily connect with others from different cultures and backgrounds. This has fostered a global community, promoting cultural exchange and understanding. The internet allows us to learn from and connect with people across the world, breaking down barriers and building bridges. In today's digital landscape, the internet has truly revolutionized the way we live and work. It has paved the way for endless chances and allowed us to connect with the world in ways we never thought possible.

The internet will continue to shape our behaviours and perceptions, bringing us closer together as a global community in the ever-evolving digital world. The internet has given us many ways to communicate with people around the world. This has not only brought us closer together, but also allowed us to learn from and share with other cultures. We can easily access a lot of information and knowledge with just a click, which helps us understand different cultures and promote exchange. Furthermore, businesses have greatly benefited from the internet's global reach. Companies can now expand their markets and drive economic growth by connecting with customers and clients worldwide. New opportunities for businesses of all sizes, from small start-ups to large corporations, have emerged in the global marketplace.

The internet has truly transformed our world, breaking down geographical barriers and bringing us all closer together. With its vast potential for communication and commerce, it has created a global community that is constantly evolving and advancing. As we explore cyberspace, the internet will continue to shape the world.

As cyberspace continues to expand, it also presents new challenges and concerns. With the increasing amount of personal information stored and shared online, privacy and security have become major concerns. Fake news and cyber bullying are big problems for the safety of the internet. The spread of false information can have severe consequences, from influencing public opinion to causing harm to individuals or groups. Cyber bullying, on the other hand, can have a detrimental effect on mental health and well-being.

It's important to use the digital world responsibly and ethically for the benefit of society. It is our responsibility to ensure that the internet remains a safe and inclusive space for all individuals.

Cyberspace isn't a physical place, but a network of data and communication channels created by electronic systems. It is not just a virtual realm, but a vast interconnected world of information and communication. It is a dynamic and ever-evolving landscape, shaped by the advancements in technology and the collective efforts of its users. Cyberspace means the digital world, including websites, online platforms, communication networks, and all the information and services you can access through the internet.

Types of Cyberspace

a) **Public cyberspace** is a vast and ever-growing space that encompasses the entire online world. It is a virtual universe that is accessible to anyone with an internet connection. This digital realm is constantly evolving and expanding, allowing for endless possibilities and opportunities. Public cyberspace has always been important, from dial-up internet to fast broadband.

The rise of public cyberspace has fundamentally changed the way we communicate, learn, and interact with one another. It has opened up new avenues for education, entertainment, and commerce. We can access information and connect with people worldwide with just a button click. However, with this accessibility comes the need for caution and responsibility. We need to be careful of our online activities and the effects they can have on ourselves and others. In today's society, public cyberspace is not just a tool, but a way of life. It has revolutionized the way we work, play, and socialize.

The internet has connected us in new ways, but it also presents new challenges and threats. It's important to be mindful and responsible as we navigate this complex and dynamic environment to ensure a safe and positive experience for everyone.

b) **Private cyberspace** is a virtual environment that allows for exclusive online interactions among a specific group of individuals. It can be accessed through private networks, intranets, encrypted communication channels, and secure online platforms. This creates a secure space for confidential communication and sharing of information within a limited community.

In this era of information technology, private cyberspace plays a critical role in protecting sensitive data and communication. Organizations can create their own private networks or intranets to facilitate internal communication and information sharing. This helps prevent unauthorized access and ensures that only authorized individuals have access to the network. Additionally, private cyberspace also includes encrypted communication channels and secure online platforms. These platforms provide a safe and secure environment for confidential communication, especially for organizations that deal with sensitive information. By using encryption, the data is protected from being intercepted and accessed by unauthorized parties. Private cyberspace is a crucial aspect of maintaining privacy and security in the digital world.

The dark web is a hidden part of the internet. It is not indexed by traditional search engines, making it difficult for regular internet users to access. The dark web's anonymity has led to its reputation as a centre for illegal activities and secret markets. These marketplaces provide a platform for users to engage in illegal transactions, often anonymously. To access the dark web, specialized software and knowledge are required. The software has Tor, a browser for anonymous internet browsing through a network of servers. Anonymity is very important for users who engage in illegal activities on the dark web. It makes it extremely difficult for law enforcement to trace their actions.

However, the dark web is not solely used for illegal purposes. It is also a platform for whistleblowers and activists to freely communicate and share information without worrying about censorship or surveillance. Thus, the dark web has both positive and negative implications, making it a controversial topic in the online world.

d) Virtual Reality (VR) is an exciting technological innovation that has revolutionized the way people interact with digital spaces. The term Virtual Reality refers to immersive virtual environments created using VR technology. This technology lets users explore and interact with digital spaces realistically, creating a unique and immersive experience. One of the most popular applications of VR technology is in gaming. Gamers can now enter and interact with virtual worlds, making the gaming experience more realistic and engaging. VR technology has also been used in entertainment, education, training, and simulation. VR simulations have been used for medical training, allowing students to practice procedures in a safe environment.

The term "cyberspace" is often used in conjunction with VR technology. VR cyberspace refers to the virtual environments created using VR technology. These digital spaces can range from realistic simulations of real-world locations to completely imaginary worlds. Users can navigate and explore these spaces using VR headsets and controllers, making the experience more interactive and immersive. With the constant advancement of VR technology, the possibilities for VR cyberspace are endless.

AR (Augmented reality) cyberspace is an exciting new technology revolutionizing our world. AR allows us to add digital information and virtual objects to the real world, giving us a new and improved way of perceiving reality. This can be done with smartphones, tablets, or AR glasses, where users can see computer-generated elements integrated into their surroundings. This technology has a multitude of applications, including informational, gaming, and marketing purposes.

One of the most exciting aspects of AR cyberspace is its ability to enhance our perception of reality. By merging the physical and digital worlds, we are able to experience a new level of immersion and engagement. Imagine walking down the street and seeing virtual signs and ads in front of you, or playing a game where characters and objects are part of your real-life surroundings. This technology could change how we interact with our environment and access information. However, as with any new technology, there are also potential concerns and challenges that come with AR cyberspace.

Privacy and security are big concerns since personal data can be collected and used without our knowledge or consent. Some people may have access to AR technology while others don't, which can create a new type of inequality. We need to carefully think about and handle the implications as we explore and develop this new technology.

f) Cyber-Physical Systems (CPS): CPS is the next generation of technology, bringing together the physical and digital worlds seamlessly. The concept is revolutionary as it combines physical processes with cyber technologies to create interconnected systems that monitor, control, and interact with the physical world.

This opens up a whole new realm of possibilities, with endless potential for improving our daily lives. CPS is great because it brings together different systems and devices, creating a unified and efficient ecosystem. CPS examples exist in our daily lives. Smart grids control energy usage and industrial automation systems optimize production processes. With CPS, these systems are not only connected, but also intelligent and adaptive. This means that they can learn and improve over time, making them more efficient and effective. Imagine a world where your car can talk to traffic lights for a safe trip, and your home devices can adapt to your habits. CPS is making this a reality.

The potential of CPS is endless, and it is constantly evolving and improving. Integrating physical processes with cyber technologies can transform industries, improve efficiency, and enhance the quality of life for individuals. CPS will transform how we live and work with technology. Cloud computing has revolutionized how people do business and use technology. Due to remote work and global connectivity, cloud computing has become essential for people and organizations.

This innovative approach involves delivering computing services over the internet, eliminating the need for physical infrastructure. This technology allows users to access resources and applications from anywhere, making it a highly convenient and efficient solution.

One of the most common uses of cloud computing is for data storage. As more data is created, secure and reliable storage solutions are more important than ever for businesses and individuals. By leveraging cloud storage, users can store and access their data from any device with an internet connection.

This eliminates the need for physical storage devices and reduces the risk of data loss. Cloud computing is commonly used for SaaS and IaaS solutions, offering users various applications and tools to improve productivity and efficiency. However, as with any technology, there are also potential risks associated with cloud computing.

Security and privacy concerns are often cited as the main drawbacks of this approach. As data is stored and accessed remotely, there is a risk of unauthorized access and data breaches. Users must carefully choose and use security measures to protect their data when using cloud computing. Cloud computing is valuable for people and organizations because it helps streamline operations and stay connected in today's digital world, despite its challenges.

Amplitude of Cyberspace

The amplitude of cyberspace is incredibly vast, and as technology continues to evolve, so does its reach and scope. The digital world is part of every aspect of our lives, from communication and accessing information to doing business and interacting with people. It has become an essential part of our daily routines, and it's hard to imagine a world without it.

The digital world also offers a wide range of activities and services that were previously unimaginable. Online shopping, virtual meetings, and social media are some of the conveniences and opportunities that cyberspace has brought to us. Now we can access information and resources from anywhere in the world, connecting us to people and cultures that were once out of reach.

1 - Cyberspace facilitates real-time communication through various channels, such as email, instant messaging, video conferencing, and social media platforms. These channels have made it easier for people to connect with others from anywhere in the world, at any time. Today, people are more connected than ever thanks to technology and the internet. The ability to communicate in real-time has had a significant impact on how businesses operate. Remote work has made cyberspace essential for businesses to stay connected with employees and clients. It has also allowed for faster and more efficient communication between team members, regardless of their physical location.

This has led to increased productivity and collaboration among team members, resulting in better outcomes for businesses. Furthermore, cyberspace has also revolutionized the way we interact with our loved ones. We can now easily video call our distant family and friends with a single click, making it feel as if they are right beside us. Social media platforms have made it easier to stay connected with friends and family, even if we live far away.

2 - The rise of e-commerce has improved business-customer connections, making shopping more convenient and efficient. This has not only benefited businesses, but has also had a positive impact on consumers. Customers can now buy products and services from anywhere and at any time, which expands their options and increases competition among businesses. E-commerce has helped small businesses grow by allowing them to reach more customers and compete with bigger companies. Moreover, e-commerce has also revolutionized the way in which people work. Thanks to online marketplaces and platforms, people can now start businesses with fewer resources and lower costs. This has led to a surge in entrepreneurship and enabled people to make successful careers out of their passions and hobbies.

E-commerce has created new job opportunities in digital marketing, web development, and customer service, offering a more diverse job market. Overall, the rise of e-commerce has had a profound impact on the way we live and conduct business. The global economy has changed due to the interconnected world. It has given us more choices and created new job opportunities. As technology improves, e-commerce will keep changing and impacting our world in unpredictable ways. By clicking a button, people can buy things from home and businesses can reach more customers. This has transformed the traditional way of shopping, making it easier and more convenient for everyone involved. Online shopping has changed the way we buy and sell things, and it has also led to the rise of digital payments.

From buying groceries to booking flights, everything is now just a few clicks away. This trend of virtual transactions is expected to keep growing as more people see the benefits. With the world constantly evolving, it's safe to say that e-commerce and digital payments are here to stay. With digital payments, you can use a mobile phone or a computer to make seamless and secure payments.

Virtual transactions are now safer for businesses and consumers, thanks to a significant reduction in the risk of theft and fraud.

Cyberspace is a huge digital information repository that has changed the way we live and interact with the world. With a simple click, we can access a lot of knowledge and resources, including the most recent news and entertainment.

Technology has improved our lives, creating numerous opportunities for learning, growth, and connection. One of the most remarkable aspects of cyberspace is its ability to connect people from all corners of the world. We can keep in touch with friends and family through social media, no matter where they are. We can also connect with like-minded individuals and form communities based on shared interests and passions. This has created a global network of individuals, breaking down barriers and fostering a sense of unity and understanding. However, with this vast amount of information and connectivity also comes great responsibility. We can use libraries, educational resources, and online courses to continuously learn and broaden our knowledge. This benefits both individuals and society as a whole by making us more educated and informed.

5 - The rise of streaming services and social media has revolutionized the way people consume entertainment. With just a few clicks, people can access an endless supply of content from the comfort of their homes. This has also opened up opportunities for new and emerging artists to showcase their talents and reach a wider audience. The impact of the entertainment industry goes beyond just providing entertainment. It has also become a major contributor to the economy, providing numerous job opportunities and boosting tourism. The success of movies, TV shows, and music also has the power to influence popular culture and shape societal norms. Entertainment is essential in our daily lives, and it keeps changing to suit people's preferences.

6 - Critical Infrastructure is a vital component of modern societies. Industries that are vital to a country's survival are the backbone of its economy. Industries like energy, healthcare, finance, and transportation rely heavily on interconnected systems in cyberspace for their daily operations. Attacks on these systems can have serious consequences for both the industries and the country as a whole. Industries are relying more on cyberspace because of technological advancements. With digital systems becoming more prevalent and efficient, it has become more cost-effective for these industries to operate through cyberspace.

7 – E-government functions, including public services, administrative processes, and civic engagement, have an online presence within cyberspace. The government has used technology in many areas to improve how it operates, which has made its services more efficient.

Most government agencies have websites which allow citizens to access services from the comfort of their homes. This has improved access to government services and reduced waiting times at government offices. The government has also made strides in using technology to improve administrative processes. Government agencies now use electronic payment systems to reduce the need for citizens to visit government offices in person for making payments. This has resulted in a more streamlined process, making it more convenient for citizens.

Additionally, the government has also embraced the use of technology in civic engagement. Social media platforms have given government's new ways to engage with citizens, collect feedback, and raise awareness about various initiatives. This has resulted in a more engaged citizenry, promoting a sense of ownership and responsibility towards the government.

2 - The Internet

The internet is an interconnected global network that provides various services and resources to people all over the world. The internet allows people to communicate, share ideas, and access information at an unprecedented scale. Users can now interact with each other in real-time, regardless of their geographical location.

Due to its massive size, the internet is divided into different classifications and categories based on specific criteria. Categories group different types of content together, making it easier for users to find what they want. For example, there are search engines designed to help individuals find information quickly and easily. Social media platforms let you share personal experiences and thoughts with people worldwide. Categorizing the internet has made it organized, efficient, and has opened up endless possibilities for users. The internet offers many resources and services, such as online shopping, banking, education, and entertainment.

The internet is an intricate and complex system that has revolutionized the way we communicate, do business, and access information. Its creation required the use of a variety of innovative and groundbreaking technologies. These technologies were carefully chosen and skilfully combined to create the powerful and interconnected network that we know today.

One of the key technologies used in creating the internet was packet switching. Data transmission involves breaking information into smaller packets and sending them through different routes to their destination. This improved the efficiency of data transfer and made the network stronger against failures and congestion.

Internet packet switching is the backbone of the internet and allows for efficient and reliable communication between devices. Packet switching works by dividing data into packets and attaching a header to each packet with information about its destination.

Packets are sent through networks and routers to find the best path to their destination. This data transmission method is more efficient than traditional circuit switching, where a dedicated circuit is established between two devices for the duration of the communication. With packet switching, multiple packets can be sent at the same time, allowing for faster and more reliable communication.

Another technology used was the development of the TCP/IP protocol. These rules made it possible for different devices and systems to communicate with each other without any issues. It also enabled the creation of the World Wide Web, which revolutionized the way we access and share information. HTML, HTTP, and DNS are also important technologies for the internet, each contributing in its own way to make the network what it is today.

The surface web has many websites, web pages, and online tools. It is the part of the internet that you can easily access with a web browser and is listed by search engines like Google, Bing, Yahoo and many others. Anyone with internet can access the surface web, which is the most popular and well-known part of the internet. However, the surface web is just the tip of the iceberg when it comes to the vastness of the internet.

Deep Web

The deep web refers to web pages and online resources that cannot be found by search engines. This includes private databases, password-protected websites, and other hidden content that is not intended for public consumption. The deep web is much bigger than the surface web, making it a mysterious and interesting part of the internet. The surface web is only a small part of the whole internet, despite being big and easy to access.

It is constantly expanding and evolving, with new websites and online resources being added every day. The surface web seems to have everything we need, but it's just a small part of the internet. The deep web is a large network of hidden content that cannot be accessed by regular users. The deep web is about 95% of the internet and keeps growing with new information. The deep web cannot be accessed through traditional search engines like the surface web. It is not indexed and can only be accessed through specific means. This makes it a haven for all types of sensitive and private information. The deep web is often linked to illegal activities like drug trafficking, human trafficking, and cybercrime due to its hidden nature.

However, not all content on the deep web is illegal. Many legit organizations and businesses use the deep web to protect their data from hackers and cyber threats. This includes password-protected websites, private databases, and subscription-based content. Accessing these resources on the deep web often requires specific credentials or authentication, which makes it difficult for the average user. Despite its shady reputation, the deep web serves a vital purpose in protecting sensitive information and maintaining online security.

It also offers a wealth of valuable and legitimate resources that are not easily accessible through traditional means. The deep web is growing, so users must understand its complexities and the risks and benefits of accessing it.

The Intranet

Intranet networks are commonly used in organizations for secure information sharing. These networks offer authorized users easy access to internal websites, email servers, and file-sharing systems.

The use of internet technologies enables intranets to offer seamless communication and collaboration between employees, regardless of their physical location. This makes it easier for teams to work together on projects, share important documents, and exchange ideas. Organizations may customize their intranet networks to fit their specific needs. This can include tailor-made tools and applications that are designed to enhance the efficiency and productivity of employees.

These networks can also serve as a central hub for important information, such as company policies, procedures, and announcements. Intranets can help organizations by providing a central location for employees to access important information. This improves communication and streamlines processes. Intranet networks are important for organizations. They allow employees to collaborate and share information securely and efficiently.

Internet technologies help these networks to enable smooth communication and serve as a central hub for important information, ultimately enhancing organization efficiency and productivity. Organizations can create a powerful tool by customizing intranets to fit their needs. This tool enhances collaboration, streamlines processes, and leads to greater success.

Extranet

Extranet is an essential tool that businesses use to communicate with their external stakeholders. It is like a private extension of an organization's intranet, which is restricted to only internal users. The extranet allows outside users like partners, suppliers, and customers to securely access and collaborate with the organization while having limited information access. This controlled environment ensures that sensitive company information is only shared with trusted stakeholders.

Extranets usually require secure login details or VPNs to protect the shared information. These measures protect the organization from potential cyber threats and unauthorized access.

Extranets are essential for organizations to securely communicate with external stakeholders, especially with the growing demand for remote work and virtual collaboration. It allows businesses to extend their intranet to external users while still maintaining a level of privacy and security. Extranets are central for businesses to communicate and collaborate with partners, suppliers, and customers in today's dynamic business environment.

Mobile Internet

The demand for mobile internet has greatly increased over the years. People now prefer to access the internet using their mobile devices.

These mobile devices include smart phones, tablets, and other wireless-enabled gadgets. Mobile internet is a fast and convenient way to access information, connect with others, and do tasks on the go. The mobile internet has become a necessity in today's world, with users relying on it for different purposes. The mobile internet allows us to check emails, make online purchases, and stay connected with loved ones while we are out and about. Users can easily access the internet anywhere due to advancements in cellular networks (3G, 4G, 5G, and upcoming 6G) and the availability of Wi-Fi hotspots.

Mobile internet has created new opportunities for businesses to reach a larger audience and offer their services on mobile devices. This has led to the development of websites, apps, and online services that are easier for users to access on their mobile devices.

The increasing demand for mobile internet will revolutionize how we use the internet, making it more accessible and efficient worldwide.

Internet of Things

The Internet of Things (IoT) is a network of connected devices with sensors, software, and internet connection. This allows these devices to collect and exchange data with each other and other systems over the internet.

IoT has revolutionized our way of life and work, with devices being used in many industries and applications. One of the most common examples of IoT devices are smart home appliances. These include devices such as smart thermostats, lighting systems, and security cameras, among others. These devices can be controlled remotely through a smart phone or other device, making our lives more convenient and efficient. Wearable gadgets like fitness trackers and smart watches are popular uses of IoT technology, helping us monitor our health and fitness in real time.

In the industrial sector, IoT devices are used extensively for monitoring and controlling various processes and systems. This includes sensors that can detect changes in temperature, pressure, and other variables, allowing for real-time adjustments and optimizations. Self-driving cars depend on IoT technology for communication and data exchange, which enhances their safety and efficiency on the roads. IoT devices keep improving and being used in limitless ways, making them crucial to our modern society.

Concept of Cyber security

General Concept

Society shapes and is shaped by advancing technology. The word "cyber" was derived from the word "cybernetics," a study of communication and control in living organisms and machines. It's a prefix connected to various activities, technologies, and systems related to the internet and computer networks. "Cyber" now includes virtual reality, artificial intelligence, and the internet of things.

It is a world that is constantly evolving, with new advancements and innovations being made every day. In today's digital age, the term "cyber" has taken on a whole new meaning. It is no longer just a prefix, but a way of life. The internet is now a crucial part of our daily lives, affecting how we communicate, do business, and find information or entertainment.

"Cyber" has truly become a symbol of the modern world and all its endless possibilities. As the world becomes increasingly interconnected and reliant on technology, the term "cyber" will continue to evolve and expand. It will continue to shape and transform society, bringing about new opportunities and challenges.

The prefix started with communication and control, but now it represents a huge and always changing digital world. "Cyber" will always remind us of the power and potential of technology, and the limitless possibilities in our future. The term "cyber" has evolved and expanded beyond its original meaning of communication and control. It now encompasses the vast and ever-changing digital landscape that is constantly expanding and evolving. This new world offers endless possibilities and opportunities for growth and advancement.

When expanding, it's essential to acknowledge the responsibility and power that comes with embracing technology and its benefits. We need to keep pushing limits and seeking progress, but we must also consider the consequences of our advancements.

Cyberspace is a network of data, information, and communication channels used for online activities like transactions, social media, and information exchange. It has created a virtual environment that transcends physical limits and allows for global connectivity. This has revolutionized the way we communicate, work, and access information, making the world more interconnected than ever before.

Technology has created different ways of communication. This helps us do things like online shopping, social media, and sharing information. These channels have opened the way for a virtual environment that transcends physical limits and allows for global connectivity. It has changed how we communicate, work, and access information, connecting the world more than ever.

The term "cyber" will continue to hold great significance and shape the way we communicate, work, and access information.

It is an ever-evolving concept that continues to shape our world and has become an integral part of our society. Cyberspace offers countless possibilities and opportunities that will keep shaping our lives, jobs, and communication in the future.

About Cyber security

Cyber security is one of the most critical concerns in today's fast-paced digital landscape. It is the protection of computer systems, networks, and data from unauthorized access, attacks, damage, or theft. Its goal is to protect sensitive and confidential information, ensuring its availability, integrity, and confidentiality. Without proper measures, businesses, governments, and individuals are at risk of cyber threats, which are constantly evolving and becoming more sophisticated.

With cloud computing, IoT, and mobile devices, cybercriminals have more opportunities to attack. There has been a rise in cyber attacks such as malware, phishing, and ransom ware that can cause serious harm to people and companies. As a result, cyber security has become a top priority for governments, businesses, and individuals worldwide. It's involves a variety of technologies, processes, and practices that work together to protect digital assets. These may include firewalls, antivirus software, encryption, and access controls, among others. Implementing the right tools and technologies is important, but education and awareness are also necessary. Human error and negligence are often the weakest links, so it's important for people to understand the risks and how to protect themselves and their organizations.

To keep our digital world safe, we should follow best practices and stay vigilant. In today's digital age, our lives revolve around technology and the internet, making network security more important than ever. It's important for people to understand the risks of cyber attacks and data breaches and to know how to protect themselves and their organizations. However, human error and negligence are often the vulnerabilities. Even with all the security measures, one mistake can still make the whole network vulnerable.

To prevent such risks, it's important for individuals to follow best practices and stay vigilant. This includes regularly updating passwords, avoiding suspicious emails and links, and being cautious when sharing personal information online. Organizations should also have strong security rules and offer regular training to teach employees about cyber security risks and how to avoid them.

It's important to note that network security is a continuous process. With new and advanced cyber threats emerging every day, it's critical to stay updated and adapt to new security measures. Protecting data and privacy is important for maintaining the network's integrity and confidentiality.

Endpoint security is important in protecting data and privacy from cyber threats. With the growth of technology and the internet, more devices are connected to the network, increasing the risk of attacks. Endpoint security relies on antivirus software, anti-malware solutions, and endpoint detection and response tools. These tools detect and prevent cyber threats like viruses, malware, and ransom ware from getting into devices. They continuously monitor and scan for any suspicious activities and provide timely alerts and responses to potential threats. By prioritizing network security and taking necessary precautions, we can create a safer digital world for ourselves and future generations. In today's world, it is important to keep up with the latest security measures to protect our devices and data from cyber threats. Endpoint security is vital for the protection of your digital assets. It focuses on securing individual devices and is essential for network security. With proper endpoint security, we can ensure the safety and privacy of our digital world.

Endpoint security is a critical aspect of overall network security that helps protect our devices and data from potential threats. By using the latest security measures like IAM (identity and Access Management), we can make sure the digital world is safe and private.

IAM controls access to systems and data, making sure only authorized people can view or change sensitive information.

It includes practices like user authentication, access controls, and user privilege management. These practices ensure that the correct individuals have the appropriate access to our devices and data. This helps prevent unauthorized access and potential data breaches. IAM helps to track and monitor user activity. This enables us to detect and respond to any suspicious or malicious behaviour. With proper endpoint security measures in place, can mitigate the risks of cyber attacks and safeguard digital assets. By implementing IAM, it can also ensure compliance with regulatory requirements and industry standards.

Encryption is crucial for endpoint security to protect sensitive data from unauthorized access. With the rise of cyber attacks and data breaches, implementing encryption measures is fundamental for safeguarding the devices and data. Encrypting information adds an extra layer of security by allowing only those with the correct decryption key to access it. In addition to protecting data, encryption also helps us comply with regulatory requirements and industry standards. Many organizations must protect sensitive information like personal or financial data. Using encryption is often necessary to meet these requirements. By implementing proper encryption techniques, can be ensured that data is secure and that in compliance with relevant regulations. Whether it's sensitive personal information or confidential business data, encryption helps to prevent unauthorized access and maintain privacy. This is essential for organizations that deal with sensitive data. A data breach can lead to financial losses and harm their reputation and customer trust. By incorporating encryption into endpoint security measures, devices and data can have one more protection from potential threats and ensure the integrity of our digital assets.

Fragmented data can cost companies millions in losses and damage their reputation with customers. Therefore, it is imperative for businesses to prioritize application security. To protect software applications, it's important to secure them against vulnerabilities. It's also necessary to review code regularly and use testing tools to find potential risks. This comprehensive approach to application security can prevent data breaches and maintain the integrity of digital assets. This not only mitigates financial losses, but also maintains trust with customers by demonstrating a commitment to protecting their privacy. By prioritizing application security and implementing encryption, organizations can safeguard their data and maintain their reputation.

Training

Security awareness training helps individuals recognize and mitigate potential threats, such as phishing attacks and social engineering. Organizations can create a security-conscious culture within their workforce by offering regular training and updates on the latest security measures. This creates an additional layer of protection, as employees are able to identify and report suspicious activities, preventing potential breaches.

Furthermore, implementing a strong password policy and multifactor authentication can further enhance the security of applications and sensitive data. Organizations can prevent unauthorized access to their systems by prompting users to update their passwords regularly and adding an extra verification step.

This deters hackers and ensures only authorized personnel can access sensitive information. Thus, investing in employee education and implementing strong security measures can greatly enhance an organization's overall security posture. Regular vulnerability assessments and penetration testing can help find and fix weaknesses in an organization's security systems. This proactive approach allows organizations to stay ahead of potential threats and ensure that their applications and data are secure.

By continuously evaluating and improving their security measures, organizations can maintain trust with their customers and protect their reputation.

Cyber security includes incident response, which means creating plans to respond to and recover from security incidents. This includes identifying and containing threats, investigating the incident, and implementing measures to prevent similar occurrences in the future. With a clear incident response plan, organizations can reduce the impact of a cyber attack and prevent it from happening again. Protecting the organization's assets and information is crucial.

It also builds customer confidence in the company's ability to address potential threats.

To minimize the impact of cyber attacks, organizations should have a plan in place. This will help them quickly and effectively mitigate any potential damage caused by such incidents. By doing so, they can also reduce the likelihood of the attack happening again in the future. Having an incident response plan is important because it helps protect an organization's assets and sensitive information.

SIEM (Security Information and Event Management) play an essential role in incident response plans by providing real-time monitoring and correlation of events. They aggregate and analyze log data from various sources, such as firewalls, intrusion detection systems, and other security tools. This allows for the detection and response to security incidents in a timely manner. By identifying abnormal or suspicious activities, SIEM solutions can help organizations quickly contain and remediate the attack, minimizing its impact.

To implement an effective cyber security training and education program, it's important to consider some key factors.

First and foremost, it is essential to establish a strong foundation of knowledge. This includes providing individuals with a comprehensive understanding of cyber security principles, concepts, and best practices. To ensure a strong grasp of the basics, it is important to cover topics like risk management, cryptography, network security, and incident response. By laying this groundwork, people will have the knowledge they need to build upon as they go through more specialized training. Besides basic knowledge, it's important to provide specific training opportunities for the different roles in the security field. This can include tracks focused on network security, application security, penetration testing, security analysis, and security policy development.

Tailoring training programs to suit the specific needs of professionals helps them acquire the skills and expertise needed to succeed in their chosen field. Encouraging and supporting recognized certifications boosts the credibility and expertise of individuals in cyber security. Certifications like Compton Security+, Certified Information Systems Security Professional (CISP), and Certified Ethical Hacker (CEH) prove someone's knowledge and skills, making them more desirable to employers.

Using hands-on labs and simulations in training programs helps people apply theoretical knowledge practically and improve their learning and skills. Practicing cyber range exercises helps participants improve their incident response skills by simulating real-world cyber scenarios in a controlled and realistic environment. To be effective, training and education on cyber security should include foundational knowledge, specialized tracks, certifications, hands-on learning experiences, and cyber range exercises. By following these considerations, organizations and individuals can create a skilled workforce to tackle evolving cyber security challenges effectively, promote continuous learning for professionals by encouraging them to stay updated on the latest threats, vulnerabilities, and security technologies. This can be done through ongoing training, attending conferences, and reading industry publications.

Encourage collaboration between schools, training providers, and industry partners to make sure security training programs match their requirements and follow best practices. By working together, these organizations can create a thorough and effective training program to tackle current and future challenges in the field. Effective security professionals require not only technical expertise but also strong soft skills like communication, problem-solving, and teamwork.

It is important to provide security awareness training for non-technical staff within organizations. This helps create a collective culture of security, where all employees understand basic cyber security principles and practices. This can greatly contribute to the overall security posture of an organization by minimizing vulnerabilities caused by human error.

It is necessary to consider ethics in training. This using red team exercises, professionals can better understand the effects of their actions and make ethical decisions in their roles, thus promoting a more responsible and ethical approach to security. Integrating ethical considerations into cyber security training is central for promoting responsible and ethical behaviour in the field. Professionals should prioritize ethical decision-making, respect privacy, and follow legal and regulatory standards to understand the impact of their actions. This leads to a more conscientious approach to security, which is essential in the ever-evolving digital scene.

One way to achieve this is by incorporating online learning platforms into training programs. These platforms offer flexible and accessible options for individuals to acquire skills at their own pace and convenience. By utilizing online courses, webinars, and virtual labs, professionals can enhance their knowledge and understanding of ethical practices in cyber security. In addition to online learning, mentorship programs can also play a crucial role in promoting ethical behaviour in this field.

Mentorship connects experienced professionals with newcomers, offering valuable insights, guidance, and career advice. This not only helps individuals develop their skills but also encourages ethical decision-making and responsible behaviour. Real-world case studies and examples can improve participants' ability to apply theoretical knowledge in practical situations, helping them handle ethical dilemmas in their roles. The government and industry should work together to support cyber security education and training initiatives. By collaborating, they can create comprehensive and well-supported programs that cater to the evolving threat landscape. This will ensure that individuals are equipped with the necessary skills to mitigate risks and protect sensitive information. Regular evaluation and updates to the training curriculum are essential for its effectiveness and relevance. This ensures that the training remains relevant and addresses current challenges.

By continuously investing in training programs and collaborating with institutions, a skilled and resilient workforce can be developed. Effective training and education are foundational elements in building a robust cyber security ecosystem. Continuous investment in training programs and commitment to ongoing learning are essential to adapt to the evolving nature of threats.

Vulnerabilities detection

Vulnerability management is an essential aspect of maintaining a robust security posture. It involves continuously identifying, assessing, and mitigating potential vulnerabilities in systems and applications. By proactively scanning for weaknesses and implementing necessary security updates, organizations can significantly reduce their risk exposure. In addition to regular vulnerability scanning, patch management is another critical aspect of vulnerability management. This process involves identifying and deploying security patches to fix any known vulnerabilities in systems and applications. Regularly scanning for weaknesses and quickly fixing them through patch management and security updates can greatly improve an organization's security.

This helps to improve security by considering both technical weaknesses and human factors that can lead to security breaches. The policies and frameworks help employees know what to do to keep the organization safe. Additionally, they help organizations stay compliant with industry regulations and avoid costly penalties and damage to their reputation.

Organizations can take advantage of secure app development, MDM (Mobile Device Management), and encryption to improve their security posture. By implementing these measures, they can effectively safeguard sensitive data and critical systems from potential cyber threats. This protects the organization and makes customers, partners, and stakeholders feel confident about the security of their data.

Cloud security is important as it protects data, applications, and infrastructure in cloud environments. Cloud security involves more than just implementing access controls and encryption. It also requires organizations to adhere to best practices for securing their data in the cloud. This may include regular monitoring and auditing, as well as implementing multifactor authentication and data backup and recovery plans. Organizations can protect their data and systems from breaches and attacks by using a comprehensive approach to cloud security. In today's digital landscape, it is vital for organizations to have a strong security posture. Investing in secure app development, MDM, encryption, and cloud security helps organizations protect their data and systems, and build trust with customers, partners, and stakeholders. Organizations must regularly assess and improve their security strategies to stay ahead of potential threats and protect their data from cyber attacks.

Threat intelligence plays a decisive role in achieving data security. By gathering and analyzing information about potential cyber security threats, organizations can anticipate and respond to emerging threats effectively. This helps them stay ahead of potential attacks and protect their data from being compromised. Threat intelligence helps businesses make informed security decisions and be prepared to defend against potential threats.

Organizations must also continuously monitor and analyze potential threats to ensure the safety of their data and systems. Investing in threat intelligence helps businesses stay ahead of potential attacks and build trust with stakeholders. This, in turn, can lead to increased customer loyalty, improved partnerships, and a strong reputation in the marketplace. When it comes to businesses, protecting their data and systems is of utmost importance. Investing in threat intelligence is crucial. Cyber security helps businesses prevent cyber attacks and build trust with stakeholders. This can lead to increased customer loyalty, improved partnerships, and a strong reputation in the marketplace. However, for businesses that use block chain technology there is an added layer of security that must be considered. Block chain technology, known for its decentralized and immutable nature, is becoming increasingly popular in various industries. However, as with any technology, ensuring its security is vital. This includes implementing secure development practices and measures to prevent unauthorized access to the distributed ledger and smart contracts.

Cyber security is not a one-time effort; it requires ongoing attention and efforts to stay ahead of potential threats. This involves using the latest security technologies, regularly updating security protocols, and continuously training employees to be aware of potential risks. Businesses can protect themselves from cyber risks by taking these actions.

Mobile devices are more popular now, so it's important to focus on keeping sensitive data and critical systems safe from cyber threats. Regular vulnerability scanning and patch management are essential steps in maintaining a proactive approach to cyber security. However, these measures must be paired with well-defined security policies and governance frameworks to achieve optimal results. Secure app development is crucial for mobile security. It involves creating apps with built-in security features. This helps to prevent malicious attacks and data breaches that could compromise the device and its data. In addition, mobile device management (MDM) is also an important aspect of mobile security.

Policies

Establishing effective cyber security measures is vital for organizations to safeguard their information assets and minimize risks. Policies are created and enforced by governments, regulators, and international bodies to ensure a basic level of security in different sectors. Without these policies, organizations would struggle to maintain the confidentiality, integrity, and availability of their information.

One of the key aspects of these policies and regulations is data protection and privacy laws. These regulations, such as GDPR (General Data Protection Regulation) set standards for the protection of personal data. They require organizations to implement measures to secure and responsibly handle personal information. This not only protects individuals' privacy but also helps prevent data breaches, which can have severe consequences for organizations.

Another important aspect is the use of frameworks. These frameworks, such as ISO/IEC (ISO/IEC (International Organization for Standardization/International Electro technical Commission), and CIS (Centre for Internet Security), provide guidelines and best practices for organizations to develop their policies. By following these frameworks, organizations can ensure that their policies are comprehensive and effective in addressing potential cyber threats. This, in turn, helps to establish a strong cyber security posture and protects organizations from cyber attacks.

Organizations must also consider industry-specific regulations when developing their policies. These regulations are tailored to address the unique risks and challenges faced by different industries. The financial sector follows regulations to protect sensitive financial information. For instance, they adhere to the Payment Card Industry Data Security Standard (PCI DSS). Similarly, healthcare organizations must comply with the Health Insurance Portability and Accountability Act (HIPAA) to safeguard patient data.

In addition to industry specific regulations, there are incident reporting requirements that organizations must follow. These requirements vary by jurisdiction but typically require organizations to report cyber security incidents promptly. It is important to ensure that authorities can respond well to incidents and that organizations take necessary steps to minimize any potential impact.

Governments also play a significant role in developing cyber security policies through national and regional strategies. These strategies are comprehensive and encompass a range of policies, initiatives, and collaborations to enhance security at a national level. Additionally, there are specific regulations focused on protecting critical infrastructure, such as energy, transportation, and telecommunications. These regulations aim to safeguard essential services from cyber threats that could have a significant societal impact.

Finally, organizations must also have robust identity and access management (IAM) policies in place. The policies explain how organizations handle user identities, access controls, and authentication to prevent unauthorized access and ensure correct permissions for users. Remote work and Bring Your Own Device (BYOD) policies are essential for organizations to maintain device, network, and data security in non-office environments. These policies focus on issues such as device security, secure connections, and data protection.

With the increasing adoption of cloud services, organizations also implement policies to address the secure use of cloud computing. These may include guidelines for data storage, encryption, and contractual agreements with cloud service providers. Organizations need policies for managing vulnerabilities in their systems and applications. This involves identifying, assessing, and fixing any vulnerability. Regular vulnerability assessments and patch management are often emphasized in these policies.

Encryption policies include encryption algorithms, key management, and data protection for data in transit and at rest. Furthermore, organizations may establish policies regarding penetration testing and red teaming activities to assess the effectiveness of their cyber defences. These policies outline the scope, methods, and reporting requirements for such testing. Regular penetration testing and red teaming help organizations find and fix system weaknesses before cyber threats can exploit them. Organizations need strong policies to protect themselves from cyber threats and prevent societal impacts.

Supply chain security policies are critical given the interconnected nature of supply chains. Organizations should have guidelines for assessing and mitigating risks within their supply chains. These policies should cover aspects such as vendor risk management, incident response and recovery, and disaster recovery planning. Employee training and awareness programs are an integral part of an organization's policies. These policies emphasize the need for cyber security training for employees and offer guidelines on recognizing phishing, practicing secure behaviour, and reporting security incidents. Regular training and awareness programs help employees stay updated on the latest cyber threats and best practices to prevent them.

Regulatory compliance audits are a necessary aspect of cyber security policies. Regulations often require organizations to undergo periodic audits to assess their compliance with security requirements. Internal teams or outside third parties can perform audits to help organizations find security gaps.

Policies addressing cross-border data transfers are essential for organizations that operate on an international scale. These policies ensure that organizations comply with legal requirements when transferring data across international borders. This includes adherence to data protection laws and international agreements to protect sensitive information. Encouraging collaboration and information sharing is another critical element of policies. Governments and industry bodies promote the sharing of threat intelligence to enhance collective defence against cyber threats. This helps organizations stay informed about security threats and promotes awareness and cooperation within and across industries.

Advanced Persistent Threats

As such, organizations must be aware of the key characteristics and considerations related to APTs in order to better protect themselves against these advanced cyber attacks.

APTs are highly targeted, focusing on specific organizations, industries, or even government entities. Threat actors conduct extensive reconnaissance to gather intelligence about the target, its infrastructure, and potential vulnerabilities. This level of specificity allows APTs to remain undetected for extended periods of time, making them particularly dangerous. APTs frequently involve the use of custom-designed malware tailored to the specific target environment. These malware variants are often created to evade traditional security measures and blend into the targeted system. In addition, APTs may also employ various techniques to avoid detection, such as using encryption and obfuscation to hide their malicious activities.

Zero-Day Exploits: APTs may leverage zero-day exploits, which are vulnerabilities in software or hardware that are not yet known to the vendor or the public. These vulnerabilities provide a valuable advantage to threat actors, as there are no available patches or defences. This allows APTs to exploit these vulnerabilities and gain access to systems and data without being detected. Organizations need to always watch for possible zero-day exploits and have plans ready to stop any attacks.

Spear Phishing: A common entry point for APTs is spear phishing, where threat actors send carefully crafted and personalized emails to targeted individuals within the organization. These emails often contain malicious attachments or links to initiate the attack. APTs may also use social engineering tactics to gain access to sensitive information, such as pretending to be a trusted source or using fake login pages to steal credentials. As such, organizations must educate their employees on how to identify and avoid falling victim to these types of attacks in order to protect against APTs.

Lateral movement within the target environment is a key tactic used in Advanced Persistent Threats (APTs). Threat actors gain initial access and then move laterally across the network, escalating privileges and accessing sensitive systems or data. This allows them to gain a foothold within the organization and maintain access over time. As such, organizations must not only prevent initial access, but also closely monitor for lateral movement to stop APTs in their tracks.

Persistence mechanisms are another tool used in APTs to maintain access to compromised systems. These can include backdoors, rootkits, or other techniques to ensure ongoing control. This allows threat actors to continue their attack even if their initial access is discovered and blocked. Organizations must recognize and eliminate persistence mechanisms to completely eliminate an APT. The ultimate goal of APTs is often the extraction of sensitive data. People who pose a threat try to steal information for reasons like spying, making money, or gaining an advantage over others. This puts organizations at risk of significant financial and reputational damage. To combat this, organizations must not only focus on preventing APTs, but also have a robust incident response plan in place to swiftly detect, contain, eradicate, and recover from an attack.

Expanding on the context provided, organizations face a constant threat of advanced persistent threats (APTs) that are often motivated by espionage, financial gain, or competitive advantage. Organizations must have strong cyber security strategies to prevent financial and reputational damage from these threats. In addition to focusing on preventing APTs, organizations must also have a proactive incident response plan ready for swift detection, containment, eradication, and recovery in the event of an attack.

One of the key components of a comprehensive cyber security strategy is leveraging cyber threat intelligence. This involves gathering and analyzing relevant data to understand the tactics, techniques, and procedures used by APTs. By having access to timely and accurate intelligence, organizations can proactively defend against potential threats.

Another critical aspect of a multi-layered cyber security strategy is network segmentation. By dividing the network into isolated segments, organizations can limit the lateral movement of APTs within their systems. This helps limit the impact of a possible breach and stop it from spreading to other parts of the network.

Additionally, proactive threat hunting is essential for identifying and mitigating APTs. This involves actively searching for signs of APTs within the network using advanced analytics, threat intelligence, and behavioural analysis to identify anomalies and potential indicators of compromise. Lastly, collaboration and information sharing with other organizations, industry partners, and government agencies can enhance collective defence against APTs. Sharing knowledge about current cyber threats helps the cyber security community improve their defences and be ready for possible attacks.

Infrastructure Protection

As technology and interconnected systems have become more essential, critical infrastructure protection (CIP) has become increasingly important in recent years. Essential systems and assets are vital for a nation's functioning, economy, and society. Without proper protection measures in place, the disruption or destruction of these critical infrastructures could have catastrophic consequences.

CIP includes the energy sector, which includes power plants and oil and gas pipelines. Renewable energy and smart grid technology are making the energy sector more susceptible to cyber attacks. This has led to a greater focus on protecting these critical assets from potential threats.

Another critical sector within CIP is transportation, which includes everything from highways and bridges to airports and seaports. Transportation is vulnerable to cyber threats and physical attacks due to its role in moving goods and people. As such, protecting these assets is crucial for maintaining the smooth functioning of our economy and society. By implementing proper security measures, we can ensure the resilience and reliability of our transportation systems.

Conducting risk assessments is essential in identifying and evaluating potential threats and vulnerabilities to critical infrastructure. This involves evaluating how cyber threats, physical attacks, and other risks affect the operation of vital systems. By conducting these assessments, we can better understand the potential risks and take proactive measures to mitigate them. It is crucial for industries to adhere to sector-specific guidelines and standards for critical infrastructure protection.

Many industries have established regulatory frameworks and best practices to enhance security and resilience. By following these guidelines and standards, we can ensure that our transportation systems are well-protected against potential threats and attacks. Ensuring smooth functioning of the economy and society inspires public confidence in the safety and reliability of infrastructure.

Continuously monitoring and updating security measures are important, along with conducting risk assessments and following guidelines. This includes staying informed about emerging threats and implementing new technologies and protocols to address them. Improving security measures helps us stay ahead of threats and make transportation systems more resilient and reliable. Protecting critical infrastructure is crucial for both security and the stability of society.

The collaboration and information sharing among different agencies and organizations is crucial in staying one step ahead of potential threats. By working together and sharing threat intelligence, we can solve security challenges and identify new threats.

This proactive approach allows implementing preventative measures and mitigates risks before they become major issues. In addition to collaboration, implementing robust cyber security measures is essential in protecting critical infrastructure from cyber threats. T

This includes utilizing advanced technologies such as firewalls, intrusion detection and prevention systems, encryption, and continuous monitoring. By constantly monitoring systems, can detect and respond to cyber incidents in a timely and effective manner.

To further enhance security measures, it is important to also prioritize physical security. To protect critical infrastructure, we need to use access controls, surveillance systems, and perimeter security to prevent unauthorized access, sabotage, or terrorist attacks. By regularly reviewing and improving our physical security measures, we can make sure that transportation systems remain strong and reliable, which ultimately helps to keep society safe and stable.

Critical infrastructure assets must be protected from various threats such as:

a) Unauthorized access;

b) Sabotage, and

c) Terrorist attacks.

This can be achieved by implementing effective access controls, surveillance systems, and perimeter security. However, simply installing these measures is not enough. Continuous evaluation and updates are necessary to ensure the resilience and reliability of transportation systems. This is critical in contributing to the well-being and stability of society.

One way to build resilience into critical infrastructure systems is by incorporating redundancy and failover mechanisms. This means having backup systems in place so that if one part of the infrastructure is compromised, other components can still work. This prevents widespread disruption and minimizes the impact of any potential attacks. Regular testing of these mechanisms is also important to ensure their effectiveness and readiness for emergency situations.

In addition, it is essential to have emergency response and recovery plans in place for critical infrastructure incidents. This includes coordination with emergency services, communication strategies, and procedures for restoring services quickly after an incident. A well-developed plan helps critical infrastructure to be better prepared for potential threats. It is important to regularly test and update these plans to ensure their effectiveness and relevance in ever-changing threat landscapes.

The strategy should be customized to meet the specific needs and challenges of each society. Location, resources, and potential threats should be considered. Organizations can protect their communities by creating clear guidelines to identify and reduce potential risks to critical infrastructure. However, it is not enough to simply have a strategy and guidelines in place. It is equally important to regularly review and update these measures in order to stay ahead of ever-evolving threats. To deal with this, we must always evaluate risks and weaknesses.

By using their accomplishments and available resources, societies can improve their capacity to recognize and address possible dangers. This helps to ensure the safety and stability of their communities. Strong strategy and guidelines are needed to protect critical infrastructure and ensure the safety and stability. Organizations can protect their communities by customizing strategies, regularly updating measures, and promoting collaboration and communication. It's essential to keep prioritizing these efforts to maintain the infrastructure that supports our daily lives. Risk assessments are crucial for managing potential risks. A thorough risk assessment provides comprehensive insight into potential threats and vulnerabilities that may have otherwise gone unnoticed. Prioritizing risks helps organizations focus on the most important issues and manage them effectively.

This ensures that limited resources are allocated wisely, effectively managing both the potential impact and likelihood of risks. Conducting a risk assessment involves evaluating all aspects of an organization's critical infrastructure, from physical to digital assets. It includes identifying potential threats such as natural disasters, cyber attacks, and human error. By identifying all possible risks, organizations can proactively develop strategies to mitigate or prevent them from occurring. Prioritizing risks also helps organizations to allocate resources and funds appropriately, ensuring that the most significant threats are addressed first.

When assessing risks, it's important to include all stakeholders, as they may have helpful information about possible risks. This collaborative approach ensures that all perspectives are considered, providing a more complete picture of potential threats and vulnerabilities:

Collaboration and information sharing is a key to maintaining the safety and security of critical infrastructure. Public-private partnerships allow government agencies, private sector organizations, and other stakeholders to collaborate effectively. By fostering collaboration, one can better understand the threats facing our critical infrastructure and develop effective strategies to mitigate them. One important way to facilitate collaboration is through the sharing of threat intelligence and best practices. This means that all stakeholders must be willing to share information with each other in a timely and transparent manner. By doing so, can be identified potential vulnerabilities and address them before they can be exploited by malicious actors.

Additionally, by sharing best practices, we can learn from each other and improve our overall security posture. Establishing mechanisms for collaboration and information sharing is a crucial step in protecting our critical infrastructure. By working together with all stakeholders, we can create a better defence against threats. Given the rise in advanced attacks, it is crucial for us to unite and build strong partnerships to safeguard and strengthen our critical infrastructure.

Resilience planning is an essential process in ensuring the smooth functioning of critical infrastructure. Developing resilience strategies is fundamental to mitigating the impact of disruptions caused by various incidents. These strategies must be comprehensive and well-thought-out in order to ensure that they are effective in their purpose. Plans should be created with a focus on identifying critical infrastructure and implementing measures to quickly recover from disruptions. The resilience of critical infrastructure is vital to the safety and security of people in our society. Planning for potential disruptions, like cyber attacks, natural disasters, or other incidents, is important for maintaining the resilience of these systems.

Plans should be regularly reviewed and updated to ensure they are up-to-date and able to adapt to changing circumstances. Share and coordinate these strategies with relevant stakeholders to ensure a cohesive response in case of a disruption. A strong resilience plan is important for both short-term recovery and long-term sustainability of critical infrastructure. It is central to remember that resilience planning is an ongoing process and must be continuously evaluated and improved upon. By implementing these strategies, we can better protect critical infrastructure and ensure the safety and well-being of our communities.

A well-prepared crisis communication plan is important for having communication protocols in place for handling emergencies, like a cyber incident. This plan must be proactive and well-defined, to avoid any confusion or delays in communication. Effective communication is crucial for maintaining public trust and protecting an organization's image. The crisis communication plan should include all necessary protocols that need to be followed during an emergency. This involves identifying important stakeholders, setting up a communication chain of command, and defining the roles and responsibilities of each person involved. Please provide a detailed list of both internal and external contacts that should be notified in case of an emergency.

It include communication methods in an emergency plan, like email, phone, or social media. It should also specify the frequency and content of updates to be provided to the stakeholders.

The plan must be regularly reviewed and updated to ensure its effectiveness and relevance. This will reduce confusion and delays in a crisis, and also build trust with stakeholders. A well-developed crisis communication plan is a fundamental element in any organization's risk management strategy.

One key aspect of protecting critical infrastructure is to provide proper training and education to those involved in its operations. Collaboration also allows for a more comprehensive and coordinated response to any security incidents that may occur. It's important to have a national risk management framework to guide decisions and resource allocation for protecting critical infrastructure.

This framework should outline a systematic approach to identifying, assessing, and mitigating risks. A unified strategy and guidelines help critical infrastructure protect itself and ensure society's safety and stability. Continuous monitoring and regular testing of critical infrastructure systems are essential to protect them from changing threats.

- Incorporating threat intelligence feeds and collaborating with international partners to address cross-border threats. By staying informed and working together, the impact of global security challenges can be mitigated. In addition to monitoring and collaboration, a systematic approach to identifying, assessing, and mitigating risks is essential.

- Implementing a framework that outlines guidelines and strategies for critical infrastructure protection. Regular exercises and simulations should be done to test the effectiveness of these measures and identify any weaknesses that need to be addressed.

- Protecting critical infrastructure requires collaboration between government agencies, private sector organizations, and other stakeholders. To ensure the reliability and safety of critical infrastructure assets, nations can prioritize security, resilience, and risk management. This framework helps make decisions and allocate resources. It aims to create a safer and more stable society.

Building Resilience

Organizations must prioritize building resilience against cyber attacks in order to safeguard their operations from potential security incidents. This involves taking proactive measures, implementing effective response strategies, and constantly improving their defences against cyber threats. One of the key aspects of cyber resilience is being prepared to withstand and adapt to cyber threats. This means having solid security protocols in place, such as firewalls, intrusion detection systems, and regular vulnerability assessments. Additionally, organizations must be ready to respond to any security incidents in a timely and effective manner.

It is important to have incident response plans, conduct regular drills and simulations, and have a dedicated team to handle cyber attacks. It is also important to constantly improve and evolve their cyber resilience strategies as cyber threats continue to evolve and become more sophisticated, organizations must stay ahead by implementing new technologies and strategies.

This means investing in modern security tools, providing regular security training for employees, and staying updated on the latest cyber threats and trends. Organizations can protect themselves from cyber criminals and potential attacks by improving their cyber resilience.

One essential aspect of enhancing cyber resilience is conducting frequent risk assessments to identify and prioritize potential cyber risks. Organizations can create a risk management plan that fits their goals and includes actions to reduce, move, or accept risks they find. This proactive approach ensures that organizations are well-prepared to handle potential cyber attacks. By educating employees on best practices for cyber security, organizations can create a culture of security awareness that helps prevent cyber attacks.

Staying updated on the latest cyber threats and trends is another essential element of continuously improving cyber resilience. As cybercriminals continue to evolve their tactics and techniques, organizations must stay informed and adapt their security strategies accordingly.

Developing a comprehensive incident response plan is critical in protecting an organization's operations from potential cyber attacks. This plan should include a detailed outline of the steps to be taken in the event of a security breach. Clear communication protocols, defined roles and responsibilities, and predetermined actions for addressing and recovering from a situation need to be established for an effective response. Investing in security tools and training is important, but having a good incident response plan is crucial for improving cyber resilience. This plan should be regularly reviewed and updated to adapt to ever-evolving security. By having a plan in place, organizations can minimize the impact of a cyber attack and quickly recover from any damages.

By staying informed and alert, organizations can improve their defence against common attack tactics like phishing and social engineering. Training can also empower employees to identify and report potential threats, allowing organizations to take proactive steps in addressing vulnerabilities.

Monitoring of networks, systems, and user activities, coupled with educating and informing employees. By taking a proactive approach, organizations can detect and respond to threats quickly, minimizing the potential impact of cyber attacks. It also creates a culture of security awareness and responsibility within the organization, strengthening its overall security posture.

Organizations can empower their workforce to defend against potential threats by educating and informing employees about the importance of cyber security. This not only strengthens the overall security posture of the organization, but also fosters a sense of accountability among employees. By being proactive about security and keeping employees well-informed, organizations can better detect and respond to threats, reducing risks and safeguarding their critical assets.

Using encryption helps organizations keep their important data safe from attackers, even if it's intercepted or stolen. In addition to encryption, organizations can also implement multifactor authentication to further enhance their security efforts. By using a combination of password and biometric scan, companies can reduce the risk of unauthorized access to their important assets.

This approach is also an effective deterrent to potential attackers, as it makes it much harder to breach the network. Organizations must have a well-established patch management process to regularly update their software, operating systems, and applications. Timely patching is central for closing potential entry points for attackers and mitigating cyber risks. Keeping systems and applications up-to-date helps organizations enhance security and safeguard sensitive information. Regular backups of important data and a disaster recovery plan are also essential.

With the increasing sophistication and frequency of cyber attacks, relying on a single security measure is no longer sufficient. Organizations must implement multifactor authentication (MFA) to ensure the protection of their critical assets. MFA requires users to enter a code sent to their phone to verify their identity. Adding extra security makes it harder for hackers to access sensitive information, even if they get login details.

In addition to MFA, organizations should also integrate cyber threat intelligence into their security operations. This means staying informed about the latest threats, tactics, and techniques used by cyber adversaries. By doing so, organizations can enhance their detection and response capabilities. They can proactively identify potential risks and take necessary measures to prevent or mitigate cyber attacks. This approach is essential in maintaining the security of critical assets and preventing significant financial and reputational damage. By implementing MFA and integrating cyber threat intelligence, organizations can do regular security audits, vulnerability assessments, and penetration testing.

To prioritize the development of a crisis communication plan, organizations must secure the supply chain and conduct regular exercises. This plan outlines the necessary protocols for communicating with stakeholders during and after a cyber attack. Transparent and timely communication is crucial for managing public perception and maintaining stakeholder trust. Organizations need to know that cyber resilience is a continuous process that requires constant improvement and adaptation to new threats. This can be achieved through a holistic approach that combines preventive, detective, and responsive measures.

Supply Chain Security

"Threats to the supply chain, such as cyber attacks, counterfeiting, theft, and natural disasters, can have serious consequences. To enhance supply chain security, it is essential to achieve end-to-end visibility across the entire supply chain. This means having a clear understanding of how goods, information, and finances flow within the supply chain. By having this visibility, potential vulnerabilities can be identified, and better risk management strategies can be implemented. Conducting comprehensive risk assessments is also vital in enhancing supply chain security. This means finding and assessing possible risks and weaknesses in the supply chain and understanding how they can affect operations, finances, and reputation.

Additionally, implementing robust supplier risk management practices is necessary. This involves evaluating suppliers' cyber security, financial stability, and overall reliability, and regularly monitoring and auditing them to ensure they comply with security standards. Following security standards and certifications like ISO 27001 and ISO 28000 improves supply chain security. These standards provide guidelines for best practices in information security management and supply chain security.

Implementing secure communication channels to protect sensitive information exchanged within the supply chain. Encryption, secure data transmission protocols, and secure communication platforms help prevent data breaches and unauthorized access. These measures protect sensitive information and maintain supply chain security by allowing only authorized parties to access it, reducing the risk of compromise. By establishing secure communication practices, companies can enhance the confidentiality, integrity, and availability of their data, safeguarding against cyber threats.

Supply Chain Resilience: Build resilience into the supply chain to mitigate the impact of disruptions. This involves adding backup systems, using different suppliers, and preparing for different situations like natural disasters or geopolitical events. By diversifying suppliers, companies can reduce their dependence on a single source and minimize the risk of supply chain disruptions. Contingency plans help to respond quickly to possible disruptions and minimize their impact on the supply chain, ensuring that the business can continue operating.

Secure software development helps prevent vulnerabilities that could be exploited by malicious actors. Implementing secure coding practices reduces the risk of security breaches and helps protect the confidentiality and integrity of company data. This also makes sure that all software in the supply chain is secure and meets security standards, improving supply chain security.

Regular assessments and audits of third-party vendors and service providers are crucial for maintaining supply chain security. Companies can reduce the risk of security breaches by making sure that their partners meet security requirements and follow established standards. It is important to monitor their security practices throughout the engagement to identify any potential vulnerability and address them promptly. In addition to implementing secure coding practices, companies should also focus on enhancing physical security measures within the supply chain.

This includes securing warehouses, transportation, and implementing measures to prevent theft or tampering. By bolstering physical security, companies can protect the physical components of their supply chain and safeguard against potential security threats. Utilizing supply chain visibility tools and technologies can also help improve supply chain security. These tools track and monitor goods in transit in real-time. They help companies detect anomalies, delays, or disruptions that may indicate security issues. This enables companies to take immediate action and mitigate any potential risks before they escalate.

Implementing strong authentication mechanisms and access controls is another essential aspect of maintaining supply chain security. Restricting access to important systems and data to authorized personnel based on their roles can lower the risk of unauthorized access and data breaches. Furthermore, having well-defined incident response plans specific to supply chain security is crucial.

Regularly testing these plans helps companies identify any gaps or weaknesses and improve their response to security incidents. This minimizes the impact of security breaches and facilitates a Swift recovery. Companies need to make sure they follow regulations to protect their supply chain and keep their data secure.

Collaborating and sharing information with other organizations, industry partners, and government agencies can enhance the security of the supply chain ecosystem. By sharing threat intelligence and best practices, organizations can stay ahead of potential threats and mitigate risks effectively. In conclusion, a holistic and proactive approach is necessary for effective supply chain security. This involves collaboration among all stakeholders in the supply chain, addressing both digital and physical security aspects. Implementing these strategies helps organizations minimize the impact of security breaches and enhance the resilience and security of their supply chains.

Cyber Security Policies

Policies are created and enforced by governments, industry regulators, and international bodies to ensure a basic level of security across sectors. Without these policies, organizations would struggle to maintain the confidentiality, integrity, and availability of their information. One of the key aspects of cyber security policies and regulations is data protection and privacy laws. These regulations, such as GDPR and CCPA, set standards for the protection of personal data. They require organizations to implement measures to secure and responsibly handle personal information. This not only protects individuals' privacy but also helps prevent data breaches, which can have severe consequences for organizations. Another important aspect of cyber security policies is the use of frameworks. These frameworks, such as NIST, ISO/IEC, and CIS, provide guidelines and best practices for organizations to develop their cyber security policies. By following these frameworks, organizations can ensure that their policies are comprehensive and effective in addressing potential cyber threats.

Organizations must also consider industry-specific regulations when developing their cyber security policies. These regulations are tailored to address the unique risks and challenges faced by different industries. The financial sector follows rules like the Payment Card Industry Data Security Standard (PCI DSS) to safeguard sensitive financial data. Similarly, healthcare organizations must comply with the Health Insurance Portability and Accountability Act (HIPAA) to safeguard patient data. In addition to industry-specific regulations, there are incident reporting requirements that organizations must follow.

These requirements vary by jurisdiction but typically require organizations to report cyber security incidents promptly. This is important to make sure authorities can respond well to incidents and organizations can take the right actions to reduce the impact. Governments also play a significant role in developing cyber security policies through national and regional strategies. These strategies are comprehensive and encompass a range of policies, initiatives, and collaborations to enhance cyber security at a national level. Additionally, there are specific regulations focused on protecting critical infrastructure, such as energy, transportation, and telecommunications. These regulations aim to safeguard essential services from cyber threats that could have a significant societal impact. Finally, organizations must also have robust identity and access management (IAM) policies in place. These policies outline how organizations manage user identities, access controls, and authentication mechanisms to prevent unauthorized access and ensure appropriate permissions for users.

Organizations need remote work and BYOD (Bring Your Own Device) policies to protect devices, networks, and data used outside the office. These policies focus on issues such as device security, secure connections, and data protection. With the increasing adoption of cloud services, organizations also implement policies to address the secure use of cloud computing. These may include guidelines for data storage, encryption, and contractual agreements with cloud service providers. Organizations need vulnerability management policies to find, evaluate, and fix vulnerabilities in their systems and applications. Regular vulnerability assessments and patch management are often emphasized in these policies. Data protection is essential for cybersecurity. Regulations and policies may require organizations to use encryption to safeguard sensitive data. Encryption policies control the use of encryption algorithms, key management practices, and data protection during transmission and storage. Furthermore, organizations may establish policies regarding penetration testing and red teaming activities to assess the effectiveness of their cybersecurity defenses. These policies outline the scope, methods, and reporting requirements for such testing. Regular penetration testing and red teaming help organizations find and fix system weaknesses before they can be exploited by cyber threats. Robust policies are crucial for organizations to protect themselves from cyber threats and prevent societal impacts.

Supply chain security policies are crucial given the interconnected nature of supply chains. Organizations should have guidelines for assessing and mitigating cybersecurity risks within their supply chains. These policies should cover aspects such as vendor risk management, incident response and recovery, and disaster recovery planning. Employee training and awareness programs are an integral part of an organization's cybersecurity policies. These policies emphasize the need for staff to be educated about cybersecurity. They also provide guidelines on being aware of phishing, practicing secure behavior, and reporting security incidents. Regular training and awareness programs help employees stay updated on the latest cyber threats and best practices to prevent them. Regulatory compliance audits are a necessary aspect of cybersecurity policies. Regulations often require organizations to undergo periodic audits to assess their compliance with cybersecurity requirements. Internal or external audits help organizations find security gaps. Policies addressing cross-border data transfers are essential for organizations that operate on an international scale. These policies ensure that organizations comply with legal requirements when transferring data across international borders. This includes adherence to data protection laws and international agreements to protect sensitive information. Encouraging collaboration and information sharing is another critical element of cybersecurity policies. Governments and industry bodies promote the sharing of threat intelligence to enhance collective defense against cyber threats. It helps organizations know about security threats and encourages cybersecurity awareness and cooperation within organizations and industries.

Crime

a) Cyber Espionage is a serious threat that involves unauthorized access to sensitive information. It is often carried out by state-sponsored actors, criminal organizations, or other entities with malicious intent. These actors have the goal of gathering intelligence and gaining a competitive advantage.

Technological measures such as firewalls, encryption, and intrusion detection systems are essential in protecting against cyber espionage. However, they are not enough on their own. Effective policy frameworks that outline security protocols and procedures must also be in place. Ongoing vigilance is also critical, as the threat landscape is constantly evolving. Regular security assessments and updates to defences are necessary to stay ahead of potential cyber espionage attempts. By implementing a comprehensive approach, organizations can better protect themselves against cyber espionage and safeguard sensitive information.

Organizations must prioritize maintaining strong cyber hygiene practices to effectively protect themselves against the ever-evolving scene of cyber espionage. This includes regularly updating software and implementing a robust patch management system to address any known vulnerabilities. Additionally, utilizing strong and unique passwords is crucial in preventing cyber attacks that rely on weak or reused credentials. However, simply implementing these measures is not enough. Ongoing vigilance is key to staying ahead of potential cyber espionage attempts. Regular security assessments and updates to defences are necessary to identify and address any new or emerging threats.

This also involves staying informed about the latest tactics and techniques used by cyber criminals and adapting defences accordingly. By focusing on cyber security, organizations can protect their information and reduce the risks of cyber threats. This includes following good cyber hygiene practices, investing in advanced security solutions, and regularly updating defences. With this proactive approach, organizations can better protect themselves against the ever-present threat of cyber espionage.

Implementing network segmentation is an effective way for organizations to further protect their sensitive information against cyber espionage. By dividing the network into smaller segments, it limits the ability for attackers to move laterally and access valuable data. This adds an extra layer of defence to the organization's cyber security strategy. In addition to network segmentation, deploying advanced endpoint security solutions is crucial in mitigating the risks of cyber espionage. These solutions include antivirus software, intrusion detection systems, and endpoint detection and response (EDR) tools.

These technologies work together to detect and prevent malware, which is a common tool used in cyber espionage attacks. Regularly updating and assessing these defences is essential to stay ahead of evolving threats. Investing in these measures may require resources, but it is necessary to protect against cyber espionage.

Today, organizations need to always protect themselves from cyber espionage and improve their defences to outsmart attackers. To achieve this, organizations must implement strong cyber hygiene practices and utilize advanced security solutions. One way to safeguard sensitive information is by using encryption to protect data both in transit and at rest. This security measure ensures that unauthorized access to the data will not make sense without the decryption keys. By utilizing encryption, organizations can greatly reduce the risk of their sensitive information falling into the wrong hands.

Organizations should prioritize the use of encryption to protect sensitive data from falling into the wrong hands. This adds extra protection to important information and can help lessen the impact of a successful cyber espionage attempt. To protect against cyber espionage, organizations should use regular training, advanced security solutions, and encryption. They should also regularly review and update their security protocols to stay ahead of evolving cyber espionage tactics. Regular security training for employees can help them identify suspicious activities and prevent social engineering attacks.

Implementing advanced security solutions such as intrusion detection and prevention systems, firewalls, and security information and event management (SEEM) can help detect and prevent cyber espionage attempts in real-time.

Another important measure to protect sensitive information is to ensure the security of the supply chain. This includes thoroughly vetting suppliers, validating the integrity of software and hardware, and implementing secure procurement practices. By doing so, organizations can prevent the insertion of malicious components or software into their infrastructure. Cyber attackers often use weaknesses in a company's supply chain to hack into their systems and steal important data. Collaborating with international partners, law enforcement agencies, and cyber security organizations to share information and coordinate efforts against cyber espionage campaigns.

Legal measures can provide a framework for prosecuting cyber espionage activities and holding perpetrators accountable. It is important to establish clear guidelines for how sensitive data should be stored, accessed, and shared within an organization. This helps prevent data breaches and ensures employees know how to handle sensitive information. Having legal measures in place can deter potential cyber espionage activities by imposing consequences on those caught engaging in such behavior. Implement continuous monitoring of networks and systems to detect and respond to cyber threats in real-time.

A robust incident response plan helps organizations swiftly contain and mitigate the impact of a cyber espionage incident.

b) Financial Fraud. Online banking scheme is a huge concern in today's digital age. With the convenience of online banking, there comes a risk of unauthorized access to personal accounts. This can happen in different ways, like phishing attacks. Fraudsters send fake emails or messages pretending to be from a bank and trick individuals into revealing their login information.

Hackers can steal money by getting access to account credentials and using them to steal money from unsuspecting victims. The consequences of online banking fraud can be devastating for individuals and businesses alike. It can cause financial losses and harm a bank's reputation and trust with customers. Banks and customers must be careful to prevent and discover fraud. Banks must invest in secure technology and constantly update their security measures to stay ahead of fraudsters and customers should always be careful and attentive when accessing their accounts online, making sure they are on a secure and legitimate website.

Despite the efforts to prevent it, online banking fraud continues to be a major issue. With the advancement of technology, fraudsters are constantly finding new ways to exploit vulnerabilities in online banking systems. People should learn about different types of online banking fraud and be vigilant for any suspicious activity. By working together and staying aware, we can help combat online banking fraud and protect our financial information.

c) Identity Theft is a serious issue that has been on the rise in recent years. As more personal information is shared online, it's easier for criminals to access our private information. This can happen in a number of ways, including through personal information theft and identity spoofing.

These two forms of identity theft are often used together to carry out fraudulent activities.

- Personal information theft involves the unauthorized access to personal information, such as Social Security numbers, addresses, and birthdates. This information can be obtained in different ways, like phishing scams, data breaches, or physical theft. If a criminal gets this information, they can use it to open credit accounts, make purchases, or even apply for loans in the victim's name. This can result in serious financial consequences for the victim and can also damage their credit score.

- Identity spoofing, on the other hand, involves pretending to be someone else online for fraudulent purposes. This can involve making fake social media profiles, sending scam emails, or creating fake websites to trick people into giving away their personal information. This type of identity theft can also lead to financial loss and can also damage the victim's reputation. It's important to be careful when sharing personal information online and to monitor our accounts regularly for any suspicious activity. To avoid falling victim to identity theft, it is important to know about these different methods of fraud.

d) Phishing and Social engineering is a common form of cyber attack where deception is used to obtain sensitive information. These attacks are designed to appear authentic, making it difficult for users to detect the fraudulent nature.

The intention is to deceive users into sharing personal, financial, or login information that can later be used for malicious purposes. Opening attachments, clicking on links, or providing personal details can all lead to becoming a victim of a phishing attack.

Social engineering is another technique used by cybercriminals to exploit sensitive information. It involves manipulating individuals into giving away confidential data or performing actions that can be exploited. This can include posing as a trusted source or using psychological tactics to gain the trust of the victim. It's possible to use different tactics, including: building a good relationship, making things seem urgent or pretending to be someone important. Social engineering attacks aim to obtain sensitive information, like login credentials or financial data, for fraudulent purposes. These cyber attacks can have serious consequences, including identity theft, financial loss, and damage to a company's reputation.

e) Malware and Ransom ware. There are many different types of malware, each designed with a specific purpose in mind. Some malware is created to destroy computer systems, while others are designed to steal sensitive information. The most common types of malware include viruses, worms, and trojan horses. These malicious programs can infect devices and cause significant damage if not detected and removed promptly.

Ransom ware is a particularly nasty type of malware that has become increasingly popular in recent years. It works by encrypting files or entire systems, rendering them inaccessible to the user. The creators of ransom ware then demand payment in order to release the encrypted data. This type of attack is especially dangerous for businesses and organizations that rely on their data for day-to-day operations. Ransom ware attacks can cause big financial losses and harm a company's reputation if not stopped fast and well.

In today's digital age, strong cyber security measures are vital to protect against malware and ransom ware attacks. This involves updating software and systems regularly, using firewalls and antivirus programs, and teaching users how to recognize and avoid possible threats.

f) Hacking and Unauthorized access are two of the most dangerous threats that people face in today's digital world. The advancement of technology has made it easier for people to access systems and networks without proper authorization.

This unauthorized access can lead to serious consequences, such as identity theft or financial fraud. Additionally, hackers can exploit this access to gather personal information or cause harm to individuals, companies, or governments.

One of the main ways hackers gain unauthorized access is through Denial-of-Service (DoS) attacks. These attacks overload systems with a lot of traffic, making it difficult for legitimate users to access them. This can be incredibly disruptive for businesses or organizations that rely on their systems for daily operations. Hackers can use DoS attacks as a distraction to access sensitive information while the system is busy dealing with the attack. To protect against these threats, it is crucial to have strong security measures in place.

g) Harassment and cyber bullying have become rampant in today's digital world, causing serious mental and emotional harm to victims. Social media has made online harassment more common, making it easier for bullies to target their victims. Harassment can take various forms, including unwanted messages, threats, or stalking. It can happen through any digital medium, such as emails, texts, or social media platforms.

The internet's anonymity has made harassers braver, making it easier for them to use fake identities and harm others. Victims of online harassment are often left feeling violated, helpless, and fearful, and the effects can be long-lasting. Cyber bullying, on the other hand, specifically targets individuals with harmful or intimidating messages, often on social media. It causes emotional distress and serious consequences on the victim's mental health, including depression, anxiety, and suicidal thoughts. Cyber bullying can be terrible, since more people can see it and it can really hurt the victim's reputation and confidence.

h) Cybercriminals networks are organized groups of individuals collaborating in illegal digital activities. These networks are typically motivated by financial gain, political objectives, or other malicious purposes. Cybercriminals often work together to share resources, expertise, and tools, making their activities more sophisticated and challenging to combat.

Technology advances and law enforcement agencies fight cybercriminal networks, but criminals also evolve to find new ways to operate. This makes it extremely difficult for authorities to completely dismantle these networks. In order to effectively combat cybercrime, international cooperation and information sharing are decisive.

Cyber security awareness is also important in preventing and identifying cybercriminal activities. Law enforcement agencies and professionals have to work hand in hand to stay on top of cybercriminal networks. They constantly identify, investigate, and prosecute individuals involved in these networks. The fight against cybercrime is a continuous battle because these networks keep adapting and finding new ways to exploit technology for their own benefit. This requires a continuous effort from authorities to stay ahead of these criminals. Besides working together and sharing information, it's crucial for individuals and organizations to remain alert and informed about cyber security risks.

Common types of cybercriminal networks:

a) Hacker groups are highly organized communities of people with extraordinary technical abilities. These groups are known for breaking the law, such as exploiting weaknesses, spying online, and causing chaos with disruptive attacks. They usually operate under the radar and are difficult to track down. One of the most notorious hacker groups is Anonymous. This group is well-known for their various activities, including hacking government agencies, corporations, and other organizations. They are famous for participating in social and political causes, using their abilities to uncover corruption and injustice. Another well-known group is Lizard Squad. This group gained notoriety for their involvement in the Christmas Day attack on Sony's PlayStation Network. Others operates worldwide like: Chaos Computer Club (CCC) – Germany, L0pht Heavy Industries – USA, Cult of the Dead Cow (cDc) – USA, Lazarus Group – North Korea, APT28 / Fancy Bear – Russia, APT29 / Cozy Bear – Russia, REvil (Ransomware Group) – Russia-linked, Conti Group – Eastern Europe, Lizard Squad – Global, Team Xecuter , The Shadow Brokers – Unknown origin

They are known for their disruptive activities that aim to cause chaos and harm to organizations and individuals. One of the biggest threats to cyber security today is the existence of APT groups, or Advanced Persistent Threats. These groups are highly sophisticated and often state-sponsored, making them highly dangerous.

They use advanced technical skills to conduct cyber espionage and steal sensitive information from government agencies, corporations, and other organizations. They are almost impossible to detect and can cause significant damage to their victims.

b) Botnets are a threat to the security of the internet. They are created by cybercriminals who use them to launch massive coordinated attacks. These attacks may be aimed at gathering sensitive data, spreading malware, or disrupting services.

To achieve this, cybercriminals take control of a large number of computers, known as bots or zombies, through malicious software. These bots can then be used to carry out malicious activities without the owners' knowledge. The criminals behind botnets are constantly evolving their tactics to stay ahead of security systems. They use various techniques to infect devices and create new bots. These techniques range from social engineering to using vulnerabilities in software.

c) Online forums and marketplaces on the deep web or encrypted platforms are gaining popularity as cybercriminals use them to trade hacking tools, stolen data, and other illegal services due to the growth of digital technology.

These forums and marketplaces serve as hubs for cybercriminals to exchange information, services, and goods. This underground market is largely unregulated, making it a safe haven for cybercriminals to operate in anonymity.

One of the most popular items on common dark net forums and marketplaces is hacking tools. Cybercriminals use these tools to gain unauthorized access to computer systems and networks. The stolen data acquired through these tools is then sold at a high price on the dark net. Being watched by Law enforcement in Dark net they moved to the deep web.

This creates a profitable cycle for cybercriminals who are often looking for quick and easy ways to make money. The dark net marketplace is also a haven for the buying and selling of stolen data. This can range from personal information such as credit card numbers and social security numbers to sensitive corporate data. This data is often sold in bulk, making it easier for cybercriminals to make a profit.

d) Hackers create and spread ransom ware to make money by disrupting the systems of people, companies, and organizations. This helps them offer their services to less skilled cybercriminals who cannot create and launch ransom ware attacks on their own. Ransom ware is a type of malicious software that encrypts a person's data and demands money in exchange for the decryption key.

This enables hackers to make a profit while their clients carry out the actual attack. Ransom ware attacks are more common and advanced, with hackers always finding new ways to take advantage of system and network weaknesses. The attacks are not just about money; they can also be used for spying or sabotage. By offering ransom ware as a service, hackers can reach a wider audience and increase their chances of success. This also helps them improve their techniques continuously, making it harder for cyber security experts to defend against these attacks.

Ransom ware as a service has made it easier for cybercriminals to launch widespread attacks and profit from them. The situation has also created an underground market where hackers can trade ransom ware, tools, and services for carrying out these attacks. Law enforcement has a hard time catching and punishing these criminals because they can work without revealing their identity and from anywhere in the world.

e) Groups involved in carding activities often have a complex network of transactions and dealings. These groups are often organized by location, and may have multiple hubs of activity in different regions. Despite being organized, these groups are hard to trace because they operate covertly and employ different methods to conceal their activities.

The people involved in these activities range from low-level scammers to high-level criminal organizations. Criminals use different ways to get credit card information, like phishing scams, hacking, or theft. Once obtained, the information can be traded, sold on the dark web, or used for fraudulent transactions.

The impact of carding activities can be devastating for individuals and businesses alike. Not only does it result in financial losses, but it also compromises personal information and can lead to identity theft. Authorities are always trying to fight against these groups, but it can be a tough battle due to their advanced techniques and always changing strategies.

f) Nation-states or state-sponsored groups are known to engage in a multitude of activities for political, economic, and military purposes. These activities range from cyber espionage, cyber warfare, and other disruptive cyber activities. These secret actions aim to gain an advantage over other nations or groups. In recent years, cyber espionage has become a prevalent issue in the world of international relations. Cyber espionage helps nations gather important information without the risk of physical conflict.

Non-state actors also engage in such activities, not just state-sponsored groups. This has led to a growing concern among nations, as it poses a threat to national security and sovereignty. However, it is important to note that not all cyber activities are malicious in nature. Many nation-states also engage in cyber activities for defensive purposes, in order to protect their own networks and systems. This is especially true for those nations that are technologically advanced, as they are more susceptible to cyber attacks.

g) Phishing groups are known for creating fake emails, websites, or messages to trick people. These groups are known to target a wide range of people, from regular internet users to high-profile organizations. Their main aim is to deceive people and make them share private information, like login details, credit card numbers, or personal identification details. One of the most alarming aspects of phishing gangs is their ability to constantly evolve and adapt their techniques. They are constantly on the lookout for new ways to manipulate their victims and stay ahead of security measures. This makes it incredibly challenging for individuals and organizations to protect themselves against these attacks.

h) Crypto currency has become a popular form of digital currency worldwide. Crypto currency's decentralized nature makes it hard to regulate, which makes it popular for fraud and money laundering. Illegal activities are successful because of specific networks designed for them. These networks consist of technology experts with the skills to navigate the complex crypto currency world. These networks collaborate with each other to carry out fraud in a sophisticated and organized manner. They use different methods to deceive, manipulate, and steal from unsuspecting individuals who are investing in crypto currency. Many of these networks are based in countries with weak regulations and are constantly evolving their techniques to avoid detection. As a result, it has become increasingly difficult to track and stop these networks from carrying out their illegal activities.

i) Groups affiliated with nation-states conduct cyber espionage activities, which could include stealing intellectual property, political intelligence, or military secrets. Espionage is a growing and risky strategy that countries use to obtain classified information from other nations. Cyber espionage is not only limited to state-sponsored groups, but also includes private organizations and individuals. The activities are targeted and planned to access sensitive data without being detected. However, these attacks can have a significant impact on governments, industries, and individuals.

Cyber spying can lead to loss of sensitive data, compromise of important infrastructure, and disruption of national security. As technology continues to advance, so do the methods used for cyber espionage. This includes the use of malware, phishing scams, and other sophisticated tactics to gain access to networks and systems. It is important for organizations and governments to stay alert and enhance their cyber security to defend against such attacks. Successful cyber espionage attacks can have devastating consequences. It is crucial to always stay ahead of those trying to infiltrate and steal valuable information.

j) Cyber activities have become a popular tool for collectives to express their political or social beliefs. These activities often involve hacktivism, which uses hacking for activism, and DDoS attacks to disrupt websites and online services.

Different groups have used these strategies to raise awareness about topics like climate change, social justice, and corruption. Hacktivism has become an effective way for collectives to express their opinions and make their voices heard. By hacking into websites or computer systems, they can expose sensitive information or deface websites to send a message. This type of activism has been used by groups like

Anonymous have targeted governments and corporations to protest against their actions and policies. On the other hand, DDoS attacks have been utilized by collectives to disrupt online platforms and services. By overloading websites with traffic, they can effectively take them down, causing inconvenience and financial damage. Overall, cyber activities have become an effective form of protest for collectives to promote their political or social agendas. Some may think these actions are controversial and illegal, but they have been effective in raising awareness and drawing attention to important issues. It is important, however, for these groups to use these tactics responsibly and ethically.

Internet of Things – IOT

The Internet of Things, or IoT, has completely changed the way technology is seen in daily lives. From smart phone to industrial automation and industrial automation, IoT has opened up endless possibilities for improving efficiency and functionality. One of the key components of IoT is the use of sensors. These sensors are embedded in various devices and are responsible for collecting and transmitting data in real-time.

This data can then be analyzed to gain valuable insights and make informed decisions. With the help of IoT, industries can optimize their processes, reduce costs, and improve productivity. Smart factories to connected supply chains, IoT has revolutionized the way businesses operate. It has enabled real-time monitoring and control of machines, allowing for increased efficiency and reduced downtime.

One major area where IoT has made a significant impact is in the field of predictive maintenance. By utilizing sensors and data analytics, machines can now self-diagnose and predict when they will require maintenance or replacement. This has resulted in huge cost savings for companies, as they are able to avoid unexpected breakdowns and costly repairs. IoT enables manufacturers to monitor their products remotely, detecting and solving problems proactively.

Another exciting application of IoT in the industrial world is the use of drones for monitoring and inspection purposes. Drones with sensors and cameras are useful for inspecting large or inaccessible areas, providing important data for maintenance and repairs. In addition, they can be used to monitor environmental conditions and detect potential hazards, enhancing workplace safety.

The interconnected network of devices and people has opened up endless possibilities for innovation and convenience. With IoT, we can remotely monitor our homes, track our fitness, and even automate mundane tasks. As more and more devices are connected, the amount of data being collected and shared is increasing exponentially. This raises questions about who has access to this data and how it is being used. Given the risk of hacking and data breaches, it's crucial to have proper measures in place to safeguard our personal information.

1- Q-learning is a well-known and popular algorithm in the field of reinforcement learning. This algorithm is commonly used by agents to make decisions in an environment in order to maximize a cumulative reward. It is commonly used in different situations where an agent takes actions in a state space to achieve a goal.

One of the main advantages of Q-learning is its ability to learn from experiences and improve its decisions over time. The concept of Q-learning is based on the principle of trial and error. The agent takes different actions in a given state and observes the corresponding rewards. The agent updates its Q-values using this information. Q-values represent the expected rewards for each action in a specific state. The Q-values are updated until the agent learns the best policy for the maximum cumulative reward. Once this optimal policy is learned, the agent can make decisions more efficiently and effectively in the given environment. In addition, Q-learning can handle complex environments with a large state space and a high number of possible actions. This makes it suitable for various real-world applications, such as robotics, gaming, and finance.

Q-learning has significantly advanced artificial intelligence by enabling the development of intelligent agents that can learn and make decisions independently. With its potential for solving complex decision-making problems, the impact of Q-learning is expected to continue growing in the future.

2 - MMTC, or Molecular Communication for the Internet of Things, is a new technology that could change the way we communicate in the future. By using molecules as carriers for information, MMTC enables devices to communicate with each other at the nano scale level. This means that even the smallest of devices, such as sensors and actuators, can exchange information and work together seamlessly. The use of molecules as carriers for information is not a new concept. In fact, it has been used by living organisms for millions of years to communicate and coordinate their actions. With nanotechnology advancements, scientists can use natural phenomena to create better IoT communication systems.

This has opened up new possibilities for applications in areas such as healthcare, environmental monitoring, and smart cities. MMTC has an advantage over traditional wireless communication methods, like electromagnetic waves. These traditional methods are not suitable for communication at the nano scale level, as the wavelength of electromagnetic waves is too large to interact with nano scale devices. By using molecules instead, MMTC can achieve reliable and efficient communication even in complex and dynamic environments. With the continued development and implementation of MMTC, the future of the IoT looks brighter than ever before.

3 - Deep Reinforcement Learning learn by trial and error. This method is very effective for solving complex problems in fields like robotics and gaming. The integration of deep neural networks with Q-learning, known as DRL, has been particularly impactful in this field. A famous DRL technique is Deep Q Networks (DQN). It has been successful in managing complicated state spaces and enhancing agents' learning performance. Combining deep neural networks and Q-learning allows the agent to handle large amounts of data, extract relevant features, and make decisions based on a reward system.

Overall, the integration of deep neural networks with Q-learning has opened up new possibilities for problem-solving in various industries. This combination helps decision-making to be more efficient and effective, allowing advancements in fields like autonomous vehicles and artificial intelligence.

4 - **Transfer learning** is a powerful technique that greatly improves the efficiency of machine learning. By training a model on a specific task, it can then be easily adapted to related tasks. This is especially helpful in MMTC (Multimedia Multimodal Task Computing) scenarios, where there are many different tasks and data types. Transfer learning enables a model to use its existing knowledge to learn new tasks faster and more accurately, instead of starting from scratch each time.

One of the key benefits of transfer learning is its ability to adapt to new tasks. The model has been previously trained on a related task, providing a strong foundation for further development. Through this process, the model can quickly learn the nuances of the new task while still maintaining its previous knowledge. This saves time and improves performance by allowing the model to better understand the data. Transfer learning is also crucial in MMTC scenarios, where there is a vast amount of diverse data. By using transfer learning, models can improve understanding of relationships between different data types and tasks, leading to more accurate predictions. This is crucial in fields like computer vision and natural language processing, where the data can be complex and diverse.

5 - Meta-learning

Meta-learning is a type of machine learning that focuses on training models to learn how to learn. This is achieved by developing algorithms that can learn from experience and adapt to new tasks and environments quickly. Meta-learning is very popular in artificial intelligence because it can greatly improve machine learning performance. One major benefit of meta-learning is its ability to quickly adapt to new environments.

This is particularly useful in scenarios where the environment is constantly changing, such as robotics or self-driving cars. Meta-learning algorithms can learn from experiences and use that knowledge in new situations, enabling good performance even in unfamiliar environments. Another advantage of meta-learning is its potential to improve the performance of machine learning models. By training models to learn how to learn, they can become more efficient at picking up patterns and making predictions, resulting in better performance. This has significant implications for a wide range of applications, including natural language processing, computer vision, and predictive modelling.

6 - Multiple Machine Learning (ML) technologies into a single system. One way is to use an ensemble technique, which combines different ML models to make more accurate predictions. Another method is through transfer learning, where a pre-trained ML model is fine-tuned for a specific task. Additionally, federated learning allows for the training of ML models across multiple devices without sharing sensitive data. These are just a few examples of how multiple ML technologies can be integrated to achieve better results. One of the main benefits of integrating different ML technologies is the ability to handle complex and diverse data types. For example, a system may need to process both structured and unstructured data, such as text, images, and videos. By combining various ML models, the system can better handle the different data types and make more accurate predictions. This is very useful in applications like natural language processing, where various ML techniques can be applied for tasks such as sentiment analysis, text classification, and named entity recognition.

Another advantage of integrating multiple ML technologies is the potential for faster and more efficient training. You can distribute the workload among multiple models instead of relying on just one model. This will decrease the total training time. This is especially important in time-sensitive applications where real-time predictions are required. Using different ML technologies together can produce better results, as each model may perform well in different areas. This can help reduce bias and improve the overall accuracy of the system.

- **Supervised Learning** is an important step in training machine learning models. It refers to the process of training the model using labelled data. This helps the model to gain an understanding of the data and its characteristics. The model learns to recognize patterns and makes predictions based on the data. The labelled data provides the model with the ground truth to learn from. For most machine learning models, reinforcement learning is the next step. In this step, the model learns from its own mistakes and improves its predictions over time. But before the model can start learning from its own decisions, it needs to have a solid foundation.

This is where supervised learning comes in. It prepares the model by providing it with a basic understanding of the data and its features. This pre-training process is crucial for the success of the model in reinforcement learning. In conclusion, supervised learning is an essential step in training machine learning models. It sets a strong foundation for the model to learn from and improves the accuracy of its predictions. By using labelled data, the model gains an understanding of the data and learns to recognize patterns. This allows the model to make more accurate predictions when it moves on to reinforcement learning.

The model needs supervised learning to understand the data and get better at making predictions.

- **Clustering**, a popular unsupervised learning technique can be used to identify hidden patterns in molecular communication. By grouping molecules into distinct clusters, scientists can better understand their behaviour and potential interactions. Another technique, dimensionality reduction, is particularly useful when working with large datasets. It identifies the most important features of molecules for communication, helping researchers focus on relevant information.

Both of these methods can provide valuable insights into the complex world of molecular communication. In addition to providing a better understanding of molecular communication, these techniques can also aid in drug discovery and development. By identifying clusters of molecules that have similar properties, scientists can potentially find new drug candidates that target specific pathways. This can lead to the development of more effective and targeted treatments for diseases. Dimensionality reduction helps by identifying the most important features of molecules, making it easier to find potential drug targets. Furthermore, these unsupervised learning techniques have the potential to revolutionize the way we study and understand molecular communication.

By discovering hidden patterns and connections, researchers can find new areas of study and make important discoveries. As technology and data advance, they will become more important in understanding molecular communication and its role in biological processes.

- **Ensemble Learning** is a powerful technique that has been widely used in machine learning. It involves combining predictions from multiple models to enhance overall system robustness and performance. Different models have different strengths and weaknesses. By combining them, we can create a more accurate prediction. Ensemble Learning is very helpful for complex and noisy data sets where a single model may struggle to capture all the patterns and relationships in the data.

One of the most popular Ensemble Learning methods is called "bagging", which stands for "bootstrap aggregating." This method involves training multiple models on different subsets of the data and then combining their predictions.

Another popular method is called "boosting", which involves training models sequentially, with each new model focusing on the data points that were previously misclassified. This approach helps to improve the overall performance of the system by giving more weight to the hard-to-predict data points.

Ensemble Learning has become a staple in many machine learning applications, including image and speech recognition, natural language processing, and even in finance and healthcare.

By combining the strengths of multiple models, Ensemble Learning has been shown to outperform single models and improve the overall accuracy and robustness of the system. However, it is important to note that Ensemble Learning is not a magic bullet and requires careful selection and combination of models to achieve optimal results.

- **Explainable AI** (XAI) has become increasingly important in modern machine learning. With the emergence of deep learning, black box models have become more prevalent and have revolutionized the field. However, with this advancement comes the challenge of understanding the decisions made by these models. This is particularly important in sensitive scenarios, such as molecular communication, where the stakes are high and the consequences of incorrect decisions can be catastrophic.

The concept of XAI aims to address this issue by providing transparency and interpretability to the decision-making process of machine learning models. By doing so, not only can we gain a better understanding of how these models work, but we can also identify potential biases and errors that may exist within the system. This is especially important in sensitive domains like molecular communication, where even the smallest mistakes can have serious consequences. One of the key goals of XAI is to bridge the gap between human and machine understanding. By providing explanations for the decisions made by the model, XAI allows us to trust and rely on these complex systems more confidently.

This is essential in sensitive scenarios like molecular communication, where the decisions made by the model can have a direct impact on human lives. By expanding our understanding of XAI, we can ensure the safe and responsible use of AI in critical domains.

As the field of molecular communication continues to advance, researchers have encountered new and complex challenges. One such challenge is the presence of molecular noise, which can greatly affect the accuracy and reliability of the communication system. Noise can originate from different sources, like chemical reactions and diffusion processes. Dealing with it can be particularly challenging in a changing environment. Researchers are always developing new ways to reduce molecular noise and enhance the system's performance. In addition to dealing with molecular noise, there is also a need for highly efficient communication protocols in molecular communication. This is because molecules have limited resources and can only carry a certain amount of information. Therefore, it is crucial to design protocols that can effectively utilize these resources and transmit information efficiently.

The environment can affect molecular communication performance. When designing communication protocols, researchers should consider environmental factors like temperature changes, pH levels, and the presence of other molecules. Despite these challenges, researchers are constantly pushing the boundaries of what is possible in the field of molecular communication.

They are using artificial intelligence and machine learning to improve communication systems. Breakthroughs bring us closer to using molecular communication for drug delivery, environmental monitoring, and nanotechnology. One of the key developments in IoT is the concept of edge measurement. This refers to collecting and analyzing data at the edge of a network, instead of sending it all to a central location.

This not only helps to reduce network congestion, but also allows for more efficient and real-time decision-making. With so many connected devices and systems, cyber-security has become a major concern. As the number of IoT devices continues to grow, so does the potential for cyber attacks and breaches.

A Cyber attack

Advanced Persistent Threats (APTs) are known for their long-term and persistent nature. These cyber attacks are not conducted on a whim, but are rather the result of thorough planning and execution. Cyber attackers often employ complex techniques and specialized tools to gain access to and hide within targeted computer systems for a long time. This allows them to achieve their objectives, which could range from data extraction to espionage or even disruption of operations.

One of the key characteristics of APTs is their advanced tactics, techniques, and procedures (TTPs). These are carefully designed to stealthily infiltrate and remain undetected within targeted systems. This requires a high level of skill and expertise from the threat actors, as well as significant funding.

APTs are not the work of individual hackers, but rather well-organized and well-funded groups with specific objectives and motivations. It is important to note that APTs are not random attacks, but rather have specific targets and objectives. This is why they exhibit a high level of sophistication in their planning and execution. Threat actors often have a deep understanding of their target's systems and use this knowledge to bypass security measures and avoid - APTs are highly targeted attacks that are carried out by skilled threat actors. These attacks are not random and are instead planned and executed with a specific objective in mind. As a result, the level of sophistication in these attacks is much higher compared to other types of cyber threats.

The primary reason why APTs are so difficult to detect is because of their tailored nature. Since threat actors have a deep understanding of the target's systems, they can bypass security measures and avoid detection. This makes it challenging for organizations to protect themselves against APT's. Threat actors are always changing their methods, which makes it harder for regular security measures to stop their attacks. One of the key factors that contribute to the success of APTs is the use of social engineering tactics.

Threat actors often use social engineering to gain access to a target's network or systems. This can include phishing emails, fake websites, or even physical infiltration. By manipulating human behaviour, threat actors can exploit vulnerabilities and gain access to sensitive information. Organizations need to invest in robust security measures and educate their employees on how to identify and avoid social engineering attacks. This makes APTs particularly dangerous, as they can cause significant damage or loss of sensitive information before being detected.

During a cyber attack, mobilization is vital in mitigating the impact of the threat and restoring normalcy. It involves a coordinated and organized response from individuals, organizations, and government agencies. This response is essential in minimizing the damage caused by the cyber threat and recovering from the attack.

One of the key aspects of mobilization during a cyber attack is communication. It's important to communicate effectively so that everyone knows what's going on and can work together towards a shared goal. This includes sharing information about the attack, coordinating response efforts, and providing updates on the progress of the restoration process. Without clear and consistent communication, mobilization efforts can become chaotic and ineffective.

Another important aspect of mobilization is having a well-defined plan in place. The plan must define the roles and responsibilities of each party involved and include the necessary steps to reduce the impact of the cyber attack. A well-prepared and practiced plan can greatly improve the response to a cyber threat, minimizing the damage and expediting the recovery process. It also ensures that everyone involved knows what is expected of them, reducing confusion and allowing for a more efficient response.

An Incident Plan (IRP) is essential for preventing and mitigating the impact of cyber attacks. It is a detailed plan that outlines the necessary steps to be taken in case of a cyber attack. The plan should include well-defined roles and responsibilities, communication protocols, and technical measures to contain and eradicate the threat. The IRP should be regularly updated to ensure its effectiveness in handling any cyber attack. This includes conducting regular drills and simulations to test the plan and identify any areas of weakness. The plan should also be reviewed and updated based on the latest cyber threats and trends.

Having a well-defined IRP in place can significantly reduce the response time during a cyber attack minimizing the damage and financial loss to the organization. It also ensures that all employees are aware of their roles and responsibilities, leading to a coordinated and effective response. Furthermore, the communication protocols outlined in the plan ensure that all relevant parties are informed and involved in the response process. Overall, an IRP is crucial for organizations to have in place to effectively handle cyber attacks and protect their sensitive data and assets.

Communication Protocols are an integral part of any organization. It is essential to establish clear communication channels within the organization to ensure smooth functioning. Apart from this, communicating with external stakeholders is also vital. Transparency is the key to prompt communication. When there is transparency, affected parties can be informed of any changes or updates in a timely manner. This also helps in coordinating efforts and avoiding any confusion. Clear communication channels and transparency build trust and foster positive relationships. This not only benefits the organization but also its stakeholders. Furthermore, effective communication can help in resolving conflicts and avoiding misunderstandings. To sum it up, establishing communication protocols is crucial for any organization to function efficiently. It not only helps in sharing updates and coordinating efforts but also builds trust and fosters positive relationships. By following these protocols, organizations can ensure effective communication both within and outside the organization.

Collaboration is a key element when it comes to successful mobilization. It involves working together with different entities, such as government agencies, law enforcement, cyber security experts, and affected organizations. These organizations must establish pre-existing relationships and collaboration frameworks in order to respond quickly and effectively to any given situation. This allows for a cohesive and organized response that can help mitigate the impact of any potential threat. Collaboration is especially crucial in the world of cyber security, where the threat landscape is constantly evolving. In order to stay ahead of cyber attacks, it is essential for all relevant parties to work together and share information. Identifying risks and coordinating response after an attack.

Furthermore, collaboration helps build trust and understanding between different entities, which can be beneficial in the long run. In summary, collaboration plays a vital role in mobilization efforts. It enables different entities to work together and respond effectively to any given situation. By establishing pre-existing relationships and collaboration frameworks, organizations can ensure a faster and more efficient response to potential threats. Collaboration is essential in the ever-changing field of cybersecurity to stay ahead and protect against attacks.

In today's interconnected world, it's very important for organizations and government agencies to collaborate against cyber attacks. One key strategy to combat these threats is through information sharing. Organizations and agencies sharing threat intelligence and attack information helps identify patterns and attribution, leading to a better understanding of the threat scene.

A unified and effective response to cyber attacks can lead to a more secure cyber ecosystem. However, while information sharing is crucial, it is also important to do so responsibly. Organizations need to be careful with sensitive information and make sure to have the right protocols to protect it. Additionally, it is important to establish trusted channels for information sharing to avoid the dissemination of false or misleading information. By following these guidelines, information sharing can be a powerful tool in the fight against cyber threats.

Deploying technical measures is one of the key steps in mitigating cyber threats. These measures help to prevent the attack from spreading and causing further damage. Isolating affected systems is crucial in containing the attack and preventing it from spreading to other systems. It also allows for easier identification and removal of the threat. Applying patches is another important step in mitigating cyber threats. It helps to close any vulnerability that the attacker may have exploited and prevents future attacks. Implementing network security measures, such as firewalls and intrusion detection systems, is also crucial in protecting against cyber threats.

These measures can help to detect and block any malicious activity on the network, preventing the attack from spreading further. Rapid response is essential in containing the spread of a cyber attack. The longer it takes for the attack to be contained, the more damage it can cause. This is why it is important to have a well-defined response plan in place and to act quickly. The response team needs to quickly find the source of the attack and take appropriate action to stop it. They should also have the necessary tools and resources to respond effectively. Regular drills and simulations can help to ensure a rapid and effective response in the event of an actual attack.

In addition to technical measures, it is also important to have a comprehensive incident response plan in place. This plan should outline the roles and responsibilities of each team member, communication protocols, and recovery procedures. It should also include a post-attack analysis to identify areas for improvement and prevent similar attacks in the future. Organizations can better handle cyber threats and minimize their impact by using technical measures and having a defined incident response plan.

Forensic Analysis is a critical element in the world of investigative science. It is the process of examining and analyzing evidence in order to establish facts and support conclusions. This scientific approach is used to find the truth behind crimes and other incidents. Forensic Analysis is a multidisciplinary field that encompasses various sciences such as chemistry, biology, and physics. The use of Forensic Analysis has evolved over the years and has become an integral part of modern criminal investigations. It involves collecting, preserving, and analyzing evidence in a controlled and systematic manner to uncover the truth. This can range from examining fingerprints and DNA evidence to analyzing digital data and conducting ballistics tests.

Forensic analysis is used in non-criminal cases, like identifying natural disaster victims and determining accident causes. The accuracy and reliability of Forensic Analysis have made it an important tool in the justice system. It provides crucial evidence that can prove the guilt or innocence of a suspect and has helped solve countless cases. However, it is important to note that forensic analysis is not infallible and can be subject to human error. It is a constantly evolving field and new techniques and technologies are being developed to improve its effectiveness. Forensic analysis is crucial for pursuing justice and has a large impact on investigative science.

Conduct a thorough forensic analysis to understand the nature of the cyber attack, identify the entry point, and gather evidence. This information is essential for improving cyber security measures and, if applicable, for legal actions.

Cyber security incidents can have varying levels of impact depending on the nature of the attack. For this reason, it is essential to ensure that the response to these incidents complies with relevant laws and regulations. It's important to follow these legal requirements to reduce the impact of a cyber incident on the organization and its stakeholders. Organizations need to know the laws and regulations that apply to their industry and location in order to comply with them. This includes understanding reporting requirements and legal obligations that may differ depending on the severity of the incident. For example, a data breach may have different reporting requirements than a malware attack. It is imperative that organizations are aware of these differences and take appropriate action in accordance with the law. Failure to comply with these regulations can result in financial penalties, legal consequences, and reputational damage for the organization.

By sharing accurate information on time, the organization can show its dedication to fixing issues and improving its reputation among the public. In the age of social media, news and information spread fast. A single mistake can greatly affect an organization's reputation. Effective public relations can also help an organization navigate through crises and difficult situations. A solid PR strategy helps organizations manage the narrative and control information flow. This can help mitigate any potential damage to the organization's reputation and maintain the trust of the public.

Being transparent and open builds trust with the public. It shows that an organization is ready to acknowledge and resolve issues. This can go a long way in building a positive relationship with the public and ensuring the organization's long-term success. Public relations are important for managing crises and promoting organizations and their products or services. By effectively communicating the organization's message and values, PR professionals can help build brand awareness and generate positive publicity.

This can lead to increased trust and credibility in the eyes of the public, ultimately benefiting the organization's bottom line. A good public relations strategy is vital for any organization to succeed in today's competitive market and maintain a positive reputation.

After a big cyber attack, it's important to address the immediate threat and work on long-term recovery and resilience. We need to fix any affected systems and improve cyber security to avoid similar incidents in the future. This is important because cyber attacks are becoming increasingly common and can cause significant damage to businesses and organizations. One way to ensure recovery and resilience is by developing strategies that can minimize the impact of future attacks. This could involve regularly backing up important data, implementing multifactor authentication, and regularly updating software and systems.

Resilience strategies should consider both technical aspects and the human element. Train employees to identify and prevent cyber attacks. Promote a culture of cyber security in the organization. By involving all stakeholders, organizations can create a more comprehensive and effective resilience plan.

The attack

1 - Targets and Impact: Cyber security is an ever-growing concern, especially when it comes to critical infrastructure. In today's digital world, everything is connected and vulnerable to cyber attacks. These malicious attacks can come in many forms and can target various critical infrastructures, from power grids to financial institutions. Cyber attacks aim to disrupt vital services and create chaos, causing significant harm and potential loss of life.

-Power grids are a prime target for cyber attacks. Without electricity, our daily lives would come to a standstill.

- Transportation systems are also at risk, as they play a vital role in moving goods and people.

- Communication networks are another target, as they are essential for keeping people connected and informed.

- Financial institutions are also vulnerable, with the potential to cause significant economic damage.

Cybercriminals are now more advanced in their attacks. Critical infrastructure must have strong cyber security measures. Protecting critical infrastructure from cyber attacks is not an easy task. It requires constant vigilance, advanced technology, and skilled professionals. Organizations must invest in the latest cyber security tools and resources to safeguard their critical infrastructure against these threats.

Government agencies must also work together to develop and implement strict regulations and guidelines to secure critical infrastructure.

2 - Military systems are essential to the protection of a nation's people and territory. They are designed to ensure the strength and success of military operations. However, with the rise of technology, these systems have become increasingly vulnerable to attacks. In fact, attacks on military networks, command and control systems, and defence capabilities have become commonplace in recent years.

These attacks have had severe consequences, not only for the military, but for the nation as a whole. Compromising military systems not only affects operations, but also jeopardizes national safety and security. If a country's command and control system is attacked, it can cause chaos and confusion in the military, making it hard to coordinate and carry out operations effectively. This can lead to serious consequences, such as loss of life and territory. If a nation's defence capabilities are compromised, it becomes weaker in defending itself against external threats, making it vulnerable to potential attacks. Nations must prioritize protecting their military systems to ensure people's safety and security. To stay ahead of potential threats, it's crucial to keep updating and strengthening military systems due to the growing complexity of cyber attacks. Governments should invest in measures to prevent and reduce the impact of attacks on their military systems.

3 - Physical attacks

Not only the United States and its allies, but also the Japanese were involved in using electromagnetic interference (EMI) tactics during World War II. In fact, the Japanese were also utilizing these tactics in their own battles. This added an extra layer of complexity to the already intense conflict between the two nations. Japanese used EMI tactics to disrupt enemy communication and navigation systems, making it hard for them to coordinate and launch effective attacks. One of the most notable instances of the Japanese using EMI tactics was during the Battle of Midway. Japanese jammed American carriers' radio frequencies using high-frequency signals, hindering pilot communication and attack coordination. This caused confusion and disarray among the American forces, ultimately contributing to their defeat in the battle. This expansion reveals how the Japanese used EMI tactics in World War II and how it affected the outcome of specific battles. The use of EMI tactics by the Japanese was not limited to just communication and navigation systems. They used these tactics to disrupt radar and sonar systems, making it hard for the United States and its allies to find Japanese ships and submarines. This gave the Japanese a tactical advantage, allowing them to carry out surprise attacks on their enemies. The Japanese effectively used EMI tactics to help their military operations during World War II.

DDoS attacks aim to disrupt the availability of a website or service through a cyber attack. To perform this attack, a server is flooded with a high volume of traffic, causing it to crash or stop responding. Attacks are carried out by a network of hacked computers called a botnet, controlled by the attacker. DDoS attacks are a big worry for businesses and organizations because they can cause a lot of financial loss and harm their reputation. The deluge of traffic from botnets or compromised devices can be considered a form of cyber warfare. By flooding systems, attackers can cripple the infrastructure of an organization or a nation, causing chaos and confusion. This is especially concerning for government agencies, financial institutions, and large corporations, as they are prime targets for such attacks.

As the Internet of Things (IoT) grows, attackers can exploit more devices and use them for their botnets. This makes it even more challenging for organizations to defend against such attacks. Additionally, the tactics used by attackers are constantly evolving, making it difficult to anticipate and prevent them. The consequences of these attacks extend beyond financial and reputational damage. They can also have a significant impact on the safety and well-being of individuals. For example, a cyber attack on a hospital's systems could disrupt critical medical services, putting patients' lives at risk.

One of the main challenges with DDoS attacks is their ability to scale and cause widespread damage. The increase in Internet of Things (IoT) devices, like smart home devices and connected appliances, has led to a higher risk of large-scale DDoS attacks. These devices are often vulnerable to being hijacked and used in botnets, making them a prime target for attackers. As a result, businesses and organizations must constantly be vigilant and implement robust security measures to protect against these attacks. In addition to causing disruption and financial losses, DDoS attacks can also be used as a diversion tactic.

While the organization is dealing with the attack, the attacker might do other bad things like stealing important data or installing harmful software. Organizations need a good plan to quickly handle and prevent DDoS attacks and monitor their network for suspicious activity.

DNS hijacking is a common cyber attack that involves changing the DNS records of a website to redirect users to a malicious server. Hackers or cybercriminals can do this to steal important information, spread harmful software, or gain access to a network without permission. This attack can cause serious problems such as financial loss, damage to reputation, and even legal trouble. DNS hijacking is usually done by taking advantage of weaknesses in the DNS system. The DNS system is in charge of converting domain names into IP addresses. Attackers can take control of a website's DNS records in several ways, such as hacking the DNS servers, intercepting DNS requests, or tricking users into giving away their login information through phishing.

After the DNS records are changed, attackers can send users to a fake website that looks just like the real one, making it hard for users to notice the attack.

To prevent DNS hijacking, organizations should use security measures like DNSSEC and DNS filtering. DNSSEC verifies the authenticity of DNS records with digital signatures. DNS filtering prevents access to malicious websites by filtering out malicious domains.

BGP hijacking, also known as Border Gateway Protocol hijacking, is a serious threat to network security. This attack allows hackers to redirect internet traffic through their own networks by taking advantage of vulnerabilities in BGP routing protocols.

This can have disastrous consequences, as it can lead to traffic interception, data theft, or even service disruption. The potential impact of BGP hijacking is far-reaching. Attackers can intercept and change important information by rerouting traffic through harmful networks. This information includes login details, credit card numbers, and confidential business data.

They can also disrupt the delivery of critical services, causing major disruptions and financial losses. BGP hijacking can be used for espionage, giving attackers access to sensitive information without detection. To prevent BGP hijacking, network administrators must secure and update their BGP routing protocols regularly to fix any known vulnerabilities.

They should add more security measures like route filtering and monitoring to find and reduce any suspicious routing changes. Organizations should educate employees about BGP hijacking risks and how to recognize and report suspicious activity.

Zero-day exploits and malware are a major concern in the world of cyber security. These attacks are often used by attackers to exploit vulnerabilities in network protocols, software, or hardware. This allows them to infiltrate critical infrastructure or compromise key service providers. This can have devastating consequences, as attackers can gain unauthorized access to systems, disrupt operations, or steal sensitive information.

One of the main ways attackers use zero-day exploits and malware is by deploying malware or conducting targeted attacks. This means that attackers create and distribute malicious software that can infect computers and networks. Malware, once installed, can be used to access sensitive information, disrupt operations, or take control of the affected system. These attacks are very dangerous because they are hard to detect and can cause a lot of damage before being found.

Supply chain attacks are a type of cyber attack that can pose a significant threat to businesses and organizations. These attacks happen when attackers go after a company's supply chain, which covers all the processes and systems involved in making and delivering products and services. Attackers can compromise important systems and cause outages by injecting malware into commonly used software or firmware. One of the biggest concerns with supply chain attacks is the potential for widespread impact. Because these attacks target widely used software or firmware, the damage can affect a large number of organizations and individuals.

This can have a ripple effect, causing disruptions in business operations, financial losses, and even compromising sensitive data.

Border Gateway Protocol (BGP) is used for routing information exchange between autonomous systems (ASes) on the internet. BGP is strong and commonly used, but it has vulnerabilities that can be exploited by malicious actors for disrupting internet traffic or carrying out attacks. Some of the vulnerabilities in BGP include:

"An AS advertising false routing information to its neighbors." This method diverts traffic that is destined for other ASes through the attacker's network. This type of hijacking is a serious threat to the security and stability of the Internet. It can cause a variety of issues, including traffic interception, data interception, and denial of service.

There are a few different ways that attackers can hijack routes. One common method is by announcing IP prefixes that they do not actually own. This deceives other networks and ASes into thinking that the malicious AS is the ideal route to reach a specific destination. This can result in all traffic being redirected through the attacker's network, giving them the ability to intercept and possibly alter or steal important information. Another way that route hijacking can occur is through BGP (Border Gateway Protocol) manipulation.

Attackers can use BGP to create false routing information, making traffic go through their network instead of the correct destination. Additionally, there are several ways that route hijacking can be used to cause harm. For example, attackers can use this method to intercept sensitive information, such as login credentials or financial data. They can also use it to launch denial of service attacks by redirecting a large amount of traffic to a target network or server. This can overwhelm the network and cause it to crash, rendering it unavailable to legitimate users. Route hijacking is a serious threat that network administrators must be aware of and take precautions to prevent.

When route leaks occur, the consequences can be quite severe. This is because an AS, or Autonomous System, is responsible for routing internet traffic to different destinations. Improperly announcing routes between providers or peers can cause unintended traffic flows. This can result in slow traffic, overcrowding, and security issues due to using less efficient networks.

One of the main reasons why route leaks are such a big problem is because they can cause suboptimal routing. This means that traffic is not being routed in the most efficient way possible, leading to delays and congestion. Fast and reliable internet connections are crucial for businesses to carry out their daily operations. In addition, route leaks can also have security implications. Exposing internal networks to unauthorized access can put businesses at risk of cyber attacks and data breaches.

Session hijacking is a malicious method used to gain unauthorized access to a network by intercepting and manipulating network traffic. This is done by compromising the BGP sessions between routers to inject unauthorized routing updates or manipulate routing information. Successful attacks can redirect network traffic to harmful websites. This allows attackers to steal important data and disrupt regular network operations. It is a significant threat to network security and can cause severe damage if not properly addressed. BGP session hijacking happens when vulnerabilities in the Border Gateway Protocol (BGP) are exploited. BGP is responsible for exchanging routing information between autonomous systems (AS).

Attackers can exploit various weaknesses in BGP to manipulate routing tables and redirect traffic to their desired destinations. This can be done by injecting fake routing updates, redirecting routes, and even impersonating legitimate routers. Attackers can change routing information and direct traffic to their malicious sites without being detected by gaining control of the BGP sessions.

Prefix aggregation is an important optimization technique used by Internet Service Providers and Network Operators to reduce routing table size and improve network performance. Aggregation has been used as a means of reducing traffic engineering costs and improving routing efficiency. It involves breaking down IP prefixes into smaller, more specific sub-prefixes and announcing them individually.

Network operators can advertise specific routes to other networks, ensuring that traffic follows the best path. One of the key benefits of prefix aggregation is its ability to reduce routing table size. By announcing smaller sub-prefixes, network operators can reduce the number of entries in their routing tables. This leads to improved performance, as routers can process route updates and forwarding decisions much faster. However, aggregation can also have negative consequences if not properly managed. For instance, it can lead to routing table growth, increased routing overhead, and potential route instability. Network operators should thoroughly think about the risks and benefits of prefix aggregation before using it in their networks.

The Border Gateway Protocol (BGP) is a core component of the Internet, responsible for routing traffic between different networks. It is important to properly configure BGP router settings for a stable and efficient routing system. Even experienced network administrators can make mistakes when configuring BGP. These mistakes can cause problems like route flapping, black-holing, or unintended route propagation.

One of the most common misconfigurations in BGP router configurations is incorrect route filters. These filters are used to control which routes are advertised or accepted from neighbouring routers. A mistake in configuring these filters can result in incorrect routes being propagated, causing routing anomalies. A common mistake is when a router advertises a route that it does not have in its routing table. This can lead to traffic being sent to the wrong destination, causing disruptions in network communication. Incomplete route advertisements are also a source of misconfiguration in BGP routers. This occurs when a router fails to advertise all of its available routes to its neighbouring routers. As a result, traffic may be directed to a different path than intended, leading to routing anomalies. These misconfigurations, if left undetected, can have serious consequences for the overall functioning of the Internet.

BGP is a routing protocol for communication between different Autonomous Systems on the internet. Internet connectivity is important, but the weak authentication methods are worrying. Without authentication, BGP is at risk of spoofing attacks, which can seriously undermine the internet's integrity and security. Spoofing attacks occur when malicious actors impersonate legitimate ASes and inject false routing updates into the BGP routing table. These updates can then be propagated to other routers, leading to incorrect routing decisions and potentially disrupting internet traffic. This can result in denial of service attacks, data interception, and other cyber threats.

4 - Software attacks

a) **SQL injection**, also known as SQL, is a form of cyberattack that targets web applications. These applications interact with databases by executing SQL queries to store, retrieve, or modify data. Attackers exploit weaknesses in input fields like login forms or search boxes to insert harmful SQL commands into the application's database. They can then use this access to cause significant harm. As a result, SQL injection is a serious threat to the security of web applications and their underlying databases. Attackers can use SQL commands to access or manipulate sensitive data in the application's database.

This can have severe consequences for both the organization hosting the application and its users. It is crucial for developers to properly sanitize user inputs and implement security measures to prevent SQL injection attacks.

b) **Cross-site scripting**, or XSS, attacks inject code into web pages to exploit vulnerabilities in web applications. These scripts can be used for harmful activities like stealing user information, taking control of sessions, vandalizing websites, or redirecting users to dangerous sites. Attackers often target web pages with high traffic in order to reach a large number of potential victims. One common type of XSS attack is called reflected XSS, where malicious code is sent from a web application to the user's browser. This happens when a user enters data into a website form and the data is not properly cleaned before being shown on the page. Attackers can insert their own code into the page, which could compromise the user's information or lead them to a harmful website. Stored XSS is a type of attack where malicious code is stored on a web server and then executed when a user visits a page or takes a specific action.

This type of attack is more dangerous because it can affect many users and continue even after the vulnerability is fixed.

DDoS attacks can cause serious harm to online services or businesses. Attackers use advanced techniques to flood their intended target with an overwhelming amount of traffic, rendering it unreachable or unresponsive. Hackers use botnets, which are networks of compromised devices under their control, to carry out attacks. These devices are usually infected with malware, allowing the attacker to control them remotely and coordinate their efforts. These attacks have become increasingly common in recent years, with many high-profile websites and services falling victim to DDoS attacks.

d) Man-in-the-middle attacks are a common type of cyber attack that can have devastating consequences. Attacks happen when someone intercepts and changes communication between two parties without them knowing. In this way, attackers can gain access to sensitive information, manipulate communication, or even impersonate legitimate parties. These attacks work by putting the attacker between the victim and the intended recipient, allowing them to listen to the communication.

This can be done in different ways, like hacking a Wi-Fi network or creating a fake website that looks real. Once in position, the attacker can change the data being sent, making the parties think they are talking to each other when they are really talking to the attacker. Man-in-the-middle attacks are a big threat to both people and organizations because they can result in the theft of personal information, financial loss, and harm to reputation.

e) Phishing attacks trick users into giving sensitive information using different tactics. These attacks occur when malicious actors impersonate legitimate entities through fraudulent emails, websites, or messages. Phishing attacks aim to trick users into giving away personal information like login details or financial data. This information can then be used for identity theft, financial fraud, or unauthorized access to accounts.

The success of phishing attacks relies heavily on social engineering techniques, which exploit human psychology and trust. Attackers use urgency, fear, and authority to manipulate victims into acting without thinking critically. This can result in users clicking on malicious links, downloading infected attachments, or providing sensitive information without realizing the consequences.

f) Zero-day exploits are a major concern for software vendors and security researchers alike. These attacks are so dangerous because they target vulnerabilities that have not yet been discovered or patched. This means they are able to bypass traditional security defences and leave systems vulnerable to exploitation. It's crucial for vendors to promptly update these vulnerabilities because attackers exploit the time it takes to find and fix them. Zero-day exploits are not only effective, but they can also be incredibly costly. The longer vulnerability remains unpatched, the more time attackers have to exploit it.

Strategic Objectives

In the world of modern warfare, one of the most powerful weapons at a nation's disposal is the ability to launch mass critical cyber attacks. The attacks aim to disrupt and create chaos by targeting a country's infrastructure, economy, and military capabilities.

Their goal is not to directly harm individuals, but rather to cripple the country as a whole. These cyber attacks are not limited to just one area, but instead aim to attack multiple key sectors of a nation.

Attacks on infrastructure can hinder vital services like electricity, water, and transportation, causing inconvenience in people's daily lives. Targeting the economy can harm a country's financial stability, leading to panic and economic turmoil.

Attacking a country's military can make it defenceless and prone to more attacks.

The use of mass critical cyber attacks in war has become a major concern for governments around the world. These attacks could cause serious and long-lasting damage to a country's infrastructure, economy, and military.

Cyber operations can also be used for spying, acquiring confidential information, and sabotaging computer systems. These activities are far-reaching and can be carried out by individuals, groups, or nation states. The potential for damage is enormous, not only to the targeted system, but also to the economy, politics, and society. Another area of concern is information warfare, which is the use of cyber operations to influence public opinion. This can be done by spreading misinformation, planting fake news stories, and manipulating perceptions online.

The goal is to sway public opinion to favour one side or to discredit the other. This method has caused chaos and confusion in political campaigns, elections, and other controversial issues. As more people rely on the internet for news and information, the impact of information warfare is becoming increasingly significant. Moreover, with the rapid growth of social media, cyber operations have become a powerful tool for propaganda and psychological operations.

Cyber attackers can manipulate people's thoughts and emotions by creating personalized content using advanced algorithms and targeting specific demographics. This can have a wide range of consequences, from causing social unrest to instigating violence. As technology continues to advance, the potential for cyber operations to shape and control public opinion will only increase.

1 - **Attribution Challenges.** Cyber operations are a double-edged sword due to their level of anonymity. This allows attackers to hide their identity or even use false flags to throw investigators off their trail. With such a complex and interconnected network, it is difficult to pinpoint the origin of a cyber attack. This makes it challenging to determine who is responsible for the attack. The ability to attribute cyber attacks to a specific actor is central in holding them accountable and taking appropriate action. However, this task is becoming increasingly difficult due to the ever-evolving strategies of attackers.

They are able to cover their tracks and create confusion, making it challenging for investigators to determine responsibility. This can lead to a lack of consequences for the attackers and a sense of impunity for their actions. Despite these challenges, attribution is not impossible. It requires advanced technological tools, in-depth analysis, and collaboration between various organizations. With these efforts, it is possible to trace the source of a cyber attack and hold the responsible party accountable. It's important to recognize the challenges in attribution and keep working to improve our methods and strategies.

The use of cyber capabilities in armed conflict has always been a contentious issue. However, it is important to note that even in this modern technological age, international law still applies. Cyber capabilities must only be used in proportion to the situation and while distinguishing between civilian and military targets. These are decisive in mitigating the effects of any conflict and protecting the innocent. The principle of proportionality ensures that any actions taken with cyber capabilities are reasonable and necessary. This means that any use of such capabilities must not cause excessive damage or harm to the enemy. It also means that the benefits of such actions must outweigh any potential harm caused.

Similarly, the principle of distinction between civilian and military targets is a fundamental principle of international law. It dictates that cyber capabilities must be directed only at legitimate military targets and not at civilians or civilian infrastructure. Today, it's very important to follow international law, especially when using cyber capabilities.

As such, any use of these capabilities must be carefully considered and executed with the utmost care. It is crucial to uphold the principles of proportionality and distinction to reduce harm and conduct conflicts fairly and ethically.

The growing dependence of society on technology necessitates the establishment of norms and rules of behaviour in cyberspace. However, achieving consensus on these issues is a daunting task for the international community.

With various countries having different cultural, political, and economic backgrounds, reaching a mutual agreement is easier said than done. Moreover, the rapid advancement of technology poses new challenges and complexities in defining what constitutes appropriate behaviour in cyberspace. As more devices become connected, the potential for cyber attacks and malicious activities also increases. It is important for the international community to unite and create rules to handle emerging cyber threats effectively.

Despite the challenges, there have been efforts made by different organizations and countries to address these issues. The United Nations Group of Governmental Experts is working on creating rules for how countries should act in cyberspace. Efforts require ongoing discussion and collaboration between countries to establish common rules and norms for governing cyberspace.

Escalation Risks

Cyber operations have become a significant threat in modern times. With the advent of technology, cyber attacks have become more sophisticated and complex. They can have far-reaching implications and can even lead to traditional military conflicts. It's not just about stealing information anymore; it's about disrupting entire systems and causing chaos.

As the world becomes more interconnected, the risk of unintended consequences also increases. With the rise of cyber attacks, governments have started taking them more seriously. They have realized that a cyber attack can have the same impact as a physical attack, and sometimes even more. In fact, cyber operations have become a critical component of modern warfare. This has also raised concerns about the potential for escalation in traditional conflicts. A simple cyber attack can quickly turn into a full-blown military conflict if not handled properly.

It is more difficult to reduce the risks of cyber operations due to the connection between cyber and physical systems. A single cyber attack can have a domino effect, causing disruptions in various interconnected systems. This not only puts critical infrastructure at risk but also the lives of civilians. As technology continues to advance, it has become imperative for governments to work together to prevent and mitigate cyber threats. The consequences of not doing so could be catastrophic

Cyber Defence **and Resilience**

Enhanced cyber security measures the ever-growing threat of cyber attacks has become a global concern and one that cannot be ignored. Countries must be prepared for attacks in the digital world's rapid expansion. Not only do these attacks threaten national security, but they also put citizens and their personal information at risk.

Cyber security should be a top priority for all nations. It is vital that governments invest in the necessary resources to ensure their cyber security measures are top-notch. To prevent attacks, we need defence mechanisms and a skilled team to respond to breaches. Additionally, resilience strategies must be developed to minimize the impact of attacks and aid in the recovery process. These measures are important for protecting a nation's infrastructure, economy, and the privacy and security of its citizens. In today's digital age, it is no longer a question of if a cyber attack will happen, but when. Nations must take proactive steps to protect themselves and their citizens from these threats.

Governments must prioritize cyber security as a necessary responsibility to protect their nation and people. Effective counter mass critical cyber attacks require the collaboration of nations in information sharing, joint defence, and coordinated responses. Today, a cyber attack can start in one country and easily spread to others due to global connectivity.

To protect against threats, countries should share information, collaborate on defence, and coordinate responses to attacks. This collaborative effort is fundamental for the safety and security of all nations involved. Through information sharing, nations can learn about potential threats and vulnerabilities, allowing them to better prepare and defend against attacks.

Collaborating in defence strengthens the response against cyber attacks, making it harder for hackers to breach security. And in the event of an attack, coordinated responses can help mitigate the damage and prevent further spread. In today's digital age, cyber attacks are a looming threat that can have devastating effects on nations and their citizens. The only way to effectively counter these attacks is through a united and collaborative effort.

Nations must put aside their differences and work together towards a common goal of protecting against cyber threats. Nations must trust and cooperate with each other, while willingly sharing information and resources.

Mobilization

The mobilization process in case of a cyber attack requires a swift and efficient response from all parties involved. This includes individuals, organizations, and government agencies, all working together to mitigate the impact of the threat and restore normalcy. In order to achieve this, there are several key aspects that must be considered and put into action.

First and foremost, communication is the key. For successful mobilization, everyone needs to be informed and communicate effectively. This means having clear lines of communication and established protocols for sharing information and updates. Having a point of contact for each party will help make the process smoother and ensure everyone is in sync.

Another important aspect of mobilization is having a plan in place. Having a plan in place for dealing with a cyber attack is essential. Identify vulnerabilities, establish protocols for responding to threats, and assign roles and responsibilities to each party involved. Having a plan in place will help expedite the response and minimize the impact of the attack.

1. Incident Plan (IRP) is an essential element of any organization when it comes to cyber security. It is a detailed plan that outlines the necessary steps to be taken in case of a cyber attack. The plan also outlines the roles and responsibilities of each person in the organization to ensure a coordinated and efficient response to the attack. This helps to minimize the impact of the attack and prevent further damage to the organization. One of the most critical aspects of the IRP is its communication protocols. During an attack, it is important to communicate effectively so that everyone involved knows what is happening and can respond accordingly.

Include clear communication channels in the IRP, like email addresses and phone numbers, to ensure everyone understands each other. In addition to communication protocols, the IRP should also outline technical measures to contain and eradicate the threat. This involves isolating affected systems, implementing backup and recovery procedures, and using cyber security tools to stop the attack from spreading. Having these measures in place can significantly reduce the impact of the attack and help the organization recover quickly. Overall, a well-defined IRP is crucial in ensuring that organizations are prepared to respond effectively to a cyber attack.

2. Communication protocols are a key to keep running smoothly. By setting up clear channels of communication, everyone is able to stay informed and on the same page. This is especially important during times of change, crisis, or conflict. Without prompt and transparent communication, misunderstandings can arise and progress can be hindered. It is important to remember that communication is a two-way street. It is not just about giving out information, but also actively listening and receiving feedback. This allows for better coordination of efforts and ensures that all parties are on board with the decisions being made. Sharing updates is important to build trust and maintain a sense of community within the organization.

Additionally, effective communication can also help mitigate potential conflicts. By keeping all parties informed and involved, issues can be addressed and resolved in a timely manner. This creates a more collaborative and productive work environment. Establishing and maintaining clear communication protocols is an essential aspect of successful organizations, and should not be overlooked.

When cyber attacks occur, it's critical for various entities to collaborate in order to respond and reduce the damage effectively. This collaboration often involves government agencies, law enforcement, cyber security experts, and affected organizations. Having pre-existing relationships and collaboration frameworks in place can greatly speed up the response process and make it more effective. Collaborating allows for a more comprehensive approach to addressing the attack. Each entity brings their unique expertise and resources to the table. This can greatly increase the chances of successfully mitigating the attack and minimizing its impact. Furthermore, collaboration also enables a more proactive approach to cyber attacks.

4. Containing an threat is to deploy a number of technical measures. Measures to deal with this problem can involve different strategies. Usually, they include isolating the affected systems, applying patches, and improving network security. Since time is of the essence, a rapid response is crucial to ensure the spread of the attack is contained.

Once the threat has been identified, it is important to immediately isolate any affected systems. This can help prevent the threat from spreading to other systems and causing further damage. In addition, applying patches to vulnerable systems can help prevent the threat from exploiting any known vulnerabilities. Implementing network security measures like firewalls and intrusion detection systems can prevent threats from accessing the network and causing more damage.

These technical measures are essential in containing a cyber threat, but they must be implemented quickly and effectively. A quick response is vital to reduce the impact of the attack.

5. Forensic Analysis is an essential step that should be taken following a cyber attack. A thorough investigation is needed to determine the full extent of the attack, how it happened, and any evidence that can be used in legal proceedings. This analysis is very important for understanding the attack and for improving cyber security to prevent future incidents. During a forensic analysis, experts will carefully examine the systems and networks that were affected by the attack. They will look for any vulnerabilities or weaknesses that were exploited and determine the entry point of the attack.

This information can then be used to strengthen security measures and prevent similar attacks from happening in the future.

War

Information warfare and influence operations are tactics that have been used throughout history to shape the opinions of the masses. Today, tactics in the digital age involve using information, disinformation, and psychological tactics to achieve strategic goals. This involves shaping public opinion and guiding decision-making through channels like social media, news, and online platforms. These actions can greatly affect national security and can be used by governments, organizations, or individuals to achieve political, military, or economic objectives.

One of the main goals of information warfare and influence operations is to shape perceptions. This can involve spreading false or misleading information to create a certain narrative or to discredit opposing viewpoints. By doing so, these operations aim to manipulate public opinion and influence the decisions of individuals and organizations. Bots and fake accounts are commonly used on social media to reach a larger audience and seem more authentic. This has become increasingly popular in recent years. It is harder now to determine what information is true and what is false. This makes it easier for these operations to achieve their goals.

1 - **Information warfare** is often used to gain a competitive advantage through various methods such as disrupting communication, shaping public opinion, undermining trust, and sowing discord. These tactics are used to manipulate information in order to gain an upper hand in a particular situation. It aims to control information flow, influence public perception, and undermine trust in institutions.

One of the main reasons for the rise of information warfare is the increasing reliance on technology and the internet. There is a lot of information available, which makes it easier for people and organizations to spread false information to achieve their goals. This can have serious consequences, not only for individuals but also for society as a whole. It's important to be alert and able to recognize and counter these tactics to protect ourselves and our communities. It is a constantly evolving concept, with new tactics and strategies being developed every day. As technology continues to advance, so do the methods used in information warfare.

2- Disinformation is a significant threat to democracy in the modern world. It is spreading false information to manipulate or influence people. This can be serious because people might make decisions based on false or biased information without realizing it. This is a big problem in politics because it can influence people's opinions and affect the democratic process. Propaganda is like disinformation, but it's used to promote a particular agenda or ideology.

It involves the selective dissemination of information in order to manipulate public opinion and promote a specific viewpoint. Disinformation deceives, while propaganda shapes beliefs and attitudes. It can be used by governments, corporations, and other organizations to advance their own interests and suppress opposing viewpoints. Both disinformation and propaganda are powerful tools that can be used to control public opinion and manipulate people's perceptions. They can be very dangerous in politics, as they can have a big impact on elections and other important decisions.

3 - Social media manipulation has become a common tactic used by many to sway public perception and influence opinions. Social media has made it easier for people and groups to spread their message and influence public opinion on specific topics. Influence operations use these platforms to spread a narrative, promote specific viewpoints, and use algorithms to reach particular audiences.

Social media manipulation is often done by using bots, trolls, and fake accounts. Fake accounts are often made to make it seem like someone has a lot of followers or to make a message seem more popular than it really is. Fake accounts can manipulate public opinion and control the narrative on a specific topic by exaggerating the impact of information. This tactic is especially effective when targeting vulnerable or easily influenced audiences. Social media manipulation has serious consequences, as it distorts the truth and creates a false reality. It can also create division and polarize societies by amplifying certain viewpoints and silencing others.

4 - State-sponsored actors use cyber espionage to infiltrate computer systems, networks and databases to gather intelligence. This type of information warfare allows them to gain a strategic advantage and potentially influence decision-makers. Cyber espionage can have serious consequences of disrupting economies and compromising national security. One of the main challenges of cyber espionage is the difficulty in tracing the source of the attack. It is very difficult to identify the attacker's real identity because of advanced techniques like encryption and spoofing. This makes it easier for state-sponsored actors to carry out their espionage activities without fear of being caught.

Moreover, cyber espionage not only poses a threat to governments and national security, but it also affects businesses and individuals. Stolen information can be used to get ahead in business or to exploit individuals for money or control.

5 - Attribution is a decisive aspect of identifying the source of information warfare activities. However, it is not always a simple task. Adversaries often use various techniques to obscure their identities and make it difficult to trace back to them. One of the common techniques used is the use of proxies or false flags to mask their involvement. This makes it challenging for authorities to accurately determine the source of these activities.

The use of proxies allows adversaries to distance themselves from any potential consequences of their actions. By using intermediaries, they can carry out attacks without directly being linked to them. This creates an extra layer of complexity in identifying the true instigators of information warfare. Similarly, false flags are also used to mislead investigators and point them in the wrong direction. This tactic tricks investigators into wasting time and resources by making them believe that the attack came from a different source.

These attribution challenges highlight the need for advanced techniques and strategies to accurately identify the source of information warfare activities. It requires expertise and specialized tools to trace back to the true instigators behind these attacks. These malicious attacks are capable of wreaking havoc on our systems, causing chaos, destruction, and potential devastation.

Technology is very important in modern warfare, and cyber operations are now a key part of the battlefield. The implications of a massive critical cyber attack in the context of war cannot be overstated. The attack can cause widespread disruption and damage on a scale far greater than traditional military tactics. In fact, it's been said that the next world war may not be fought with guns and bombs, but with lines of code and computer viruses.

In a wartime scenario, every aspect must be carefully considered and planned for. The impact of a massive critical cyber attack can be far-reaching and have long-lasting implications. From disabling vital communication systems to compromising sensitive data, the consequences of such an attack can be devastating.

6 - Psychological operations (PSYOP) are strategic actions that manipulate a person's psychological state to shape their behaviours and beliefs. This form of warfare aims to influence individuals or groups through media, propaganda, and communication methods. It is a powerful tool used by governments and militaries to achieve their objectives. PSYOP involves understanding the psychological vulnerabilities of the target audience and exploiting them to achieve desired outcomes. This can include using fear, guilt, or other emotions to influence decision-making.

These operations can have a significant impact on the target audience's perceptions and actions. However, they can also be controversial as they involve manipulating people's thoughts and feelings.

Critical infrastructure is vital for society to function. It includes power, transportation, communication, and financial systems. These are often the targets of cyber attacks, which aim to disrupt services and cause chaos. The impact of such attacks can be devastating, causing widespread damage and even loss of life. Attacks on critical infrastructure can have serious consequences, affecting more than just the targeted systems. TPower grid disruptions can cause blackouts and make essential services inaccessible. Attacks on transportation systems can lead to travel delays and disrupt supply chains.

Communication networks are vital for emergency responses and maintaining connections with loved ones, making them prime targets for cyber attacks. To combat these threats, governments and organizations must prioritize the protection of critical infrastructure. This includes implementing robust cyber security measures, conducting regular risk assessments, and developing contingency plans in case of an attack. The consequences of a successful attack on critical infrastructure can be catastrophic, making it imperative to stay vigilant and prepared.

8 - Cyber weapons are the new weapons of mass destruction. Crypto currency scams are a big worry for governments worldwide due to their growing complexity and evasiveness. These weapons are used to conduct attacks, which can range from simple spam emails to sophisticated zero-day exploits. Zero-day exploits are attacks that take advantage of vulnerabilities in software that have not yet been discovered by the developers. These attacks are very dangerous because they can cause a lot of damage before developers have a chance to fix the vulnerability. One of the most dangerous cyber weapons is the remote access Trojan (RAT). This malware lets attackers have full control over a victim's computer, granting them access to sensitive information, like passwords and financial data. A RAT can be used to remotely control a victim's webcam or microphone, allowing the attacker to spy on them.

This type of cyber weapon is often used for espionage and can have devastating consequences for individuals and organizations.

Denial-of-service (DoS) attacks are another type of cyber weapon that is frequently used to disrupt the operations of a target. These attacks flood a network or website with so much traffic that it becomes overwhelmed and cannot function properly. This can cause major disruptions for businesses and organizations, leading to financial losses and damage to their reputation.

9 - Cyber sabotage, which is a deliberate attempt to disrupt or damage computer systems or networks. This can have a devastating impact on critical infrastructure, such as power grids, financial systems, or transportation networks. It is a form of cyber attack that can cause chaos and destruction on a large scale. The motive behind such attacks can vary from financial gain to political or ideological reasons. The consequences can be severe and lasting for both the systems and the people who depend on them. To protect ourselves and society from cyber sabotage, we need to understand the threat and take proactive measures.

Autonomous Computer Networks

In recent times, there has been a growing trend towards building autonomous computer networks, which are networks that are designed with individual nodes or devices having a high level of self-governance and decision-making capabilities.

An autonomous network is a network that doesn't need human intervention. It allows nodes to organize themselves and adapt to changes in the network. This means that nodes in the network can communicate and work together without external assistance. This is done through dynamic routing protocols, self-healing mechanisms, and peer-to-peer communication protocols that allow nodes to find and connect with each other on their own. One of the key benefits of an autonomous network is its ability to self-heal.

This means the network can find and fix problems without human help. This is possible thanks to self-healing mechanisms that can find and solve issues before they become big problems. This leads to a more reliable and efficient network with less downtime and seamless operation. Another important aspect of an autonomous network is its dynamic routing protocols. These protocols help nodes find the best path to send data considering network congestion and link availability.

Also ensures that data is routed through the most optimal path, resulting in faster and more efficient data transfer. Additionally, peer-to-peer communication protocols enable nodes to directly communicate with each other, without the need for a central server. It allows for faster and more direct communication, improving the overall performance of the network.

These networks do not depend on a central authority for their operation. Instead, each node can function independently, making decisions based on its own needs and requirements. Autonomous computer networks can work well without a central authority or control, which is one of their main advantages. Each node can make decisions based on its own needs, without waiting for instructions from a central source. This makes the networks very strong, so they can keep working even if some parts are damaged or attacked.

Another important aspect of autonomous computer networks is their ability to adapt and self-heal. Using advanced algorithms and artificial intelligence, these networks can detect and solve problems or weaknesses automatically, without human intervention. This makes the network more efficient and reliable. Any issues can be found and fixed quickly, without causing major disruptions.

Autonomous computer networks are a promising development in networking. They offer a more flexible, resilient, and efficient network infrastructure. They are self-governing and decentralized, not needing a central point of control or authority. This structure ensures that there is no single point of failure, making the network more resilient and fault-tolerant. As a result, decision-making and coordination are distributed among the network nodes, allowing for a more efficient and autonomous operation.

This decentralized approach also provides more flexibility and scalability for the network. Without a central point of control, the network can adapt easily to changes and expand its capabilities without disrupting the entire system. It allows for better performance and faster response times, making it an ideal solution for large-scale networks. Moreover, autonomous networks also offer increased security and privacy. With decision-making and coordination distributed among nodes, it becomes more challenging for malicious actors to attack the network. This added layer of security protects the network from potential threats and ensures the privacy of its users.

Autonomous networks are a modern technology that allows for self-configuration. This means that network nodes can automatically configure themselves without any human intervention. This revolutionary concept has greatly improved the functionality of networks. With the use of autonomous networks, there is no longer a need for manual configuration or constant monitoring. This has greatly reduced the workload of network administrators and has made networks more efficient. Furthermore, autonomous networks allow for nodes to establish connections with other nodes without any manual intervention.

Network nodes can communicate with each other and establish connections without any human involvement. It has greatly improved the speed and efficiency of network communication. It also reduces the risk of human error, as all connections are established automatically. In summary, autonomous networks have greatly improved the functionality and efficiency of networks. With the ability to self-configure and establish connections, there is no longer a need for manual intervention. This has reduced the workload of network administrators and has greatly improved the speed and efficiency of network communication. Autonomous networks are a revolutionary technology that has transformed the way networks operate.

Autonomous networks are essential for modern technology, especially for complex systems that need high reliability. These networks are designed to function without human intervention, making maintenance and management easier. When designing these networks, it is important to consider potential failures and attacks that may occur. This is why redundancy, fault tolerance mechanisms, and distributed consensus algorithms are often used in the design of autonomous networks. These features ensure that the network can continue to function even in the face of unexpected challenges.

Redundancy is important in autonomous networks because it stores critical information in multiple locations. If one node fails, there are several backups to take its place without compromising the network's functionality. In addition, fault tolerance mechanisms are implemented to detect and correct failures in the network. This ensures that any issues that arise can be quickly addressed before they have a significant impact on the network.

Consensus algorithms ensure all network nodes agree and work together towards a common goal. This helps improve the network's overall functionality and makes it harder for potential attacks to disrupt its operations. Overall, autonomous networks are constantly evolving and improving to become more resilient to failures and attacks. Technology advances and networks become more advanced too. They are now an important part of our lives. They are an essential part of modern infrastructure. In order to accommodate a large number of nodes, these networks are designed to be highly scalable. As the network grows, it can adapt to changes in size and structure without losing performance.

This is important because these networks are built to handle large amounts of traffic and data. Without scalability, the network would quickly become overwhelmed and unable to function properly. One of the key benefits of autonomous networks is their ability to adapt to changes in network size and topology. Advanced algorithms and protocols enable the network nodes to communicate and work together. As the network grows, algorithms and protocols adapt and optimize the network to maintain efficient operation.

They are designed to be able to handle a variety of different devices and services. This means that as new technologies emerge, the network can easily integrate them without significant changes to the overall infrastructure. This flexibility allows for easy integration and ensures that the network stays up-to-date and adaptable to modern technology. Autonomous networks are important in our interconnected world and support the growth of our digital society.

In order to ensure that the network is secure, various measures can be put in place. Cryptographic protocols are one such measure that can be implemented. These protocols provide a secure way of transmitting data over the network by encrypting it. This makes it difficult for anyone to intercept and view sensitive information. In addition to cryptographic protocols, access control mechanisms can also be utilized. These mechanisms allow for only authorized users to access the network, ensuring that no malicious activities can take place.

Another key security measure that can be implemented is the use of intrusion detection systems. These systems watch the network for any suspicious activities and can alert the network administrator right away if they detect any unauthorized access. This allows for quick action to be taken in order to prevent any potential security breaches.

Additionally, firewalls can also be utilized to block any unauthorized access attempts. With these security measures in place, the autonomous network can be protected against any potential threats. In today's fast-paced digital world, security is a top priority. With the rise of autonomous networks, it is essential to ensure that they are secure.

In a war scenario, autonomous computer networks could play several critical roles, both in offensive and defensive capacities: In times of compromised traditional communication infrastructure, autonomous computer networks have taken on the task of meeting user needs. The networks boast of decentralized communication protocols, which make the entire process hassle-free and efficient. This advancement has further enabled troops to maintain connectivity and exchange information securely, in turn, aiding the overall process. Military personnel can use these networks to stay connected and share important information, without worrying about infrastructure damage or compromise.

Decentralized communication protocols ensure fast and secure communication with confidentiality. Autonomous computer networks' ad-hoc networking capabilities have helped improve communication and coordination among military units. Ad-hoc networks are dynamic and self-organizing, enabling troops to establish and maintain connections in challenging environments. This feature has helped military units stay in constant communication, regardless of circumstances, to ensure effective coordination and execution of operations. Additionally, ad-hoc networking can serve as a backup communication system if the main networks fail, which is valuable for the military.

Autonomous networks are on the rise, and they have the potential to change the way intelligence gathering is done. These networks consist of unmanned aerial vehicles (UAVs), satellites, and ground-based sensors, all working together to gather intelligence. This technology allows for constant surveillance of enemy movements and strategic locations. The networks can even process and analyze the data they collect, providing real-time situational awareness to military commanders.

With the use of these autonomous networks, military commanders are now able to have a better understanding of their surroundings. They no longer have to rely on human agents for intelligence gathering, which can be dangerous and time-consuming. The networks can run all the time, collecting and analyzing data much faster, giving military commanders an advantage in the field. This advanced technology also allows for more accurate and detailed information, giving commanders a more complete picture of the situation.

With the ability to operate independently, these networks can be used to carry out cyber warfare operations with ease. From launching cyber attacks against enemy infrastructure to disrupting communication networks, the potential for damage is immense. The main concern with autonomous computer networks is their ability to invade enemy systems and gather information or cause damage.

With no human intervention required, these networks can cause chaos and destruction on a large scale. The development of advanced autonomous cyber weapons adds an even more dangerous element to this type of warfare. These weapons have the ability to identify and exploit vulnerabilities in enemy networks, making them nearly impossible to defend against. This means that if an enemy can defend against one attack, the weapon can quickly find another way to cause damage. Governments and organizations must invest in strong cyber defences and keep up with the latest technology advancements.

Autonomous networks have improved logistics and supply chain management by increasing efficiency and resilience. These networks can monitor inventory levels independently to ensure that supplies are always available. Transport routes have improved delivery speed and accuracy, making it easier to supply troops in tough environments.

One of the most significant benefits of autonomous networks is their ability to optimize distribution networks. By utilizing advanced algorithms and real-time data, these networks can efficiently allocate resources and reduce waste. This not only improves the overall efficiency of the supply chain but also helps to minimize costs and maximize profits.

With such high automation, military supplies chains can function smoothly, ensuring that troops receive the required resources and equipment on time. Autonomous networks can improve efficiency and resiliency. They can also enhance safety and security in military supply chains. These networks can quickly identify and address potential risks or disruptions by monitoring inventory levels and coordinating transportation routes. In dangerous situations, delivering resources on time is very important for the safety of troops and the success of missions.

Autonomous computer networks can control unmanned weapon systems, like drones, unmanned ground vehicles (UGVs), and autonomous weapons platforms, along with cyber warfare. These systems can autonomously identify and engage enemy targets, providing firepower and reconnaissance capabilities without risking human lives. As technology advances, autonomous systems can now do complicated tasks without human intervention.

These systems have been used in various military operations, providing a significant advantage on the battlefield. They can collect information, follow and monitor targets, and make decisions about when and where to attack.

Advancements in technology raise ethical concerns regarding the use of autonomous weapons. There is also a risk of system malfunction or hacking by enemy forces. The use of autonomous weapon systems has its advantages, but there is a growing debate on their ethical implications in warfare. Not having people involved in making decisions raises worries about accountability and the potential for these systems to make mistakes or cause unnecessary harm.

Military leaders are also worried that these systems may be hacked and used against their own forces. Regulations and protocols must be established to ensure responsible and ethical use of autonomous weapon systems as technology advances.

Autonomous computer networks can be efficient and reliable communication channels between military commanders and troops on the battlefield. Using modern technology, these networks transmit important mission objectives and help coordinate troop movements. Real-time updates are provided to keep everyone involved in the battlefield informed, even with its ever-changing and unpredictable nature. Moreover, autonomous computer networks are able to handle disruptions and enemy attacks in a way that traditional systems simply cannot.

These networks are resistant and can still work even if certain nodes are compromised due to redundancies and distributed data storage. This ensures that command and control functions do not fail, and that orders continue to get relayed and executed.

Finally, these networks are also able to adapt to changing conditions. This level of flexibility is essential on a battlefield, where circumstances can change at a moment's notice. Autonomous networks allow commanders to easily change their strategies and communicate new orders, helping troops to respond and adapt quickly. This level of agility can be the difference between success and failure in high-pressure situations.

Autonomous computer networks solve the problems of resilience and redundancy in military communication and infrastructure. These networks can work independently without constant human input by using decentralized architectures and self-healing mechanisms.

This means that autonomous networks can respond quickly and efficiently to network disruptions or attacks, ensuring that critical operations can continue without interruption. One of the key advantages of autonomous networks is their ability to dynamically reroute traffic. In case of a network disruption, the network can quickly find another route for communication and information to keep flowing freely.

Furthermore, autonomous networks also have the ability to repair damaged nodes on their own, without the need for human intervention. Reducing human error and having a faster response time are both cruçial in military operations. In addition to these benefits, autonomous networks also offer a high level of connectivity.

By constantly adapting to changes in the network, these networks maintain a strong and reliable connection, even during disruptions or attacks. This means that military operations can continue seamlessly, without any interruptions or delays.

In the event of a nuclear attack, the world as we know it could be completely destroyed. With the damage or destruction of traditional communication infrastructure, there is a greater need for alternative ways to communicate. This is where autonomous computer networks come into play. These networks could be the key to maintaining communication and coordination among military units, government agencies, and emergency responders. However, the challenges that come with using autonomous computer networks in such a situation cannot be ignored. These networks would need to be extremely resilient to nuclear electromagnetic pulses (EMPs) and be able to operate in a highly degraded and hostile environment.

Despite the challenges and uncertainties, it is important to consider the potential benefits of having autonomous computer networks in place during a nuclear attack. These networks can save lives by enabling communication and coordination for necessary actions.

Sensors and satellites can be deployed to detect and track incoming nuclear missiles. Early warning would alert military and civilian authorities and help them prepare. These sensors have to be able to analyze data and distinguish real threats from false alarms. Additionally, the warnings should be disseminated quickly to decision-makers.

To develop such a system, autonomous networks of sensors and satellites could be used. These networks would be able to detect potential nuclear missiles and track them as they approach. They would have the capability to analyze sensor data and identify legitimate threats, while disregarding false alarms.

Once a threat is confirmed, the system would autonomously send out warnings to the relevant authorities. It would improve national safety by creating an early warning system for possible nuclear attacks. With this technology, authorities would have more time to prepare and respond, potentially minimizing the impact of a nuclear strike. It would also reduce the risk of false alarms, preventing unnecessary panic and confusion. Additionally, the use of autonomous networks would ensure a Swift and efficient response, as the system would be able to identify and disseminate warnings in a timely manner.

Additionally, this technology can be implemented to manage crisis situations in real-time. In the event of a rapidly evolving threat environment, autonomous computer networks are an ideal solution. Their capability to assess the situation and adapt to changing conditions in real-time is crucial to ensuring successful outcomes. With their autonomous decision-making abilities, these networks can effectively respond to any crisis with speed and efficiency. These networks also serve as a vital tool for military and political leaders in times of conflict. They provide a comprehensive picture of the situation at hand, allowing for informed decision-making and strategic planning.

Moreover, their decentralized nature allows for a more efficient and effective chain of command, ensuring Swift and coordinated responses to any crisis. With this advancement in technology, the potential for successful outcomes in critical situations is greatly increased.

Strategic Defence Systems are a vital aspect of national security, particularly in times of conflict. Missile defence systems protect against nuclear missiles and are central for defence against attacks. Interception missiles and anti-ballistic missile systems works together to detect and track multiple targets. They coordinate interception operations to maximize the chances of success.

In order to achieve this level of efficiency, these systems must be completely autonomous. This means they must operate without human intervention, making real-time decisions and adapting to changing situations. To respond to any threat, advanced technology and complex algorithms are needed to optimize resource allocation on the network. The deployment of these strategic defence systems is a fundamental step in ensuring the safety and security of a nation.

These systems can intercept and destroy nuclear missiles before they reach their targets, acting as a deterrent against potential attacks. They use advanced technology and their autonomous capabilities to defend against modern warfare.

After a nuclear attack, the importance of autonomous computer networks is highlighted in the recovery process. These networks could help in coordinating emergency response efforts, managing humanitarian assistance operations, and restoring critical infrastructure. Autonomous networks can assess damage and help prioritize response activities and allocate resources effectively. This would be an essential step in minimizing the impact of the attack on affected populations.

Using autonomous computer networks after an attack can lead to a faster and more organized recovery process. These networks can process a lot of data, make decisions based on it, and identify areas needing attention and allocate resources. This would not only save time, but also ensure that resources are utilized effectively in the wake of a disaster.

In addition to aiding in emergency response efforts, autonomous computer networks would also be essential in restoring critical infrastructure. These networks can analyze damage to infrastructure and prioritize repairs to restore critical services quickly. This would not only aid in the recovery process, but also guarantee that populations affected by a nuclear attack can access essential services afterward.

By analyzing diplomatic, military, and intelligence information independently, these networks could assess the intentions and capabilities of potential adversaries, providing decision-makers with a better understanding of the situation. In addition to analysis, these networks could also play a important role in crisis communication and conflict resolution. By providing recommendations for de-escalation strategies, they could help prevent potential conflicts from escalating to dangerous levels.

This would be especially important in times of high tension and uncertainty, where quick and accurate decision-making is vital. Using autonomous computer networks in escalation management can greatly enhance decision-makers' ability to handle complex international situations.

Protecting autonomous networks from EMPs requires a combination of physical hardening, system redundancy, and operational procedures like one way to protect sensitive electronic components and infrastructure from the potentially devastating effects of EMPs is to utilize conductive materials in the form of metal enclosures or Faraday cages. These materials act as a barrier, either blocking or absorbing the electromagnetic radiation that can cause serious damage. By implementing these measures, the impact of EMPs can be greatly reduced, allowing critical systems to continue functioning.

Another method for mitigating the effects of EMPs is through proper shielding. This involves the use of conductive materials that are specifically designed to dissipate or redirect electromagnetic energy. By strategically placing these materials around vulnerable components, the energy from EMPs can be diverted away from critical systems, preserving their functionality.

While shielding and conductive materials can help protect against EMPs, it's important to note that these measures are not foolproof. In order to truly protect against the damage caused by electromagnetic pulses, a multi-layered approach must be taken. This includes a combination of shielding, backup systems, and emergency protocols to minimize the impact of EMPs and keep vital infrastructure and equipment running.

Grounding systems are designed and maintained to provide a low impedance path for current flow to earth, helping to dissipate induced currents and reducing the risk of damage from EMPs. This is achieved by creating a conductive connection between electrical equipment and the earth's surface. Proper grounding is essential in protecting electronic equipment and infrastructure from the harmful effects of EMPs. During an EMP event, large amounts of electromagnetic energy are released and can cause significant damage to electronic equipment. The grounding system protects sensitive electrical components by safely directing induced currents into the ground. By doing so, it prevents the currents from damaging the equipment and ensures its proper functioning. Installing TVS or surge protectors on power lines, data cables, and communication interfaces is important for protecting sensitive electronic components. These devices are essential in limiting voltage spikes that can pose a significant threat to electronic systems.

Voltage spikes caused by electromagnetic pulses (EMPs) can cause irreparable damage to electronic systems if left unprotected. TVS and surge protectors are designed to clamp excessive voltages and divert transient currents away from sensitive electronic components. They act as a barrier between the EMPs and the electronic systems, ensuring that the voltage spikes do not reach and damage the components. TVS and surge protectors play a vital role in safeguarding electronic systems from EMPs. Without these devices, electronic components are left vulnerable to voltage spikes, which can lead to system failures and downtime. These devices are designed specifically to handle high voltages and excessive currents. They are essential for any EMP protection strategy.

By installing TVS and surge protectors, you are taking proactive measures to safeguard your electronic systems against EMPs. This helps to minimize the risk of downtime and financial losses caused by EMPs. In conclusion, installing TVS and surge protectors on power lines, data cables, and communication interfaces is a critical step in protecting electronic systems from EMPs.

These devices act as a first line of defence against voltage spikes, diverting them away from sensitive electronic components.

Designing autonomous networks with redundancy and diversity can help mitigate the impact of EMPs. With technology advancing quickly, it's important to be prepared for unexpected events. This can be achieved through the deployment of multiple redundant systems, the use of diverse communication links, and the implementation of failover mechanisms.

The implementation of various redundant systems can help in mitigating the impact of EMPs. If one system fails, another system takes over to ensure critical functions and communication is still working. Redundancy allows time for repairs without completely shutting down operations. Additionally, using diverse communication links such as satellite, landline, and wireless connections can further strengthen the network's resilience. In case of an EMP attack, even if one communication link is disrupted, the others can still work, ensuring communication and critical functions remain intact.

Implementing failover mechanisms can help prevent disruptions by smoothly transitioning to backup systems in case of failure. With these measures in place, the impact of EMPs can be significantly reduced, allowing for continued operations and minimal downtime.

When dealing with the danger of an electromagnetic pulse (EMP), it is important to have strong networks that can withstand the powerful energy surge. This is where the selection and utilization of electronic components specifically designed for such scenarios comes into play. These hardened components are able to endure the intense and destructive effects of EMPs, allowing autonomous networks to continue functioning even in the face of such a catastrophic event.

One such example of a hardened component is the radiation-hardened integrated circuit (IC). These ICs are designed to withstand high levels of radiation and electromagnetic interference, making them ideal for use in situations where EMPs may occur. In addition, durable power supplies and strong communication equipment are crucial for strengthening the resilience of autonomous networks.

These specialized components are able to operate under extreme conditions, ensuring that crucial functions of the network remain intact.

Concept of Artificial Intelligence

General Concept

Generically it is the ability of a machine or computer system to think and make decisions like a human. It has been a topic of fascination for decades and has been the subject of many science fiction stories.

Artificial Intelligence is a concept that revolves around algorithms. AI is the study and development of computer systems that can perform tasks that typically need human intelligence. ESE (Enterprise Systems Engineering) systems are programmed with algorithms that allow them to learn, reason, and make decisions based on data and patterns. The ultimate goal of AI is to create machines that can think, learn, and act like humans.

AI is based on algorithms, which are instructions that a computer follows to complete a task. These algorithms are created by humans and are designed to mimic human thought processes. They can be used to analyze large amounts of data, recognize patterns, and make decisions based on that data. Technology advances have made algorithms more powerful, enabling AI systems to do tasks that were once considered impossible for machines. AI has a wide range of applications, from self-driving cars to virtual assistants like Siri and Alexa.

It is also used in industries such as healthcare, finance, and manufacturing. AI systems can process and analyze data faster than humans, making them useful in many fields. Despite the progress made in AI, there is still much to be explored and developed. AI technology is continuously advancing and expanding its potential, making it an exciting and ever-evolving field.

However, with the rapid advances in technology, AI has become a reality in our everyday lives. From virtual assistants like Siri, to self-driving cars, AI has become an integral part of our society. With the rise of AI, there has been a debate about its potential impact on humanity.

Artificial Intelligence is a vast field that has gained immense popularity in recent years. It encompasses the creation of intelligent machines that can think, learn, and adapt like humans. These machines can understand complex data, make decisions, and even mimic human behaviour. This cutting-edge technology has revolutionized various industries and continues to evolve with each passing day. OAI is designed to help humans with tasks that need advanced thinking. These tasks may include data analysis, problem-solving, and decision-making.

The development of AI has opened up new possibilities for automation, which has resulted in increased efficiency and productivity. It has allowed people to give boring and repetitive tasks to machines, giving them more time to focus on important things.

The advancement in AI technology has led to breakthroughs in numerous fields, including healthcare, finance, and transportation. Intelligent machines have been used to diagnose diseases, optimize financial investments, and even drive cars. These developments have made our lives easier and have shown us the potential of AI. AI is getting better and will change how we live and work. With AI, the possibilities are limitless, and the future looks promising.

This field focuses on creating machines that can imitate human cognitive abilities such as learning, problem-solving, understanding language, and processing sensory information.

Algorithms are a fundamental part of computer science and have become increasingly important as technology advances. Artificial intelligence and machine learning are increasingly important for enabling computers to quickly and efficiently analyze and process large amounts of data.

They are essentially sets of instructions that guide computers in solving complex problems or completing tasks on their own. These instructions are carefully designed and tested by computer scientists to ensure accuracy and efficiency. They can range from simple calculations to complex decision-making processes, depending on the problem at hand.

Algorithms are used in many different things, like search engines and self-driving cars. They keep getting better as new problems come up. As technology continues to evolve, the need for more advanced algorithms will only increase.

The internet and big data have increased the need for algorithms to organize information. They provide structure and organization to an otherwise overwhelming amount of data and allow us to extract valuable insights. Algorithms are essential for computers to complete tasks on their own.

The use of algorithms is the foundation of Artificial Intelligence (AI). It has led to advancements in this field.pt. These algorithms are essentially sets of instructions that allow computers to solve problems or complete tasks on their own. AI technology relies on following specific rules to achieve a desired outcome, making them fundamental to its functioning. AI has become essential in our society due to the rapid development of computing power and the vast availability of data. From voice assistants to self-driving cars, algorithms have become the driving force behind these technological innovations. They allow machines to learn from data, recognize patterns, and make decisions without human intervention. This opens up new possibilities and has the potential to revolutionize our way of life and work.

It's a part of computer science that focuses on making smart machines that can do tasks humans usually do. This includes learning, problem-solving, and decision-making. AI has been a concept for a long time, but recent technological advances have made it very important. AI's main goal is to simplify our lives by automating repetitive tasks, allowing us to focus on more important matters.

Also plays an essential role in several fields:

- AI is transforming the healthcare sector. Machine learning algorithms are being used to analyse vast datasets of medical records, identifying patterns and predicting patient outcomes with remarkable accuracy. AI-powered diagnostic tools can detect diseases such as cancer at earlier stages, allowing for more timely and effective treatments. Companies are also using AI to create personalised treatment plans that respond to the specific needs of each patient.

- Financial sector: analysing market data in real time and executing transactions at lightning speed. AI is also being used to detect fraud, assess credit risk and personalise financial products and services. Robotic advisors, driven by AI algorithms, are also gaining popularity, offering automated investment advice and portfolio management to individuals with varying risk profiles.

- Autonomous cars, powered by AI and sensor technology, are set to revolutionise road safety and personal mobility. AI algorithms are also optimising traffic flow, reducing congestion and improving efficiency in urban environments. In the field of logistics and supply chain management, AI is playing a crucial role in optimising routes, forecasting demand and automating warehouse operations, resulting in faster delivery times and lower transport costs.

- AI-powered robots are increasingly being used in factories, carrying out repetitive, dangerous or highly precise tasks. AI is also used to monitor and optimise manufacturing processes, identifying inefficiencies and reducing downtime.

Narrow AI is a type of AI that focuses on solving problems within a specific field. It is not as advanced as general AI, as it lacks the broad cognitive abilities of a human. ANI is limited to the specific tasks it is programmed for and cannot apply its knowledge to new situations. However, it is still able to perform its designated tasks with a high level of accuracy and efficiency. ANI can be seen in various forms, such as virtual personal assistants, image recognition systems, and language translation services.

These are all examples of ANI that are widely used in our daily lives. Virtual personal assistants like Siri and Alexa understand and respond to user commands, while image recognition systems identify and categorize objects in images. Language translation services, on the other hand, use ANI to translate text from one language to another. Despite its limitations, ANI plays a crucial role in today's society.

It has greatly improved efficiency and productivity in various industries, from healthcare to finance. As technology continues to advance, we can expect to see even more advancements in ANI and its applications. However, it is important to note that ANI is not capable of achieving true consciousness and self-awareness like general AI.

Artificial General Intelligence (AGI), also known as Strong AI, is the next level of AI development. It is the ultimate goal of creating artificial intelligence, as it would be equivalent to human intelligence. AI would be able to understand, learn, and apply knowledge to various tasks, very much like a human being. It is a massive leap forward from the current AI, which is limited to specific tasks. AGI aims to create a system that can perform any intellectual task a human can do.

This requires the development of a machine that can think like a human. In other words, AGI should be able to reason, make decisions, and solve problems. This is a big step for artificial intelligence, even though we still have a long way to go, the progress is promising.

The potential applications of AGI are vast and varied. From autonomous vehicles to medical diagnosis and scientific research,

AGI can revolutionize many industries. It can also lead to significant improvements in the quality of life for humans.

Types of AI

Artificial Narrow Intelligence It is the most basic form of artificial intelligence and is designed to perform specific tasks with a high degree of accuracy. ANI is commonly used in various applications such as robotics, natural language processing, and image recognition.

ANI is designed to work within a predefined set of rules and can only perform tasks that it has been programmed to do. ANI cannot think or make decisions outside the limits set by its creators, unlike humans.

This makes ANI very limited in its capabilities, but also highly efficient in performing its designated tasks. ANI, despite being less advanced than other types of AI, is still important in various industries. Its ability to perform repetitive tasks with precision and speed makes it an indispensable tool in various fields, including manufacturing, healthcare, and finance.

One of its key functionalities is that it can identify the brand, model, and license plate numbers of cars in the street, making tracking and filtering easier and more efficient. What would have been a tedious and time-consuming task for a human is now made simple by using filters in the program. This saves valuable time and effort for law enforcement agencies and other organizations. In addition, Sight Hound's AI capabilities extend beyond the mere recognition of vehicles. It is also capable of identifying and recognizing people based on their facial characteristics.

With its advanced algorithms, the program can determine a person's age, sex, ethnicity, and even their mood, just by analyzing their facial features. This can be extremely useful in various scenarios, such as identifying suspects in a crime or monitoring a person's emotional state in a healthcare setting.

Additionally, the program also has the ability to automatically redact personally identifiable information, such as faces and license plate numbers, further protecting the privacy of individuals.

As technology continues to advance, ANI is becoming more sophisticated and is being integrated into a wider range of applications, making our lives easier and more efficient.

While humans have tried to create machines with general intelligence, they have yet to succeed. However, the possibility of building an AI that can think, perceive, and understand like humans is highly anticipated. Such a machine would be independent, versatile, and capable of forming connections across different domains. With the advancement of technology, machines could potentially surpass humans in terms of performance, speed, and accuracy.

In addition, these machines would eliminate human error and fatigue, making them more efficient than humans. In addition, they would also have the ability to experience emotions and have consciousness. These qualities would make machines just as capable as humans, if not more. In contrast to the current AI machines that mainly focus on processing information at a faster rate, AGI would be able to strategize, think abstractly, and tap into deep thoughts and memories like humans.

This would enable machines to create abstract ideas, analyze complex situations, and make decisions based on reasoning, problem-solving, and learning capabilities.

Furthermore, AGI would also have its own imagination and creativity, which would allow them to generate new ideas and think outside the box. In order to prove that AGI has been achieved, machines would have to pass the famous Turing Test. This test is designed to determine whether a machine can engage in a conversation with a human in a way that it cannot be distinguished from another human.

Artificial General Intelligence (AGI) is a term used to describe a machine or computer that has the ability to perform any intellectual task that a human being can. This means that AGI has the ability to think, learn, reason, and even feel emotions just like humans do.

Unlike traditional machines or computers, which are programmed to perform specific tasks, AGI is designed with a more generalized intelligence that can be applied to a wide range of tasks and problems.

The concept of AGI has been around for quite some time and has been portrayed in science fiction movies and novels. However, it wasn't until recent advancements in technology that the idea of AGI became a realistic possibility. The pursuit of achieving AGI is a complex and formidable task that demands the collaboration of experts from diverse fields, including computer science, neuroscience, cognitive psychology, and philosophy.

One of the biggest challenges in creating AGI is replicating the human brain and its many intricate processes. The human brain is capable of processing vast amounts of information and making complex decisions based on that information. Replicating this level of intelligence in a machine has proven to be no easy feat. With rapid advancements in technology and a growing interest in AI, researchers and scientists are making significant strides toward achieving AGI.

Artificial Super intelligence (ASI) is a hypothetical agent with intelligence beyond any human brain. This technology poses some serious questions to humanity, since its development could potentially change the face of the entire world. The rise of ASI might even lead to the end of humanity, as the artificial intelligence could become self-aware and perceive us as a threat to its existence.

ASI concept has been around for decades, now becoming more feasible with technology. The idea of AI surpassing human intelligence is both fascinating and terrifying.

Given the immense potential of ASI, it is vital for humankind to approach its development with utmost caution and meticulous deliberation. The impact of ASI on society and the world as a whole is still unknown, but it is crucial for us to continue exploring and expanding our knowledge in this field. As we push the boundaries of technology, we must also be mindful of the potential consequences and ensure that we are creating a future that benefits everyone.

Professor Bostrom from the University of Oxford provides a concise and accurate definition of this term. He believes that a "superintelligence" is intelligence that exceeds the abilities of the most brilliant human minds in every aspect, ranging from scientific advancements to social aptitude. This definition also raises questions about the implementation of such super intelligence.

It could be achieved through a digital computer, a network of interconnected computers, or even through culture of cortical tissue. Furthermore, it also raises whether this super intelligence would possess sentience and subjective experiences.

The idea of ASI has been a topic of debate and fascination for many years. It has been a subject of many sci-fi movies and books, sparking the imagination of people all over the world.

ASI, or Artificial Super intelligence, is essentially an intellect that surpasses human intelligence in every possible way. Its potential implementation and the existence of sentience within such a being are still subjects of wide interpretation. The concept of ASI has captured the interest of people worldwide and has sparked debates about its potential impact on society and ethics. As technology continues to advance, the possibility of creating ASI becomes more and more realistic, making it a topic that will continue to be explored and discussed in the future.

Reactive machines fall into the first type of classification for artificial intelligence systems. Unlike the other types, they are limited in their abilities as they do not have the ability to form memories or use experiences to make decisions. This is why they are called "reactive" machines, as they only react to the current situation at hand.

They have no understanding of their environment, which restricts their applications to simple tasks that they were specifically programmed for. One defining characteristic of reactive machines is that their operation will always remain the same, regardless of where and when they are used. This means that they do not have the ability to learn or grow, and are confined to their programming.

Reactive machines may seem limited in their capabilities, but they have proven to be useful in certain tasks. Their inability to form memories or learn from experiences means that their actions are consistent and predictable, making them suitable for tasks that require repetitive precision. However, their lack of adaptability and growth also limits their potential for more complex tasks and decision-making. As technology advances, it will be interesting to see how reactive machines will evolve and potentially bridge the gap between reactive and more advanced artificial intelligence systems.

Limited memory systems are essential in the development of modern Artificial Intelligence. With its ability to analyze historical data and make informed decisions, limited memory is the foundation of AI applications.

Deep learning, which is prevalent in today's AI endeavours, relies heavily on limited memory systems. By feeding the computer large amounts of data, deep learning algorithms are able to create knowledge and make predictions based on patterns and trends. An excellent example of this is image recognition AI. This type of AI is trained by being exposed to thousands of labelled images, allowing the program to recognize and label objects accurately. As the AI encounters more images, its accuracy increases, making it incredibly reliable. This process is similar to how humans learn and make decisions based on experiences. By incorporating limited memory systems, AI is becoming more advanced and is able to perform tasks that were once thought to be exclusive to human intelligence.

With the continuous advancements in technology, AI is becoming increasingly essential in our daily lives.

Deep learning, which is a subset of machine learning, is an incredibly powerful technique that enables computer systems to acquire knowledge and skills from vast amounts of data and real-world interactions. This process involves training neural networks with vast amounts of data and subsequently enabling the network to make predictions on new data. Machine learning is essential for the development of truly intelligent artificial intelligence systems that can navigate complex, real-world environments. This machine learning approach has revolutionized the AI field, ushering in breakthroughs in computer vision, natural language processing, and robotics. Deep learning has also played a critical role in the development of self-driving cars, virtual assistants, and personalized recommendation systems.

By continually learning from data and experience, these systems can enhance their performance over time, rendering them more accurate and efficient. However, despite its much advancement, deep learning still faces challenges in areas such as interpretability and generalization. As researchers continue to enhance and perfect their techniques, we can anticipate witnessing even more remarkable applications of deep learning in the future.

The main objective of deep learning is to develop highly intelligent machines capable of processing immense volumes of data while comprehending and engaging with the world significantly.

H2O is an extremely versatile platform for machine learning, capable of supporting a wide range of deep learning systems. These systems include some of the most popular and cutting-edge technologies in the field, such as Cafe, Torch, and Theano. This means that H2o users have access to a vast array of tools and resources to help them build, train, and deploy their deep learning models.

Furthermore, the platform offers seamless integration with various systems, allowing users to switch between them easily and take advantage of their unique features and capabilities. This flexibility is particularly useful for data scientists and developers who may need to compare and contrast different models and algorithms to find the best solution for their specific problem. With H2O, users can easily perform tasks without the inconvenience of switching between multiple platforms or tools, ultimately saving valuable time and effort. Not only is H2O compatible with various deep learning systems, it also offers a unified interface for efficiently managing and monitoring all your models.

Regardless of which system people's use, they can keep track of their experiments, progress, and make adjustments as needed all within the H2o platform. This makes it an incredibly powerful and convenient tool for anyone seeking to leverage the full potential of deep learning in their projects.

Whether a user is a seasoned data scientist or just starting out, H2O is the perfect platform to bring deep learning ideas to life.

AI Cyber Security System

The first step in any artificial intelligence project is to identify the problem that needs to be solved. This can range from simple tasks like image recognition to more complex tasks like natural language processing or game playing. By clearly defining the problem, developers can focus their efforts on finding the most effective and efficient solution.

One of the most central aspects of developing an AI system is collecting the necessary data. This data is used to train the algorithm and teach it to recognize and understand patterns and relationships. The quantity of data required may vary significantly depending on the task at hand, but it is crucial to have a substantial amount in order to attain precise and dependable outcomes. Without enough data, the AI system may struggle to make accurate predictions or decisions.

Collecting data is crucial for any AI system. It is equally vital to ensure that the gathered data is of the utmost quality and accurately represents the real-world scenarios that the AI system will encounter. Only then can we truly harness the power of AI and make informed decisions based on reliable insights. This can involve cleaning and organizing the data, as well as identifying any biases or gaps that may exist. By carefully optimizing the data, developers can enhance the performance and accuracy of the AI system, resulting in more successful outcomes.

Data pre-processing is an essential step in data analysis and machine learning. Before feeding data into an algorithm, it often needs to be cleaned and transformed to ensure that it is in a usable format. This process is known as data pre-processing. It encompasses tasks such as removing irrelevant or duplicate data, addressing missing values, and transforming data into a format better suited for the algorithm's use. One important aspect of data pre-processing is feature extraction. It process involves identifying and selecting the most relevant features or characteristics from the data to be used as input variables for the algorithm. This step is essential in reducing the dimensionality of the data and improving the accuracy and efficiency of the algorithm. Feature extraction techniques can vary depending on the type of data and the specific problem being solved. Some common methods include principal component analysis, cluster analysis, and feature selection algorithms. Overall, data pre-processing and feature extraction are crucial steps in the data analysis process. They ensure that the data is in an appropriate format for the algorithm to utilize and that the most significant features are chosen to make precise predictions or decisions. Without these steps, the algorithm may not perform as well or may even produce erroneous results.

Choosing the ideal algorithm for a particular task is an important part of any AI project. Each algorithm is specifically designed for certain types of problems, with unique strengths and limitations. For example, predicting numerical values is better suited for linear regression, while image recognition may require a convolution neural network. To ensure that the algorithm will effectively address the analyzing problem, it is essential to understand its capabilities and limitations.

Linear regression, for instance, excels when the relationship between variables follows a linear pattern, whereas a convolution neural network demonstrates superior capability in identifying intricate patterns within images. It is equally important to take into consideration the magnitude and intricacy of the accessible dataset, since certain algorithms might encounter difficulties when dealing with extensive or intricate data.

Once selected an algorithm, it is important to properly implement and fine-tune it for optimal performance. This requires a deep understanding of the algorithm's inner workings, its parameters, and how to properly evaluate its results. It may also be necessary to combine multiple algorithms to achieve the desired outcome. Ultimately, the right algorithm will greatly impact the success of AI projects.

The training of the model is a critical step where the algorithm learns to make predictions. This is done using a labelled dataset, where the correct outputs are already known. The algorithm adjusts its internal parameters based on the input data and the corresponding correct outputs.

The training process comprises multiple iterations, during which the algorithm progressively learns to minimize the disparity between the anticipated outcomes and the real outcomes. During training, the algorithm goes through a series of mathematical calculations to understand the patterns and relationships within the data. It then uses this information to make predictions on new, unseen data.

The training process is iterative, which means that the algorithm repeats the same steps multiple times, adjusting its parameters each time to improve its predictions. This process continues until the algorithm reaches a point where it can accurately predict the outcomes with minimal error. The training process is decisive as it determines the accuracy and reliability of the model. A properly trained model will have the capability to accurately predict outcomes on new data, whereas an inadequately trained model could yield unpredictable or untrustworthy results.

The process of validating a trained algorithm model is an essential step in ensuring its reliability and effectiveness. This step involves testing the model on a separate dataset, which has not been used during the training process. This is done to ensure that the model can generalize well to new, unseen data. By testing the model on this new dataset, we can evaluate its performance and identify any potential weaknesses or limitations. During the testing phase, the model is exposed to data it has not encountered before. This step is crucial as it replicates real-world conditions in which the model must make predictions on new and unseen data.

The model's performance is then evaluated based on its ability to accurately make predictions and handle unexpected data inputs. If the model performs well on this new dataset, it can be deemed reliable and proficient in generalizing to various datasets. The testing phase is fundamental in determining the overall effectiveness of the trained algorithm model. It provides a comprehensive depiction of the model's performance in real-life scenarios and aids in detecting any potential issues that may arise. By ensuring that the model can generalize effectively to new, unseen data, we can greatly increase our confidence in its ability to make accurate predictions and solve complex problems.

Once satisfied with the model's performance, it is then ready to be deployed for real-world use. This means that the model is now capable of accepting new input data and making predictions, classifications, or decisions based on that data. This is where the true value of AI systems lies: in their ability to deliver precise and efficient solutions to real-world problems. In order to ensure that the model continues to perform at its best, a feedback loop is often implemented. The model's performance is continuously monitored, and any potential issues or areas for improvement are identified. This allows the model to be retrained with new data or fine-tuned to improve both its accuracy and generalization.

This iterative process is fundamental in the development of AI systems because it enables constant improvement and adaptation to changing environments. Overall, the deployment and refinement of AI systems is a continuous process that involves constant monitoring and iteration.

The effectiveness of an AI system relies on more than just the algorithm alone. In fact, it is dependent on a variety of factors that work together to create a successful outcome. These factors encompass the quality and diversity of the data utilized for training, the selected features, and the overall system design. Each of these components plays a crucial role in the performance of the AI system.

When it comes to choosing the right algorithm, it's important to consider the specific task at hand. This is because different algorithms and techniques are better suited for different tasks. The characteristics of the problem must be carefully analyzed in order to select the most appropriate algorithm for the task. The design of the AI system is also a crucial aspect to consider. This includes not only the algorithm, but also the overall architecture and structure of the system.

The design should be well-thought-out and tailored to the specific problem it is meant to solve. A poorly designed system can lead to inaccurate results and hinder the effectiveness of AI.

Amplitude of AI

Machine Learning (ML) is a part of AI that focuses on data-driven learning systems. These systems can learn and improve from experience without being explicitly programmed by taking advantage of algorithms and statistical models. This enables ML to develop systems capable of analyzing data and making decisions or predictions without the need for explicit programming.

Machine Learning is also widely used in various applications such as email filtering, pattern recognition, computer vision, and much more. ML is the driving force behind the development of self-driving cars, voice-controlled assistants, and smart home systems. It is also used in the medical field to help doctors diagnose diseases and detect patterns in medical data.

This technology is constantly evolving. With the advancements in computing power and the availability of large datasets, machine learning is becoming increasingly powerful and efficient. It is also being used in financial institutions to detect fraudulent activities, as well as in e-commerce to enhance customer behavior and boost sales.

The rapid ascent of machine learning has not only fostered the emergence of deep learning, an intriguing branch of ML, but has also propelled the advancement of artificial neural networks that can adeptly acquire knowledge from massive datasets. This breakthrough has empowered machines to accomplish tasks that were once exclusively within the realm of human capabilities. Now, they can effortlessly conquer image recognition and handle natural language processing with unparalleled precision.

Although machine learning offers numerous advantages, it is not exempt from challenges. One major obstacle is the presence of biased data, which can have significant consequences. Additionally, machine learning models require constant monitoring and maintenance to ensure their accuracy and effectiveness. These challenges highlight the importance of addressing biases in data and the critical need for ongoing vigilance in maintaining machine learning systems. However, with its potential to revolutionize various industries and improve our daily lives, the future of ML looks very promising.

It is a subset of AI that involves the development of algorithms and models that enable systems to learn from data and improve their performance over time without being explicitly programmed.

Deep learning has experienced a surge in popularity in recent years, mainly due to its remarkable success rates in tasks such as image and speech recognition. Deep Learning is a powerful form of machine learning that leverages neural networks with multiple layers, known as deep neural networks, to analyze and process data.

This allows for more complex data to be processed, leading to more accurate results. One of the key benefits of deep learning is its ability to recognize patterns and features within data that may not be immediately obvious to the human eye. This feature is especially valuable for tasks like image and speech recognition, where there is often a significant amount of data to analyze.

Deep learning algorithms can extract and interpret intricate patterns with exceptional precision and reliability by leveraging deep neural networks. Another advantage of deep learning is its ability to continuously learn and improve over time.

As the system is exposed to increasing amounts of data, it becomes capable of adapting and enhancing its performance, thus making it highly flexible and versatile. This makes it suitable for a wide range of applications, from self-driving cars to automated customer service systems. With its increasing popularity and ongoing advancements, deep learning is poised to revolutionize the way we process and analyze data, paving the way for even more advanced technologies and solutions in the future.

Natural Language Processing (NLP) represents a rapidly evolving field of artificial intelligence focused on developing systems capable of understanding, interpreting, and generating human language.

The main objective of NLP is to empower computers with the ability to understand and decipher the intricate nuances and complexities of human language. This will empower them to carry out various tasks, including chatbot interactions, language translation, and sentiment analysis. By achieving this goal, computers can communicate with humans in a more natural and intuitive way, making human-computer interactions seamless and efficient.

One of the primary challenges in NLP is to train machines to accurately process and interpret human language, which is inherently ambiguous and dependent on context. Take, for instance, how a single word can yield various interpretations depending on the context, just as a sentence can be subject to different meanings influenced by the speaker's tone, expressions, and gestures. In order to tackle these challenges, NLP researchers employ a multitude of techniques, encompassing natural language understanding, natural language generation, and machine learning. These techniques empower machines to analyze, comprehend, and generate language in a remarkably human-like way. As a result, they become capable of accomplishing complex tasks like language translation and sentiment analysis.

NLP has many real-world applications, including virtual assistants, chatbots, language translation services, and sentiment analysis tools. Given the rising demand for intelligent automation and enhanced human-computer interactions, the significance of NLP is expected to continue growing in the future.

As machines become more proficient in understanding and generating human language, they will be able to assist us in many different ways, making our lives easier and more efficient. Thus, the advancements in NLP have the potential to revolutionize the way we communicate and interact with technology.

4- Computer vision is a rapidly growing field, with countless applications that are changing the way we interact with technology. By leveraging sophisticated algorithms and cutting-edge machine learning techniques, computers are able to interpret and analyze visual data, making decisions and taking action based on what they "see."

This is a significant advancement, as computers are now able to accomplish tasks that were once thought to be unique to humans. One of the most notable applications of computer vision is in facial recognition technology. With this powerful tool, computers are able to recognize and analyze human faces, even in large crowds. This has revolutionized security systems, and has also been used to help find missing persons and identify criminals.

Another area where computer vision has had a major impact is in object detection. By analyzing images and videos, computers can now identify and locate objects within a scene. This has been applied in a variety of fields, from self-driving cars to medical imaging. Thanks to computer vision, machines can now perceive and interact with the world, enhancing their autonomy and efficiency. As technology advances, the potential for computer vision is endless, and it will continue to play a crucial role in shaping our future.

5 - Robotics is a rapidly growing field that combines artificial intelligence with physical systems. This integration has given way to machines that are able to interact with and manipulate their environment. This is where AI comes into play, providing the necessary algorithms for machines to make complex decisions and take action. The hardware aspect of robotics encompasses the tangible creation of robots capable of effectively completing tasks in the physical realm.

These robots come in all shapes and sizes, from small drones to large industrial machines. They are equipped with sensors, motors, and other components that allow them to move, sense, and interact with their environment. The software component of robotics is equally important, as it provides the intelligence that drives the machines. AI algorithms allow robots to analyze data, learn from their experiences, and make decisions that lead to optimal outcomes.

The ultimate goal of robotics is to create machines that can operate autonomously, without the need for human intervention. This would allow these machines to perform tasks that are too dangerous, difficult, or tedious for humans to do. From manufacturing to healthcare, there are countless applications for robotics that can improve efficiency, safety, and quality of life. As technology continues to advance, we can expect to see even more impressive developments in the field of robotics.

Expert Systems are a form of Artificial Intelligence (AI) that aims to emulate the decision-making process of a human expert in a specific field. These systems employ a technique called rule-based reasoning, which entails inputting data and information into the system and analyzing them according to a predetermined set of rules. This enables expert systems to think and make decisions much like humans, by analyzing all the available information and then selecting the best course of action.

The aim of expert systems is to solve complex problems that would normally require the expertise of a human. By using this technology, organizations and businesses can save time and resources by automating certain decision-making processes. For example, an expert system could be used to diagnose medical conditions, provide legal advice, or make financial decisions.

This allows experts to focus on more critical and specialized tasks, while the system handles routine and repetitive tasks. One of the main advantages of expert systems is their capability to learn from their own decisions and enhance their performance over time. By analyzing past decisions and their outcomes, the system can continuously refine its rules and logic, making it more accurate and efficient in the long run.

This not only leads to better decision-making but also reduces the risk of errors and improves overall performance. With the rapid advancements in AI technology, we can anticipate that expert systems will become increasingly sophisticated and play a prominent role in various industries in the future.

Ethics in cyberspace

Individuals, organizations, and societies each play a unique role in shaping the landscape of the cyber world. As technology continues to evolve and advance, it is imperative that these entities collaborate to promote the essential values necessary for a secure and fair online environment.

Privacy, security, fairness, and transparency are fundamental values that should take precedence in order to uphold a healthy and functional cyberspace. Privacy is the right of individuals to control their personal information and how it is shared. In this era of digitization, where an immense quantity of personal data is being collected and stored, safeguarding individuals' privacy has become increasingly vital.

Security, on the other hand, refers to the measures taken to protect individuals and organizations from cyber threats and attacks. In today's increasingly interconnected world, the internet has become an indispensable part of our daily lives. With this growing reliance, it is vital to continually update and enhance our security measures to counter emerging threats effectively.

Fairness and transparency are also essential values that must be upheld in the cyber world. Fairness ensures that all individuals and organizations have equal access to the resources and opportunities available online, while transparency promotes openness and accountability in the use of technology.

A special remark:

1 – Privacy in cyberspace is a essential aspect of modern society. With advancements in technology, the concept of privacy has evolved, requiring a delicate balance between convenience and individual rights. As the digital age progresses, so do the challenges to maintaining personal privacy. It is decisive to continually evaluate

and enhance privacy measures to keep up with the ever-changing scene of technology.

One of the greatest obstacles to personal privacy in the digital world is the continual gathering and utilization of personal data by corporations and organizations. The rise of social media and online shopping has led to a constant sharing of personal information, which can be exploited for targeted advertising and other purposes.

This raises concerns about the potential exploitation and misuse of personal data, highlighting the need for stronger privacy measures.

A - Every citizen that uses the internet in its personal life exposes:

1 - Identity Information like:

* **Name:** Full names, nicknames, or usernames.

* **Date of Birth:** Birthdates used for age verification and personalization.

* **Gender:** Information about an individual's gender identity.

2 - Contact Information:

* **Email Addresses**: Used for communication and account verification.

* **Phone Numbers**: Contact details for communication and account recovery.

* **Physical Addresses:** Residential or mailing addresses.

3 - Financial Information:

* **Credit Card Details**: Information used for online transactions.

* **Bank Account Information**: Details for electronic fund transfers.

* **Income Information**: Data related to an individual's financial status.

4- Online Account Credentials:

* **Usernames and Passwords**: Login credentials for various online accounts.

* **Security Questions and Answers**: Information used for account recovery.

5 - Social Media Data:

* **Profiles and Usernames**: Information displayed on social media profiles.

* **Posts and Comments**: Content shared by individuals on social platforms.

* **Friend Lists**: Lists of connections on social networks.

6 - Biometric Data:

* **Facial Recognition Data**: Facial features used for identification.

* **Fingerprint Data**: Biometric information for authentication.

7 - Health and Medical Information:

* **Medical Records**: Health history and treatment details.

* **Fitness Data**: Information related to physical activity and health monitoring.

8 - Location Data:

* **GPS Coordinates**: Real-time or historical location information.

* **Check-Ins**: Location-based check-ins on social media or other platforms.

9 - Internet Browsing and Search History:

* **Browsing History**: A record of websites visited.

* **Search Queries**: Keywords used in online searches.

10 - Behavioral and Usage Data:

* **Purchase History**: Information about products or services bought online.

* **App Usage Data**: Data generated by the use of mobile or web applications.

* **Online Activities**: Patterns of online behavior and interactions.

11- Education and Employment Information:

* **Educational Background**: Academic history, degrees, and qualifications.

* **Work History**: Employment details, including job titles and responsibilities.

12 - Preferences and Interests:

* **Shopping Preferences**: Information about preferred products and brands.

* **Content Preferences**: Types of content individuals engage with online.

B - Every company that uses the internet in its activity exposes:

1 - Customer Data:

* **Personal Information**: Names, addresses, contact details of customers.

* **Transaction History**: Records of purchases, orders, and financial transactions.

* **Customer Preferences:** Information about product or service preferences and buying behavior

2 - Financial Data:

* **Revenue and Expenses:** Financial performance metrics and records.

* **Budgets and Forecasts**: Financial projections and planning data.

* **Tax Information**: Details related to corporate taxes and compliance.

3 - Employee Data:

* **Personal Information**: Employee names, addresses, contact details.

* **Payroll Information**: Salary, bonuses, deductions, and tax details.

* **Performance Reviews**: Employee evaluations and performance metrics.

* **Training Records**: Information about employee training and development.

4 - Product and Service Data

* **Product Information**: Details about products or services offered.

* **Inventory Data**: Stock levels, tracking of goods in supply chains.

* **Product Development**: Plans, prototypes, and development data.

5 - Intellectual Property:

* **Patents and Trademarks**: Information related to patents and trademarks.

* **Copyrighted Material**: Protection of original creative works.

* **Trade Secrets**: Confidential business information, formulas, processes.

6 - Marketing and Sales Data:

* **Lead Information**: Data on potential customers and prospects.

* **Marketing Campaigns**: Information about marketing strategies and campaigns.

* **Sales Reports**: Data on sales performance and revenue.

7 - Operational Data:

* **Supply Chain Information**: Details about suppliers, logistics, and distribution.

* **Production Data**: Manufacturing processes, production schedules.

* **Quality Control Data**: Information on product quality and testing.

8 - Website and Analytics Data:

* **Website Traffic**: Data on website visits, user behavior, and interactions.

* **SEO Metrics**: Search engine optimization data for online visibility.

* **User Analytics**: Insights into user engagement and preferences.

9 - Security and Access Data:

* **Access Logs**: Records of user access to systems and applications.

* **Security Incident Data**: Information on security breaches or incidents.

* **Authentication Data**: User login and access credentials.

10 - Compliance and Legal Data:

* **Regulatory Compliance Records**: Documentation demonstrating adherence to industry regulations.

* **Legal Documents**: Contracts, agreements, and legal correspondence.

11 - Research and Development Data:

* **Research Findings**: Data from research initiatives and studies.

* **Prototypes and Designs**: Information related to product development.

* **Innovation Data**: Records of new ideas and innovations.

C - Critical data to National Security stored and managed in computers.

1 - Operational Data:

-Mission **Plans**: Details about military missions, including objectives, strategies, and tactics.

-Deployment **Information**: Schedules and locations of deployed military units.

-Logistical **Details**: Information related to the movement and supply of military forces.

2 - Personnel Information:

-Soldier **Identities**: Personal details of military personnel, including names, ranks, and positions.

-Training **Records**: Information about military training, qualifications, and skills.

-Deployment **History**: Records of past deployments and assignments.

3 - Equipment and Technology Data:

* **Weapon Systems Information**: Details about military equipment, weaponry, and capabilities.

* **Technology Specifications**: Information on advanced military technologies and capabilities.

* **Maintenance Records**: Data related to the maintenance and status of military equipment.

4 - Intelligence and Surveillance Data:

* **Satellite Imagery**: Images captured by satellites for intelligence purposes.

* **Signals Intelligence (SIGINT)**: Intercepted communications and electronic signals.

* **Human Intelligence (HUMINT)**: Information gathered from human sources.

5 - Cybersecurity Data:

* **Network Topology**: Information about the structure and layout of military networks.

* **Cyber Threat Intelligence**: Insights into potential cyber threats and vulnerabilities.

* **Incident Response Data**: Records of responses to cyber incidents.

6 - Geospatial Information:

* **Geographical Data**: Maps, coordinates, and terrain information for military operations.

* **Strategic Locations**: Information about key military bases and installations.

7 - Training and Simulation Data:

* **Simulation Scenarios**: Virtual training scenarios for military personnel.

* **Training Exercise Results**: Data from military training exercises.

8 - Communication Data:

* **Secure Communication Records**: Logs of secure military communications.

* **Radio Frequencies**: Information about authorized radio frequencies for military use.

9 - Strategic Plans and Policies:

* **National Security Strategies**: Documents outlining a country's national security priorities.

* **Military Policies**: Guidelines and policies governing military operations.

10 - Biometric and Identity Data:

* **Biometric Data**: Fingerprints, facial recognition data for identity verification.

* **Security Clearance Information**: Levels of access granted to military personnel.

11 - Emergency Response and Contingency Plans:

* **Disaster Response Plans**: Procedures for military response to natural disasters or emergencies.

* **Contingency Plans**: Strategies for responding to unforeseen events.

12 - International Collaboration Data:

* **Joint Military Exercises**: Information about collaborative military exercises with allied nations.

* **Diplomatic and** Defense **Agreements**: Agreements between countries related to defense and security.

AI Protection on Attacks

To use computers in handling such vital data poses multiple ethical dilemmas that must be addressed. Without proper safeguards in place, the potential for misuse or theft of this information is high.

This presents a moral quandary for those tasked with safeguarding this data, as they must go through the delicate equilibrium between ensuring security and potentially encroaching upon individuals' privacy. Moreover, the incorporation of computers in data management has given rise to concerns regarding the responsibility and accountability of individuals who possess access to this information.

What measures should be taken to ensure that this information is used ethically and responsibly?

How can we ensure that those who have access to this data are acting in the best interests of the country and its citizens?

To gain a comprehensive understanding of the ethical implications associated with the utilization of computers for handling important data, one must carefully contemplate the potential ramifications of cyber attacks. The loss or misuse of sensitive information can have wide-ranging impacts, ranging from individual identity theft to severe financial hardship, all the way to jeopardizing national security. There is a significant responsibility placed on those in charge of protecting this data to ensure that appropriate protocols and safeguards are in place.

This requires a delicate balancing act between security and privacy, and highlights the ethical dilemma at hand. In conclusion, the use of computers in managing vital data is a complex ethical issue that demands careful consideration. The potential consequences of a security breach must be taken seriously, and extensive measures must be implemented to prevent such incidents from happening. It is the duty of those in authority to guarantee the ethical and responsible utilization of this data, prioritizing the wellbeing of the country and its citizens above all else. Cyber security is a rapidly evolving field, with new dangers and vulnerabilities emerging daily. As a result, ensuring complete protection against cyber threats is an immense challenge and, for some, an impossible accomplishment.

No matter how advanced the technology, it is impossible to guarantee that any system or network can be completely shielded from cyber attacks. The constantly changing scenery of cyber threats makes staying ahead of them a discouraging task for cyber security professionals. To make matters worse, cybercriminals are always looking for new and innovative ways to breach systems and networks. This means that even if a system is secure today, it may not be tomorrow.

Government Ethical Justification for AI employment

The ethical considerations surrounding a government's exposure to a cyber attack are complex.

In the event of a cyber attack, to any governmental department either health (Hospitals) Justice (Courts, security forces) Education (Schools and Universities) Financial or regulatory institutions, national documents archives including Identity cards, passports issuers, social security, taxes and all the panoply of related subjects spread in a wide diversity of govern departments including energy and power suppliers considered as a national essential good for survival of the government must weigh the potential risks and consequences of their response.

One of the main concerns is the impact on innocent civilians. The government must also consider the potential for retaliation and escalation of the attack if they choose to respond aggressively. Additionally, the government must consider the potential political and diplomatic implications of their response. A cyber attack could be seen as an act of war, which could have far-reaching consequences on international relations.

The government must carefully strategize their response in order to minimize any negative effects on their alliances and partnerships. It is essential to take into account the potential economic impact of a cyber attack, as it has the power to disrupt businesses and result in substantial financial losses. Overall, the ethical considerations surrounding a government's exposure to a cyber attack require careful consideration and decision-making.

Governments have the critical responsibility of striking a delicate balance between safeguarding their citizens and protecting the interests of their nation, all while taking into account the potential repercussions of their decisions. It is crucial that they have a thorough understanding of the situation and all possible outcomes before making any decisions. After all, the safety and well-being of their citizens and the stability of their country are at stake.

National Security:

Governments have an ethical duty to prioritize the safety and security of their citizens. This responsibility is not taken lightly, as the well-being of every individual within the country is at stake. It is up to the government to safeguard its people from all kinds of threats, both foreign and domestic. To achieve this, implementing policies and procedures is essential to safeguard critical infrastructure and sensitive information from potential threats.

This is a vital aspect of national security that demands serious attention to ensure the ongoing safety of its citizens. In recent years, the rise of cyber attacks has become a major concern for governments around the world. It is no longer just a physical threat that needs to be addressed, but also a digital one. With the ever-increasing reliance on technology, protecting sensitive information has become more important than ever.

Government agencies must collaborate closely with cyber security experts to develop effective strategies and protocols aimed at safeguarding their critical infrastructure and sensitive data. Ensuring the security and stability of our nation is not only an ethical obligation but also an imperative necessity. It is of utmost importance for governments to continually reassess and enhance their security measures to stay one step ahead of potential threats. The use of AI neutralise the hackers and other malicious actors are constantly evolving and finding new ways to breach systems and steal information. The government has a critical responsibility to stay watchful and adjust to these emerging threats. It is their ethical duty to safeguard the safety and security of their citizens. Maintaining trust and ensuring people's safety is an ongoing and vital process that demands unwavering attention and ample resources.

Deterrence and Defence

Government has a responsibility to proactively address potential cyber threats, especially in today's interconnected world where our data is increasingly susceptible. This means investing in cyber security measures and developing defensive capabilities to protect against potential attacks. By doing so, governments are not only fulfilling their ethical obligations, but they are also safeguarding the privacy and security of their citizens.

To take proactive steps to prevent cyber attacks from occurring in the first place. By deterring potential attackers, governments are not only protecting themselves, but they are also protecting their citizens and their data. Ensuring the safety of its citizens and the integrity of its data is an imperative responsibility that governments must take seriously. Ultimately, ethical preparedness is about taking proactive steps to prevent cyber attacks and protect our data. This includes investing in cyber security measures using AI, developing defensive capabilities, and deterring potential attackers. By fulfilling these responsibilities, governments uphold not only their ethical obligations but also create a safer and more secure digital world for all.

Transparency and Accountability

Governments should provide clear and comprehensive information to the public regarding the risks of cyber threats and the strategies employed to counter them. This is an important aspect of any government's responsibility to its citizens. By keeping the public informed about potential risks, governments can help citizens be more aware and better prepared. Furthermore, transparency facilitates greater accountability, enhancing citizens' ability to hold their government responsible for any security breaches that may arise.

One important way that governments can communicate with the public is through regular reports and updates. Governments play a pivotal role in guaranteeing the safety of their citizens by efficiently communicating information regarding the latest threats and the proactive measures being implemented to combat them. In doing so, they aim to enlighten individuals about the risks they might face and the comprehensive strategies implemented to protect their well-being. This transparency fosters trust and awareness, empowering individuals to make informed decisions and contribute to their own safety and security. This can also help build trust between the government and the public, as transparency can be seen as a sign of good faith.

Another important aspect of transparency is the ethical imperative to be accountable for cybersecurity practices. By being open and honest about cybersecurity measures, governments can demonstrate their dedication to safeguarding citizens' private information and fostering a secure online environment. This can also help promote a sense of responsibility among government officials for ensuring the security of their citizens' data. Transparency in government communication about cyber threats is not only crucial for keeping the public informed, but it also plays a vital role in promoting trust and accountability.

International Relations

Governments are expected to adhere to international norms and laws related to cyberspace. Countries that prioritize responsible behaviour in cyberspace are more likely to foster trust and cooperation with their global partners. This is especially important in today's interconnected world, where cyber attacks can have devastating effects on businesses, governments, and individuals. Cyber security has emerged as a vital concern for nations worldwide, as they confront the escalating challenges of cyber warfare and espionage. Governments must not only protect their own networks and infrastructure, but also collaborate to create a safer and more secure cyberspace for everyone what means using AI in preventing attacks.

By adhering to international norms and laws, countries can create a solid foundation for responsible conduct, enabling them to hold one another accountable for any violations of these norms. This not only promotes ethical international relations, but also helps prevent conflicts and maintains stability in the global community. In addition, responsible behaviour in cyberspace can also have economic benefits.

By promoting a secure and trustworthy digital environment with AI employment, countries can attract foreign investment and encourage economic growth. This is particularly important for developing countries, where the absence of strong cyber security measures can impede their development and expose them to the risk of cyber attacks. Adhering to international norms and laws in the realm of cyberspace is not only a moral obligation but also a strategic manoeuvre that can yield numerous benefits for nations and the global community at large.

5 - Protection of Critical Infrastructure

Governments must implement ethical safeguards to protect critical infrastructure, such as energy, transportation, and communication systems. It is important for governments to recognize the potential harm that could occur if these systems are not properly protected. These systems play a vital role in ensuring the well-being of citizens, and neglecting to establish appropriate safeguards could result in dire consequences.

The consequences of not having proper ethical safeguards in place could range from minor inconveniences to major disasters. For instance, if transportation systems are not adequately maintained, it may lead to delays or malfunctions that would greatly disrupt the daily lives of citizens.

On a larger scale, the lack of protection in energy systems could result in power outages that have the potential to impact entire cities or regions. These consequences could have a ripple effect, causing further disruptions in other critical systems. It is the responsibility of governments to ensure that ethical safeguards are in place to protect critical infrastructure. This includes not only implementing security measures, but also regularly updating and maintaining them.

Governments need to think about how AI technology can make changes to protect against potential threats. By implementing these measures, governments can ensure the safety and well-being of their citizens and prevent any potential disasters from occurring.

6 - Privacy and Civil Liberties

Governments are often faced with difficult ethical dilemmas when trying to maintain national security. On one hand, they want to ensure that their citizens are safe from malicious cyber attacks. But on the other hand, they must also respect the privacy and civil liberties of their citizens.

Governments must consider the potential consequences of such actions before implementing them. They must also ensure that these measures are proportionate to the threat at hand and are not being used as a means of control or suppression striking a balance between AI driven cyber security and individual rights for maintaining trust between governments and their citizens. It is essential for governments to carefully consider the ethical implications of their actions and to find ways to protect their citizens without compromising their rights.

7- Response and Recovery Planning

Governments must prioritize the development of response to muse AI to avoid cyber incidents, as they are responsible for the well-being and safety of their citizens. In today's digital age, cyber attacks have become increasingly common and can have catastrophic consequences if left unchecked.

It is the responsibility of governments to safeguard not only their own systems and infrastructure but also to provide aid and support to those impacted by such attacks. In order to fulfil this responsibility, governments must prioritize the devélopment of robust and comprehensive response and recovery plans.

Not only should these plans focus on mitigating the impact of cyber attacks, but they should also prioritize providing comprehensive support and assistance to individuals and entities affected by such attacks. This is particularly important for vulnerable populations, such as small businesses or individuals with limited resources, who may not have the means to recover from a cyber-attack on their own.

Furthermore, governments must also consider the ethical implications of their response and recovery plans. Having a well-thought-out plan is not sufficient; it is imperative that the plan upholds ethical standards and takes into account the rights and welfare of all parties involved. This includes protecting personal information and ensuring that any assistance provided is done so in a fair and equitable manner. By prioritizing ethical preparedness, governments can not only mitigate the impact of cyber attacks but also uphold their responsibility to protect and support their citizens effectively.

8 - International Collaboration

Coordinated actions taken together to confront cyber threats are crucial not only in safeguarding individual nations but also in ensuring the security of the entire globe. Collaborating with other nations is not only a moral imperative, but it is also crucial in promoting a more secure and stable cyberspace for everyone. By combining strengths and resources, joint efforts can lead to improved global AI driven cyber security and prevent the escalation of cyber conflicts.

This ethical cooperation can also provide a more complete picture of the evolving cyber landscape. By harnessing the unique perspectives and expertise of each nation, collaborative efforts can be instrumental in uncovering previously unnoticed threats and vulnerabilities. This collaboration also enables the sharing of best practices and strategies, which strengthens our defence against cyber threats on a global scale. In addition, ethical cooperation can foster mutual trust and understanding among nations.

By working together towards a common goal, countries can build stronger relationships and establish a sense of accountability for cyber security. This can ultimately lead to a more peaceful and stable international environment, where cyber conflicts are less likely to occur.

9 - Public Trust

Amidst the rapid advancements in technology, governments must be held to a higher standard to ensure the utmost protection of their citizens from cyber threats. It is not only a matter of national security, but also an ethical imperative to maintain public trust.

Citizens deserve to have confidence in their government's commitment to taking responsible and effective measures to protect their personal information and ensure the safety of their digital lives.

However, it is not enough for governments to simply state that they are taking action against cyber threats. They must also be transparent in their efforts and provide regular updates to the public. This will not only show a commitment to protecting their citizens, but also build trust and confidence in the government.

As citizens become increasingly reliant on technology, the responsibility of governments to protect them from cyber threats becomes even more central. By prioritizing ethical considerations and maintaining public trust about AI use, governments can not only prevent cyber attacks, but also foster a sense of security and stability within their society. Moreover, implementing rigorous security measures and maintaining the highest ethical standards will not only protect crucial infrastructure and valuable data, but also showcase a strong dedication to the welfare and success of their citizens.

AI in Threat Detection

Utilizing advanced computer programs and machine learning techniques, these algorithms can then identify any anomalies that may occur by analyzing the data. Such anomalies are frequently warning signs of potential security threats, acting as an early-warning system for potential breaches or attacks.

This technology has become increasingly important in the world of cyber security because it enables real-time monitoring and detection of any suspicious activity. Through continuous comparison of data with established patterns, AI algorithms can rapidly detect and highlight potential threats, thereby equipping security teams with invaluable insights and timely alerts. Not only does this help prevent attacks, but it also enables faster response times in the event of a breach.

Overall, the use of AI algorithms in cyber security has revolutionized the way we approach and handle potential security threats. With its capacity to analyze and identify anomalies in large datasets, this technology serves as a crucial tool in the battle against cyber attacks. By constantly evolving and adapting, these algorithms continue to play a pivotal role in maintaining the security of systems and networks, safeguarding them from potential threats.

With the increasing complexity and sophistication of cyber attacks, traditional security measures are becoming insufficient in protecting systems and networks.

This is where AI technology comes in, enabling organizations to stay one step ahead of potential threats. By employing advanced algorithms and machine learning, AI systems can develop behavioural profiles for both users and systems. These profiles can then be employed to detect any atypical activities that could potentially signify a security breach. This allows organizations to respond to potential threats in real-time, mitigating the risk of a successful assault.

In addition, AI technology constantly evolves and adapts, making it a powerful tool in the ongoing fight against cyber attacks. As cybercriminals continuously find new ways to breach security systems, AI algorithms are able to learn and adapt to these changes, making them highly effective in detecting and preventing potential threats. This not only helps in protecting organizations from current threats, but also prepares them for future attacks.

AI technology is an indispensable tool for safeguarding systems and networks from potential security threats, thanks to its proficiency in analyzing and detecting anomalies in massive datasets.

AI technology has the ability to enhance threat detection by integrating and analyzing threat intelligence feeds. These feeds continuously update knowledge about emerging threats and attack techniques, enabling AI systems to more effectively identify and respond to the latest cyber security risks.

This not only helps in protecting organizations from current threats, but also prepares them for future attacks. With its advanced capabilities, AI technology is an essential tool in keeping systems and networks safe from potential security threats. In addition to analyzing and identifying anomalies in large datasets, AI technology can proactively monitor and detect potential threats in real-time. Through constant monitoring of network traffic and user behaviour, AI systems have the capability to swiftly identify and alert against any potentially malicious activity, preventing it from evolving into a fully-fledged attack.

This proactive approach allows organizations to stay one step ahead of potential threats and prevent them from causing any harm. Moreover, the use of AI in threat detection also helps organizations to save time and resources. AI systems have revolutionized threat detection and analysis, allowing security teams to devote their attention to other vital tasks and respond to potential threats with unparalleled efficiency.

Not only does this enhance an organization's overall security stance, but it also enables a more streamlined and effective cyber security strategy. Overall, the integration of AI technology in threat detection is crucial in keeping organizations safe from ever-evolving cyber threats.

Deep learning, a subset of machine learning, has emerged as a powerful tool in the fight against cyber threats. Through the use of deep neural networks, organizations can now effectively detect and respond to increasingly sophisticated attacks. This state-of-the-art technology enables automatic learning and adaptation to ever-changing threat landscapes, empowering organizations to remain one step ahead of cyber criminals. With deep learning, organizations can now respond to potential threats more efficiently and effectively. This not only improves their overall security posture, but also allows for a more streamlined and proactive approach to cyber security.

By leveraging this technology, organizations can identify and neutralize threats in real time, reducing the likelihood of data breaches and other cyber attacks. The integration of AI technology, particularly deep learning, in threat detection is vital for organizations to ensure their safety against constantly evolving cyber threats. By continuously learning and adapting to new and emerging threats, deep neural networks provide a strong defence against cybercriminals.

Artificial intelligence (AI) technology has revolutionized the field of threat detection, empowering organizations to efficiently identify and respond to potential threats with unprecedented effectiveness. By employing advanced algorithms and machine learning capabilities, AI models can identify patterns and behaviours that diverge from the norm, even when dealing with previously unknown or zero-day threats.

This proactive approach is crucial for staying ahead of attackers who may use novel techniques to infiltrate an organization's systems. Furthermore, integrating AI technology into threat detection not only enhances an organization's overall security posture but also enables a more streamlined and effective approach to cyber security.

Thanks to AI, security teams can now sift through large volumes of data and identify potential threats in real time, reducing the time and effort needed for manual threat detection. Not only does this save precious resources, but it also empowers organizations to swiftly and efficiently counter threats, thus minimizing the potential impact of cyber attacks. In today's rapidly evolving threat scenery, the integration of AI technology in threat detection is more essential than ever. With the ability to continuously learn and adapt, AI models are able to keep organizations safe from ever-evolving cyber threats. By harnessing the immense power of AI, organizations can strengthen their security defences and maintain a decisive advantage over potential attackers. This allows them to safeguard their systems and data with utmost certainty and confidence.

Organizations are continually at risk of cyber attacks, and given the constantly changing nature of these threats, it is essential for them to implement robust security measures. This is where AI comes in, as it has the ability to continuously learn and adapt to new threats. By leveraging the power of AI, organizations can strengthen their security defences and stay ahead of potential attackers. It is important to note, however, that while AI significantly enhances threat detection capabilities, it should not be the exclusive solution for cyber security.

A multi-layered approach that combines AI with human expertise and other security measures is the most effective way to combat a diverse range of threats. This happens because AI models can still be manipulated or exploited by malicious actors, a concept known as Adversarial Machine Learning (AML). AML plays a role in both attacks and defence in the context of cyber security. Attackers can exploit it to deceive or compromise AI models, which mean that defenders must be vigilant against potential AML attacks, and continuously monitor, assess, and improve their AI models to stay ahead of evolving threats. AI and AML are engaged in a constant battle, where organizations depend on AI to safeguard their systems and data, while attackers seek to exploit vulnerabilities in AI models.

In this ever-evolving world, where digitalization and automation reign supreme, the significance of cyber security and artificial intelligence has magnified. These two pillars of modern technology have emerged as paramount forces shaping our future. The two fields are intricately intertwined, and as they both continue to thrive and advance, their dynamic relationship will inevitably transform.

In the digital age, it's essential to understand the key points that govern the intersection of cyber security and AI. Cyber security is all about protecting sensitive information, and AI has become a central tool in this process. With the increasing number of cyber threats, AI has emerged as a powerful ally in detecting, preventing, and mitigating such attacks. Its capacity to analyze large amounts of data in real time and detect patterns and anomalies has proven to be an invaluable asset in the battle against cybercrime. This has also increased the demand for skilled professionals who can develop AI solutions to enhance cyber security.

AI possess incredible self-learning abilities and an adaptive nature that enables it to swiftly respond to emerging threats, rendering it a formidable adversary in the battle against cybercriminals. Cyber security has revolutionized the world, and its importance will only continue to grow in the future. It has the capability to analyze user and system behaviour, creating a baseline for normal operations. This enables AI to rapidly identify any abnormal or suspicious activity, thereby providing an early warning system for potential cyber threats. Throwing its self-learning capabilities, AI can continuously adapt and enhance its baseline, making it a formidable tool in the battle against cybercriminals. Furthermore, AI's adaptive nature allows it to quickly respond to new and evolving threats. Traditional ccybersecurityasures often rely on pre-programmed rules and signatures, making them less effective against constantly changing tactics used by cybercriminals.

With AI, once equipped with these constantly updated and refined rules and signatures, becomes an unstoppable adversary for cybercriminals. In conclusion, AI has revolutionized the world of cyber security with its adaptive capabilities. It plays a crucial role in early threat detection and response, providing a defense against attacks.

As technology continues to advance, the significance of AI in cyber security will soar, establishing it as an indispensable tool for safeguarding our digital realm.

AI plays a critical role in cyber security as it continually evolves to meet the ever-changing scenery of cyber threats. With its advanced capabilities, AI empowers security teams to detect and respond to potential attacks in real time, providing a stronger defence against cybercriminals.

By automating the analysis of security events and logs, AI enhances Security Information and Event Management (SIEM) solutions, accelerating the detection of security incidents and providing security teams with actionable insights. As technology continues to advance, the importance of AI in security will only increase.

The integration of AI in cybersecurity has not only enhanced protection against threats, but it has also significantly improved the efficiency of security measures. With its ability to continuously learn and adapt, AI has significantly reduced the response time to potential threats. This has not only saved time and resources but has also prevented major data breaches. However, as with any technology, there are concerns about the ethical use of AI in cybersecurity.

The potential for AI to be misused or hacked by criminals is a growing concern that needs to be addressed. One of the primary challenges in the intersection of AI and cyber security is the critical lack of skilled professionals in both domains. This scarcity of talent poses a significant obstacle to addressing the evolving threats in our digital landscape. As the demand for AI solutions in security increases, so does the need for experts capable of developing and implementing them.

This has created a new job market for individuals with expertise in both AI and cyber security, making it a promising career path for those interested in the technology sector. As the world continues to become increasingly digitalized, the importance of AI in security will inevitably expand. Therefore, integrating AI into an organization's security strategy becomes a crucial and indispensable aspect to consider.

The future holds endless possibilities for the integration of AI in security. From advanced threat detection to automated incident response, AI has the potential to revolutionize the protection of sensitive information in the digital age. As we advance in cyber security technology, it's decisive to stay updated on advancements in AI and its applications in cyber security.

The unit's security has revolutionized the way it's protected sensitive information. With the constant evolution and innovation of technology, the partnership with AI is becoming increasingly crucial. In this ever-advancing technological era, it is essential for us to remain well-informed about the latest breakthroughs in artificial intelligence and its extensive applications in the realm of security.

One of the most significant contributions of AI in cyber security is advanced threat detection. With AI, algorithms can quickly analyze large amounts of data, detecting anomalies and patterns that may indicate potential threats. This aids in preventing security breaches and mitigating the damage caused by cyber attacks. Additionally, AI also enables automated incident response, reducing the time and resources needed to respond to security incidents.

The potential of AI to transform the way we protect sensitive information in the digital age is immense. It not only enhances our ability to detect and respond to threats but also improves overall security measures.

Behavioural Analytics

AI technology can be used to establish baseline behaviour for both users and computer systems. This baseline serves as a reference point for what is considered normal activity. When there is a deviation from this baseline, it can trigger alerts for suspicious activities, aiding in early threat detection. This can help organizations quickly identify potential security breaches and take necessary actions to mitigate them before they escalate.

AI models can also detect anomalies or deviations from the norm. These anomalies can be subtle and difficult for humans to notice, but they can be a sign of potential security breaches. AI can analyze large volumes of data and identify unusual patterns or behaviours that may indicate a threat. This can save time and resources compared to manually monitoring all activities.

Furthermore, AI can continuously learn and adapt to new threats, making it a valuable tool for threat detection and prevention. As cyber threats continue to evolve, AI can stay ahead of the game by constantly updating its algorithms and learning from new data. This makes it a powerful tool in the fight against cyber attacks. In addition, AI can also help with incident response by providing real-time alerts and recommendations for mitigating potential threats. This can help organizations respond quickly and effectively to security breaches, minimizing the damage and preventing further attacks. With AI's ability to analyze and detect threats, organizations can have peace of mind knowing that their data and systems are protected.

As well, AI can continuously learn and adapt to new behaviours and patterns, making it an effective tool for threat detection. With the ability to analyze vast amounts of data in real-time, AI algorithms can quickly detect anomalies and unusual behaviours that may indicate a security threat. This allows for a more proactive approach to cyber security, rather than just relying on reactive measures.

Adding its use in threat detection, AI can also help in identifying vulnerabilities in systems and networks. By analyzing data and identifying patterns, AI can pinpoint potential weaknesses and provide recommendations for improving security. This can help organizations stay ahead of potential cyber attacks and strengthen their overall security posture. With its ability to continuously learn and adapt, AI has become an essential tool in the fight against cybercrime.

It can analyze massive amounts of data and identify patterns that humans might miss. By processing this information, AI can identify potential vulnerabilities in systems and networks. These vulnerabilities are the weak spots that attackers can exploit to gain unauthorized access or cause harm to an organization. AI's ability to continuously learn and adapt is what sets it apart from traditional security measures.

With AI's help, organizations can proactively address vulnerabilities in their systems and networks. By following the recommendations provided by AI, they can strengthen their defences and mitigate the risk of a cyber attack. This not only helps in protecting sensitive data and systems but also saves organizations from the costly aftermath of a data breach.

The advancements of technology have brought about a new era of connectivity through networks. While this has made communication and data sharing easier, it has also opened up a whole new world of vulnerabilities and cyber threats. This is where the role of AI comes in. By utilizing AI's capabilities, organizations can effectively identify and address potential vulnerabilities in their networks, thereby strengthening their defences against intromissions.

This not only protects sensitive data and systems, but also saves organizations from the costly aftermath of a data breach. With the constant evolution of cyber threats, it has become increasingly challenging for organizations to keep up with the ever-changing settings. This is where AI's role becomes even more crucial. By utilizing AI's advanced algorithms and analytical capabilities, organizations can stay one step ahead and proactively detect potential threats before they can cause harm.

Does not only increase the overall security of networks, but also saves organizations valuable time and resources that would have been spent on recovering from a cyber attack. The importance of securing networks cannot be overstated.

Organizations can effectively strengthen their defences and mitigate the risk of a cyber attack. By utilizing AI's recommendations, organizations can not only protect sensitive data and systems, but also safeguard their reputation and avoid the costly aftermath of a data breach.

As the digital scene becomes more complex and interconnected, the threat of cyber attacks looms larger than ever before. The importance of utilizing AI to defend against these attacks cannot be overstated. With its ability to analyze and detect patterns, AI can effectively strengthen an organization's defences and mitigate the risk of a potential breach.

Artificial Intelligence also offers recommendations for improving overall security measures. By utilizing these recommendations, organizations can stay ahead of potential threats and proactively address vulnerabilities before they become exploited. This level of proactive protection not only saves time and resources, but also helps to maintain the trust and loyalty of customers and stakeholders. In today's digital scene, organizations must recognize the critical role that AI plays in defending against cyber attacks.

As the threat of cyber attacks continues to evolve, it is essential for organizations to stay ahead of the game and utilize all available resources to protect their digital assets.

Adversarial Machine Learning

As technology advances, the use of artificial intelligence (AI) has become more prevalent in our daily lives. However, with its widespread use comes the risk of malicious actors exploiting AI systems for their own gain. This is known as adversarial machine learning, where attackers manipulate or deceive AI systems to carry out their nefarious activities.

This creates a never-ending cycle of attackers and defenders constantly trying to outsmart and outmanoeuvre each other. The advent of adversarial machine learning has also given rise to a new generation of attacks that are significantly more sophisticated and challenging to detect. By leveraging AI, attackers are able to find and exploit vulnerabilities in systems that were previously thought to be secure.

As companies continue to adopt AI technology, the need for heightened security measures becomes increasingly apparent. With the use of AI, attackers are able to exploit and manipulate systems in ways that were not possible before. This makes it all the more important for organizations to stay vigilant and be prepared for potential cyber threats. As AI continues to evolve and become more advanced, so do the tactics and techniques used by malicious actors. This means that organizations need to constantly monitor and update their security protocols to stay ahead of potential threats.

The use of AI in cyber attacks not only enhances their sophistication but also makes them harder to detect. Therefore, it is imperative for companies to have robust defence mechanisms in place. This calls for a comprehensive security approach, where we not only assess the technology itself, but also the procedures and policies that surround it. By taking proactive measures and implementing necessary precautions, companies can effectively mitigate the potential risks associated with AI and fully harness its true potential.

One effective way to achieve this is by implementing AI-driven endpoint protection solutions that utilize behavioural analysis to detect and prevent threats. These advanced systems enable companies to stay one step ahead of cyber attacks, equipping them with the essential tools to protect their valuable assets.

Harnessing the power of AI, companies can navigate the ever-evolving technology landscape with confidence, ensuring the highest level of security for their operations. This ensures that they are shielded from any malicious activities that may target individual devices. These solutions can identify and block suspicious processes or files, mitigating the risk of endpoint compromise. This enables companies to adopt a more comprehensive and proactive security approach, as AI systems continuously monitor and analyze potential threats. Furthermore, AI-driven endpoint protection solutions can continually learn and adapt to new threats, making them more effective than traditional security measures.

Companies can ensure that they are not only protecting their technology, but also their important processes and practices. To truly unlock the potential of AI, companies must also establish proper protocols and procedures. This includes regular training for employees on cyber security best practices, as well as implementing secure coding practices for developers. Taking a holistic approach to security, companies can not only mitigate the risks of AI but also fully leverage its benefits for their business.

This necessitates a proactive and vigilant approach, consistently emphasizing the need to stay up-to-date with the latest advancements and techniques used by attackers.

Additionally, it is important for companies to understand the specific risks and vulnerabilities associated with AI. Due to the complex and ever-evolving nature of AI, there are unique challenges and potential vulnerabilities that must be addressed. This requires a comprehensive and tailored approach to cyber security, rather than relying on generic or outdated measures.

It is critical to constantly update and adapt techniques, as well as understand the specific risks and vulnerabilities associated with AI. By doing so, we can take a tailor-made approach to protection. By adopting this approach, companies can effectively manage and mitigate the risks associated with AI while unlocking its full potential. This proactive strategy not only ensures success but also fosters unwavering trust from customers.

This means implementing strong security measures and regularly updating them to stay ahead of the game. By doing so, companies can effectively mitigate the risks associated with AI and utilize it to its full potential. To truly harness the power of AI, companies must have a solid understanding of the processes and practices surrounding it.

Moreover, companies ought to actively pursue partnerships and collaborations with other organizations in the field of AI. This strategic move can yield valuable insights and resources for the successful implementation of AI.

Skill Shortage Mitigation

The use of AI in cyber security is a game-changer for organizations worldwide. As cybercrime continues to soar, the demand for skilled professionals who can effectively combat these threats is skyrocketing. However, the shortage of such professionals has become a major concern. This is where AI steps in, offering a solution to help bridge this gap. By harnessing the power of AI in cyber security, organizations have the capability to automate monotonous and repetitive tasks, thereby freeing up human experts to tackle the most crucial and demanding facets of cyber security. Not only does this save time and resources, but it also ensures that the most skilled professionals are handling the most critical tasks.

With AI's help, organizations can improve their overall cyber security posture and stay ahead of potential threats. In addition to automating routine tasks, AI can also assist in threat detection and response. Utilizing cutting-edge machine learning algorithms, AI possesses the capability to analyze extensive volumes of data, thereby detecting patterns that could potentially signify an imminent cyber attack. This early detection can help organizations take proactive measures to prevent a breach or minimize its impact. As cyber threats continue to evolve, the utilization of AI in cyber security will be increasingly critical in safeguarding organizations from potential attacks. This cutting-edge technology has the ability to analyze vast amounts of data instantly, recognizing patterns, and pinpointing potential threats far more efficiently than conventional methods. By leveraging AI, organizations can stay ahead of cyber threats and defend against sophisticated attacks with greater precision and speed. This allows organizations to get more done with fewer resources, thereby maximizing the productivity of their human workforce.

By automating routine tasks, AI ultimately empowers human experts to concentrate on the bigger picture, enabling them to make well-informed decisions in safeguarding organizations from cyber threats. The implementation of AI in cyber security not only helps organizations to overcome the shortage of skilled professionals, but it also provides a more comprehensive and advanced approach to cyber defence. With the ever-evolving nature of cyber threats, organizations need to constantly adapt and improve their security measures.

The use of AI can assist in this process by continuously analyzing data and identifying patterns to detect and prevent potential attacks. Artificial Intelligence (AI) is a rapidly growing technology that has the potential to revolutionize cyber defence. With its ability to continuously analyze data and identify patterns, AI can offer a more sophisticated and comprehensive approach to safeguarding organizations against cyber threats. By constantly adapting and improving security measures, organizations can stay ahead of the ever-evolving nature of cybercrime.

Utilizing AI in cyber defence has immense advantages, particularly in enhancing organizations' understanding of their security posture. By analyzing data from various sources, such as network logs, user behaviour, and threat intelligence, AI can identify potential vulnerabilities and threats that might have otherwise remained undetected. This not only allows for more effective threat prevention, but also enables organizations to make better-informed decisions when it comes to their security strategy. However, it is important to note that AI is not a complete solution on its own. It must be properly implemented and integrated into an organization's security infrastructure in order to be effective. This requires a deep understanding of an organization's unique security needs and potential use cases for AI.

With proper implementation and integration, AI becomes a powerful ally in the battle against cybercrime. It equips organizations with the necessary tools to proactively defend against threats and safeguard their data and systems.

Investing in educational programs at various levels, including universities, technical schools, and online platforms. These programs should be designed to equip individuals with the necessary skills and knowledge for cyber security roles. Encouraging the development of specialized cyber security curricula and certifications is essential to ensure that professionals are fully equipped to address the unique security needs of organizations. This can also help create a pipeline of talented individuals entering the field, reducing the impact of skill shortages. Support ongoing professional development for current cyber security professionals. This can include workshops, conferences, webinars, and industry certifications to keep skills up-to-date with the latest technologies and threats.

By investing in continuous learning for existing professionals, organizations can ensure that their cyber security teams are well-equipped to handle the constantly evolving landscape of cyber threats. Establish apprenticeship and internship programs to provide hands-on experience for individuals entering the cyber security field. These programs can be valuable for developing practical skills and gaining exposure to real-world cyber security challenges. They also provide organizations with an opportunity to identify and nurture future talent, thus creating a robust pipeline of skilled professionals for the industry. With the guidance and support of experienced cyber security professionals, apprentices and interns can acquire invaluable insights and practical knowledge that will equip them for thriving careers in the field.

Foster collaboration between industry and academia to bridge the gap between theoretical knowledge and practical skills. Industry partnerships can help shape educational programs to align with the needs of the cyber security workforce, ensuring that professionals are equipped with the right skills to address the unique security needs of organizations. This collaboration can also provide opportunities for students to gain real-world experience through internships and hands-on projects, preparing them for successful careers in cyber security. By working together, industry and academia can help build a strong and diverse cyber security workforce that can effectively combat cybercrime and protect organizations from threats.

Automated Response and Remediation

AI is the technology that allows machines to learn from data and perform tasks without being explicitly programmed. In today's world, it has become a central tool in analyzing vast amounts of data in real-time. This technology has enabled organizations to promptly identify and respond to security threats as they occur. With AI, it has become possible to detect patterns and potential cyber attacks, minimizing the potential impact of such attacks.

One of the main advantages of AI is its ability to process and analyze large volumes of data at unparalleled speeds. This capability enables AI to identify patterns, trends, and insights that may not be immediately apparent to human analysts. With AI, security professionals can stay ahead of potential threats and respond to them in real time, reducing the likelihood of a successful attack. This is a game-changer for organizations that handle sensitive data and require safe their systems and networks. Furthermore, AI has empowered organizations to automate their security processes, enabling them to respond to threats faster and more efficiently. With AI, it is possible to continuously monitor networks and systems for any cyber attacks or suspicious activity, providing an added layer of security. This has become vital in today's digital scene, where cyber attacks can occur at any time and from anywhere. With the assistance of AI, organizations can proactively stay ahead of potential threats and effectively protect their data and assets. AI has sparked a revolution in the utilization of technology across various industries. One of the most significant areas of application is incident response. The advancements in AI and machine learning have revolutionized companies' incident response processes, enabling them to automate and enhance their effectiveness and efficiency like never before. This has cyber security in the digital age, where cyber security threats are constantly evolving and becoming more sophisticated.

By leveraging AI, companies can monitor their networks and systems in real-time, detecting any potential risks and threats. With machine learning algorithms, AI can analyze large volumes of data and detect patterns that might indicate a security breach. This enables companies to respond quickly and take necessary actions to prevent any damage. Furthermore, AI can automate the incident response process, reducing the workload on cyber security teams and allowing them to dedicate more time to critical tasks.

AI not only streamlines the incident response process, but it also enhances its precision. Manual methods are prone to human error, which could cause delays in detecting and addressing security breaches. This can result in significant damage and financial loss for companies. However, AI can rapidly and precisely detect patterns that indicate a security breach, enabling companies to promptly respond and avert any additional harm. Automating the incident response process leads to a reduction in the risk of human error while guaranteeing that security incidents are promptly and efficiently addressed.

Additionally, AI can continuously learn and adapt to new security threats, making it an invaluable tool for cyber security. Traditional methods often rely on pre-defined rules and patterns, which may not be effective against new and evolving threats.

AI, on the other hand, has the capacity to analyze enormous amounts of data in real time and identify anomalies that could indicate a security breach. This proactive approach allows companies to stay one step ahead of potential cyber-attacks and mitigate risks before they can cause significant damage.

With AI-powered incident response, companies can ensure that their sensitive data and systems are well-protected against cyber threats.

This is particularly critical in high-risk industries such as banking, healthcare, and government, where even a minor cyber security incident can have severe consequences.

With the rise of sophisticated cyber attacks, it has become increasingly important to have a reliable system in place to protect sensitive data. By harnessing the power of artificial intelligence, this process can be seamlessly automated, completely eradicating any potential for human error and ensuring an impeccably precise and punctual response. This is especially important in high-risk industries such as banking, healthcare, and government, where even a minor cyber security incident can have severe consequences. AI can monitor and detect potential threats that would otherwise go unnoticed by human operators. Through advanced algorithms, it can analyze large amounts of data and identify patterns that may indicate an attack.

AI is quickly becoming a crucial tool in the fight against cyber threats and data breaches. With the exponential growth of data, traditional security measures are no longer sufficient to keep pace with the constantly evolving landscape of cyber attacks. This is where AI comes in, providing a scalable solution to help organizations stay ahead of potential threats.

One of the main benefits of AI in cyber security is its ability to reduce the burden on human operators. Automating the process of threat detection and response allows human operators to dedicate their attention to other critical tasks, effectively boosting overall efficiency and productivity. This also helps to minimize the risk of human errors, which can often be the cause of data breaches or system downtime.

Furthermore, AI has the capability to identify, contain, and mitigate threats in real-time without human intervention. This means that potential attacks can be stopped in their tracks before any damage is done. This doesn't just improve the efficiency of cybersecurity operations, but also provides organizations with peace of mind in an increasingly digital world. With AI being a powerful ally, can be assured that data and systems are well-protected against cyber threats.

Phishing Detection

NLP is a powerful tool that is used to analyze and detect phishing scams. By examining the content of emails, messages, or websites, AI can identify malicious communications and block them. This is extremely beneficial in protecting individuals and organizations from falling victim to phishing attacks. AI not only can detect potential phishing attempts, but it can also analyze the content of these communications to uncover patterns and trends. This allows for a more comprehensive understanding of phishing techniques and helps in creating more effective preventative measures.

By leveraging NLP, AI can continuously learn and adapt to new forms of phishing, making it an indispensable resource in the battle against cyber threats. In addition to identifying and blocking phishing attempts, AI can also be used to gather and analyze data on these attacks. This data can then be used to identify common tactics used by hackers and provide insights on how to better protect against them.

AI is becoming increasingly sophisticated in its ability to combat cyber threats. Beyond just identifying and blocking phishing attempts, AI can also gather and analyze data on these attacks. By utilizing natural language processing and machine learning, AI is able to recognize patterns and linguistic cues commonly associated with phishing attacks.

This allows for more accurate and efficient detection and prevention of these threats. The data gathered by AI can also provide valuable insights into the tactics used by hackers. By analyzing large amounts of data from various attacks, AI can identify common patterns and methods used by cyber criminals. This information can then be used to better protect against future attacks. With the ever-evolving techniques and tactics employed by hackers, AI's ability to constantly gather and analyze data allows for a more proactive approach to cyber security.

Additionally, AI can be used to improve security measures and protocols. By understanding the common tactics and methods used by hackers, companies and organizations can implement stronger and more effective security measures to mitigate the risk of cyber attacks. This not only helps protect against potential breaches, but it also helps save time and resources by focusing on the most effective methods of defence. As the fight against cyber threats continues to evolve, AI will undoubtedly play a crucial role in keeping data and information safe.

AI technology has revolutionized the way we approach cyber security. Not only can it identify and block phishing attempts, but it can also gather and analyze data on these attacks. This valuable data can then be used to identify patterns and common tactics used by hackers, giving us insights on how to better protect ourselves against these malicious attacks. With the constant evolution of technology, the methods used by hackers are becoming more sophisticated and harder to detect.

This not only protects our personal data, but also safeguards sensitive information such as government and corporate data. Furthermore, the use of AI in the fight against cyber threats is a proactive approach that allows anticipating and preventing attacks, rather than just reacting after the damage has already been done.

Expanding the capabilities of AI, defences are a strength and make it even more difficult for hackers to breach systems. With the ever-growing capabilities of AI, there is the opportunity to take a proactive approach to security, allowing anticipating and preventing attacks rather than just reacting after the damage has already been done. This is a critical shift in mindset, as it enables us to stay one step ahead of hackers and their constantly evolving tactics.

By harnessing the power of machine learning and artificial intelligence, can be created intelligent systems that are able to detect and respond to potential threats in real-time.

This not only allows identifying and mitigating attacks before they can cause significant damage, but it also provides valuable insights and data that can inform future security strategies.

The constant advancements in technology have opened up a world of possibilities for businesses and individuals alike. However, with this rapid growth comes an increasing threat of cyber attacks.

It is crucial to stay ahead of criminals by continuously pushing the limitations and innovating in the field of cyber security. With its ability to analyze data in real-time and predict potential threats, AI can be a valuable tool in preventing cyber attacks. It can also help with automating and streamlining security processes, making it more efficient and effective. However, AI is not a replacement for human expertise and intervention. It must be carefully integrated and managed to complement and enhance our existing security measures.

Big Data Analysis

With its ability to process and interpret enormous amounts of security data in real-time, it represents a profound change in how we address security. The impact of AI on security is undeniable. Its ability to analyze data and identify patterns and anomalies that humans may miss is one of its greatest strengths.

AI works in real-time to constantly monitor network traffic and identify any suspicious activities that may indicate a potential threat. By employing machine learning algorithms, AI has the capacity to analyze vast amounts of data and identify aberrant patterns and behaviours that could signal a cyber attack or data breach.

This proactive approach to security enables security teams to promptly take action, mitigating the risk of potential harm or loss of valuable information. AI is able to quickly identify and flag any anomalies, providing security teams with valuable insights to investigate and neutralize any potential threats before they can cause harm. The advanced detection capability is crucial in today's rapidly evolving threat landscape. Traditional security methods are no longer sufficient to protect against sophisticated cyber attacks.

With AI, security becomes proactive rather than reactive. This shift is vital in staying ahead of the ever-changing cyber threat landscape. Through constant monitoring of network traffic and real-time detection of potential threats, AI plays a crucial role in identifying and addressing vulnerabilities before they can be exploited. AI's potential in security is vast, and its future looks bright.

As with any technology, there are also ethical concerns that need to be addressed. As we rely more on AI for security, it's essential to ensure that it is used ethically and responsibly. With proper oversight and regulation, AI can revolutionize security, making our world safer and more secure for everyone. AI's capabilities are not limited to just identifying potential threats and vulnerabilities. It can also provide us with valuable insights and predictions. This can help us to take proactive measures to prevent attacks.

AI algorithms are constantly learning and evolving, making them more efficient over time. This is where AI comes into play. Its ability to analyze vast amounts of data in real time, coupled with its predictive capabilities, makes it an invaluable tool for security professionals.

With AI, we can finally have a proactive approach to security, instead of just reacting to threats. It's safe to say that AI is the next big thing in the world of security, and its potential is endless. AI and big data analysis have revolutionized the field of security.

With its predictive capabilities, AI has become an invaluable tool for security professionals. It allows them to have a proactive approach to security, rather than simply reacting to threats. This shift in mindset has led to a more effective and efficient security strategy.

Moreover, AI has also greatly improved the speed and accuracy of threat detection. With its advanced algorithms and machine learning capabilities, AI can quickly identify patterns and anomalies that might be overlooked by human security professionals. This has greatly enhanced the overall security strategy, making it possible to frustrate attacks before they can cause any harm. The integration of AI in security has revolutionized the industry, making it an invaluable tool for protecting against cyber threats.

The potential of AI in the world of security is endless. By analyzing vast amounts of data in real-time, with AI tools, vulnerability management has become more efficient, accurate, and thorough than ever before. These systems are able to continuously monitor and analyze data, quickly identifying any potential risks and vulnerabilities. This proactive approach enables organizations to stay one step ahead of cyber threats and to address any issues before they can be exploited. This not only saves time and resources, but also provides a more comprehensive and thorough approach to vulnerability management.

This comprehensive approach to vulnerability detection has given organizations a more complete understanding of their system's security posture, empowering them to address potential threats proactively before any damage can occur. Furthermore, with the increasing sophistication of cyber attacks, the need for advanced security measures has become more critical than ever. AI tools have proven to be a game-changer in this regard, as they continuously learn and adapt to new threats, ensuring that organizations are always one step ahead in the fight against cybercrime.

By seamlessly integrating advanced technology and human expertise, these tools have revolutionized the way organizations manage and mitigate system vulnerabilities, making them an invaluable asset for any modern business.

This has allowed organizations to proactively identify and patch vulnerabilities before they can be exploited by potential attackers. Moreover, AI tools have significantly improved the accuracy and reliability of vulnerability assessments. By harnessing advanced algorithms and machine learning techniques, these tools can analyze vast amounts of data and pinpoint potential threats with exceptional precision.

This not only saves organizations time and effort, but also ensures that any vulnerability is identified and addressed in a timely manner, thus reducing the risk of a cyber attack. Furthermore, the utilization of AI tools in vulnerability management has significantly improved collaboration and communication among various teams within organizations.

By providing a centralized platform for vulnerability scanning and assessment, these tools enable seamless information sharing and enhanced coordination among teams responsible for system security. By providing a centralized platform for vulnerability scanning and assessment, these tools allow for easier sharing of information and coordination among teams responsible for system security. This not only helps organizations stay ahead of potential threats, but also enables them to mitigate risks effectively. Organizations are able to stay ahead of cyberattacks and mitigate risks effectively. With the continuous advancements in AI technology, these tools are expected to play an even bigger role in ensuring the security and stability of organizations in the future.

AI in Threat Detection

Artificial Intelligence algorithms, and especially machine learning, have the ability to analyze large and complex data sets, thereby identifying and establishing normal behavioral tendencies for systems, networks, or even users. Through a thorough study and analysis of the data, these algorithms have the ability to detect and recognize any anomalies that might arise, such as deviations from the established patterns. These anomalies often serve as red flags for potential security threats and can function as an early warning system for possible breaches or attacks. This technology has become increasingly important in the world of cyber security as it allows for real-time monitoring and detection of any suspicious activity. AI algorithms have the remarkable ability to swiftly detect and highlight potential threats by constantly comparing data with established patterns.

This empowers security teams with crucial insights and timely alerts, equipping them to take necessary actions with confidence. This helps prevent attacks and allows for a faster response in case of a breach. Overall, the use of AI algorithms in cyber security has revolutionized the way we approach and handle potential security threats. With its ability to analyze and identify anomalies in large datasets, this technology serves as an essential tool in the fight against cyberattacks By constantly evolving and adapting, these algorithms continue to play a crucial role in keeping systems and networks safe from potential threats.

With the increasing complexity and sophistication of cyber attacks measures are becoming insufficient in protecting systems and networks. This is where AI technology comes in, enabling organizations to stay one step ahead of potential threats. By using advanced algorithms and machine learning, AI systems can create behavioral profiles of behaviour systems, which can then be used to identify any unusual activities that might indicate a security breach. This allows organizations to respond to potential threats in real-time, mitigating the risk of a successful attack.

Moreover, AI technology constantly evolves and adapts, making it a powerful tool in the ongoing fight against cyber attacks. As cyber criminals continuously find new ways to breach security systems, AI algorithms are able to learn and adapt to these changes, making them highly effective in detecting and preventing potential threats. This not only helps in protecting organizations from current threats, but also prepares them for future attacks. With its ability to analyze and identify anomalies in large datasets, AI technology is an essential tool in keeping systems and networks safe from potential security threats.

AI technology has the ability to enhance threat detection by integrating and analyzing threat intelligence feeds. These feeds continuously update knowledge about emerging threats and attack techniques, allowing AI systems to better identify and respond to the latest cyber security risks. This not only helps in protecting organizations from current threats, but also prepares them for future attacks. With its advanced capabilities, AI technology is an essential tool in keeping systems and networks safe from potential security threats. In addition to analyzing and identifying anomalies in large datasets, AI technology can also proactively monitor and detect potential threats in real-time. By continuously monitoring network traffic and user behaviour, AI systems quickly detect and flag any suspicious activity before it becomes a full-fledged attack.

This proactive approach allows organizations to stay one step ahead of potential threats and prevent them from causing any harm. Moreover, the use of AI in threat detection also helps organizations to save time and resources. With AI systems handling the bulk of threat detection and analysis, security teams can focus on other critical tasks and respond to potential threats more efficiently. This not only improves the overall security posture of an organization but also allows for a more streamlined and effective approach to cyber security. Integration of AI technology in threat detection is crucial in keeping organizations safe from ever-evolving cyber threats.

Deep learning, a subset of machine learning, has emerged as a powerful tool in the fight against cyber threats. Through the use of deep neural networks, organizations can now effectively detect and respond to increasingly sophisticated attacks. This advanced technology allows for the automatic learning and adaptation to evolving threat landscapes, enabling organizations to stay one step ahead of cybercriminals. With deep learning, organizations can now respond to potential threats more efficiently and effectively. This not only improves their overall security posture, but also allows for a more streamlined and proactive approach to cyber security. By utilizing this technology, organizations can detect and neutralize threats in real-time, minimizing the risk of data breaches and other cyber attacks. Overall, the integration of AI technology, specifically deep learning, in threat detection is crucial for organizations to stay safe from ever-evolving cyber threats. By continuously learning and adapting to new and emerging threats, deep neural networks provide a strong defense against cybercriminals. With the ever-increasing number of cyber attacks it is imperative for organizations to invest in advanced technologies like deep learning to protect their sensitive data and maintain their reputation.

Artificial intelligence (AI) technology has revolutionized the field of threat detection by enabling organizations to identify and respond to potential threats more efficiently. By utilizing advanced algorithms and machine learning capabilities, AI models are able to recognize patterns and behaviors that deviate from the norm, even in the case of previously unknown or zero-day threats. This proactive approach is crucial for staying ahead of attackers who may use novel techniques to infiltrate an organization's systems. Moreover, the integration of AI technology in threat detection not only improves the overall security posture of an organization but also allows for a more streamlined and effective approach to cyber security. With the help of AI, security teams are able to sift through large volumes of data and identify potential threats in real-time, reducing the time and effort required for manual threat detection. This not only saves valuable resources but also enables organizations to respond to threats more quickly and effectively, minimizing the potential impact of cyberattacks. In today's rapidly evolving threat landscape, the integration of AI technology in threat detection is more crucial than ever. With the ability to continuously learn and adapt, AI models are able to keep organizations safe from ever-evolving cyber threats. By leveraging the power of AI, organizations can strengthen their security defenses and stay one step ahead of potential attackers, ensuring the safety of their systems and data.

Organizations are constantly under threat of cyber attacks and with the ever-evolving nature of these threats, it is crucial for them to have strong security measures in place. This is where AI comes in, as it has the ability to continuously learn and adapt to new threats. By leveraging the power of AI, organizations can strengthen their security defenses and stay ahead of potential attackers. However, it's important to note that while AI significantly improves threat detection capabilities, it should not be the sole solution for cyber security. A multi-layered approach, combining AI with human expertise and other security measures, is most effective in combating a diverse range of threats. This is because AI models can still be manipulated or exploited by malicious actors, a concept known as Adversarial Machine Learning (AML).

AML plays a role in both attacks and defence in the context of cyber security. Attackers can use it to deceive or compromise AI models, while defenders must also be aware of potential AML attacks and constantly monitor, evaluate, and refine their AI models to keep up with evolving threats. In this way, AI and AML are constantly locked in a battle, with organizations relying on AI to protect their systems and data, while attackers try to exploit vulnerabilities in AI models. Cyber security is all about protecting sensitive information, and AI has become a crucial tool in this process. With the growing number of cyber threats, AI has emerged as a powerful ally to detect, prevent, and mitigate such attacks. Its ability to analyze vast amounts of data in real-time and identify patterns and anomalies has made it a valuable asset in the fight against cybercrime. This has also increased the demand for skilled professionals who can develop AI solutions to enhance cyber security.

Furthermore, AI's adaptive nature allows it to quickly respond to new and evolving threats. Traditional cyber security measures often rely on pre-programmed rules and signatures, making them less effective against constantly changing tactics used by cybercriminals.

With AI, these rules and signatures can be continuously updated and refined in real-time, making it a formidable opponent for cybercriminals. In conclusion, AI has revolutionized the world of cyber security with its advanced capabilities and adaptive nature. It plays a crucial role in early threat detection and response, providing a stronger defence against cyber attacks.

By automating the analysis of security events and logs, AI enhances Security Information and Event Management (SIEM) solutions, accelerating the detection of security incidents and providing security teams with actionable insights. As technology continues to advance, the importance of AI in cyber security will only increase. As cybercriminals become more sophisticated, AI allows for a faster response to emerging threats, minimizing the potential impact of attacks.

This adaptive nature of AI also enables it to learn from past incidents and proactively identify potential vulnerabilities in a system, further strengthening the overall security posture. Thus, AI is an essential tool for protecting our digital world, providing a crucial layer of defense against cyber attacks

The potential for AI to be misused or hacked by cybercriminals is a growing concern that needs to be addressed. One of the key challenges in the intersection of AI and cyber security is the shortage of skilled professionals in both fields. As the demand for AI solutions in cyber security increases, so does the need for experts who can develop and implement them.

This has created a new job market for individuals with expertise in both AI and cyber security, making it a promising career path for those interested in the technology sector. As the world continues to become more digitalized, the importance of AI in cyber security will only grow, making it a vital aspect to consider for any organization's security strategy.

The future holds endless possibilities for the integration of AI in cyber security. From advanced threat detection to automated incident response, AI has the potential to transform the way we protect sensitive information in the digital age. As we continue to rely more on technology, it's crucial to stay updated on the latest advancements in AI and its applications in cyber security.

The potential of AI to transform the way we protect sensitive information in the digital age is immense. It not only enhances our ability to detect and respond to threats but also improves overall cyber security measures. As technology continues to advance, the integration of AI in cyber security will play a critical role in ensuring the safety and security of our digital world. Staying updated on the latest advancements in this partnership is crucial for individuals and organizations alike.

Automated Scanning

By providing a seamless integration of advanced technology and human expertise, these tools have revolutionized the way organizations manage and mitigate system vulnerabilities, making them an invaluable asset for any modern business.

This has allowed organizations to proactively identify and patch vulnerabilities before they can be exploited by potential attackers. Moreover, AI tools have significantly improved the accuracy and reliability of vulnerability assessments. By leveraging advanced algorithms and machine learning techniques, these tools are able to analyze large amounts of data and identify potential threats with high precision.

This not only saves organizations time and effort, but also ensures that any vulnerabilities are identified and addressed in a timely manner, reducing the risk of a cyber attack. In addition, the use of AI tools in vulnerability management has also enhanced collaboration and communication among different teams within organizations.

By providing a centralized platform for vulnerability scanning and assessment, these tools allow for easier sharing of information and coordination among teams responsible for system security. The increasing prevalence of cyber attacks has forced organizations to adopt new and advanced methods of protecting their systems and data. One such approach is the use of AI tools in vulnerability management. This has not only enhanced collaboration and communication among different teams within organizations, but also improved the overall efficiency of the vulnerability management process.

As a result, organizations are able to save time and resources, as well as better protect their systems and data. In today's ever-evolving cyber landscape, the use of AI tools in vulnerability management has become almost essential for organizations. These tools not only streamline the vulnerability management process, but also provide a proactive approach to addressing potential threats. By facilitating collaboration and communication among different teams, organizations are able to stay ahead of cyber attacks and mitigate risks effectively. With the continuous advancements in AI technology, these tools are expected to play an even bigger role in ensuring the security and stability of organizations in the future.

Skill Shortage Mitigation

AI (artificial intelligence) is a rapidly growing field that has found its way into many aspects of our lives. From predicting weather patterns to helping us navigate through traffic, AI has proven to be a reliable tool for providing solutions to complex challenges.

Today, AI is also being implemented in the area of cyber security, one of the most critical concerns faced by organizations worldwide. With the rise in cyber crimes, the demand for cybersecurity professionals has increased. Unfortunately, there is a significant shortage of skilled professionals who can keep up with these growing threats.

That's where AI comes into play.

The use of AI in cyber security is a game-changer for organizations worldwide. With the increasing prevalence of cybercrimes, the need for proficient experts capable of combating these threats has reached an unprecedented level. However, the shortage of such professionals has become a major concern. This is where AI steps in, offering a solution to help bridge this gap. By leveraging AI in cyber security, organizations can automate tedious and repetitive tasks, allowing human experts to focus on more critical and challenging aspects of cyber security. This not only saves time and resources, but it also ensures that the most skilled professionals are handling the most critical tasks. With AI's help, organizations can improve their overall cyber security posture and stay ahead of potential threats. In addition to automating routine tasks, AI can also assist in threat detection and response.

With advanced machine learning algorithms, AI can analyze vast amounts of data and identify patterns that may indicate a potential cyber attack. This early detection can help organizations take proactive measures to prevent a breach or minimize its impact. As cyber threats continue to evolve, the use of AI in cyber security will become increasingly crucial in protecting organizations from potential attacks. This enables organizations to get more done with fewer resources, thereby maximizing the productivity of their human workforce.

The implementation of AI in cyber security allows for proactive and predictive defences against constantly evolving cyber threats. This not only helps prevent potential breaches, but also minimizes the impact of those that do occur. By analyzing vast amounts of data and identifying patterns, AI can identify potential vulnerabilities and create more effective strategies for protection. Moreover, the use of AI in cyber security frees up valuable time and resources for organizations. With automated processes and real-time threat detection, employees can focus on more critical tasks, increasing overall productivity. Additionally, AI can continuously learn and adapt to new threats, providing organizations with a more robust and sustainable defense against cyber attacks.

The use of AI can assist in this process by continuously analyzing data and identifying patterns to detect and prevent potential attacks. Artificial Intelligence (AI) is a rapidly growing technology that has the potential to revolutionize cyber defence. With its ability to continuously analyze data and identify patterns, AI can provide a more comprehensive and advanced approach to protecting organizations against cyber threats. By constantly adapting and improving security measures, organizations can stay ahead of the ever-evolving nature of cybercrime. One of the key benefits of using AI in cyber defense is its ability to provide a more complete picture of an organization's security posture.

By analyzing data from various sources, including network logs, user behavior, and threat intelligence, AI can identify potential vulnerabilities and threats that may have otherwise gone undetected. This not only allows for more effective threat prevention, but also enables organizations to make better-informed decisions when it comes to their security strategy. However, it is important to note that AI is not a complete solution on its own. It must be properly implemented and integrated into an organization's security infrastructure in order to be effective. This requires a deep understanding of an organization's unique security needs and potential use cases for AI. With the right implementation and integration, AI can be a powerful ally in the fight against cybercrime, providing organizations with the tools they need to proactively defend against threats and keep their data and systems safe.

Invest in educational programs at various levels, including universities, technical schools, and online platforms. These programs should be designed to equip individuals with the necessary skills and knowledge for cyber security roles. Encourage the development of specialized cyber security curricula and certifications to ensure that professionals are well-equipped to handle the unique security needs of organizations. This can also help create a pipeline of talented individuals entering the field, reducing the impact of skill shortages. Support ongoing professional development for current cyber security professionals. This can include workshops, conferences, webinars, and industry certifications to keep skills up-to-date with the latest technologies and threats.

By investing in continuous learning for existing professionals, organizations can ensure that their cyber security teams are well-equipped to handle the constantly evolving landscape of cyber threats. Establish apprenticeship and internship programs to provide hands-on experience for individuals entering the cyber security field. These programs can be valuable for developing practical skills and gaining exposure to real-world cyber security challenges. They also provide an opportunity for organizations to identify and nurture future talent, creating a strong pipeline of skilled professionals for the industry. With the guidance and support of experienced cyber security professionals, apprentices and interns can gain valuable insights and practical knowledge that will prepare them for successful careers in the field.

Foster collaboration between industry and academia to bridge the gap between theoretical knowledge and practical skills. Industry partnerships can help shape educational programs to align with the needs of the cyber security workforce, ensuring that professionals are equipped with the right skills to address the unique security needs of organizations. This collaboration can also provide opportunities for students to gain real-world experience through internships and hands-on projects, preparing them for successful careers in cyber security. By working together, industry and academia can help build a strong and diverse cyber security workforce that can effectively combat cybercrime and protect organizations from threats.

Protection of Military Systems

The advent of the digital era has greatly altered the landscape of modern warfare. Gone are the days of traditional, physical combat; now, a country's military strength is largely tied to its technological capabilities. With information technology and networked systems playing a crucial role in military operations, it is no wonder that cyber security has become a top priority for national defence. The ability to protect sensitive data and prevent cyber attacks is vital in maintaining a strong defence. The interconnectedness of modern warfare has made the job of defending a nation even more complex. Cyber threats can come from anywhere, and can take on various forms - from hacking and data breaches, to malware and ransom ware attacks. As such, it is imperative that security measures are constantly updated and improved to keep up with the rapidly evolving threat landscape. This is why cyber security has become such a critical aspect of national defence ability to protect against cyber attacks can make or break a country's military operations. In today's world, a country's strength is not solely determined by its military might, but also by its technological prowess.

It is essential that governments and military organizations invest in the necessary resources to ensure the protection of sensitive data and networks. Failure to do so could have devastating consequences, not just on a nation's defence, but also on its economy and society as a whole. A strong cyber security posture is essential to protect sensitive information, critical infrastructure, and ensure the operational effectiveness of a nation's defence capabilities.

The intersection between cyber security and national defence is a complex and ever-evolving landscape. As nations become increasingly reliant on data and networks, the potential for cyber warfare and espionage also rises. Adversaries may seek to disrupt or steal sensitive information, cripple critical infrastructure, or compromise defence systems. It is imperative that governments prioritize cyber security measures to defend against these threats and protect their citizens. In summary, the protection of data and networks is vital for the national defence of any country. A strong cyber security posture is necessary to safeguard against potential attacks and ensure the operational effectiveness of a nation's defence capabilities.

These cyber threats can be perpetrated by foreign adversaries or even non-state actors with malicious intent. They can exploit vulnerabilities in military systems to gain access to sensitive data, disrupt crucial operations, or even cause physical damage. Therefore, it is essential for any country to have a strong cyber security posture in place to protect its national defence capabilities.

Governments must also be aware of the constantly evolving scene of cyber threats and stay vigilant in updating and improving their cyber security measures. This includes regularly assessing and reassessing potential vulnerabilities in their systems and staying up-to-date with the latest advancements in cyber security technology.

In the modern world, military defence is no longer just about physical weapons and soldiers. In an age where cyber threats pose just as much risk as physical attacks, AI has become a crucial tool in protecting national security. By using advanced technologies, such as AI, military systems can enhance their cyber security and better detect and respond to potential threats. This is essential for any country that wants to ensure the safety and security of its citizens. One way AI is being used to protect military systems is through automation. By automating tasks, such as routine security checks and updates, AI can free up human resources for more critical tasks. Additionally, AI can also help identify anomalies in the system that may be indicative of a cyber attack, allowing for a faster response and mitigation of potential damage. With the ability to respond in real-time, AI can help prevent catastrophic consequences for a nation's security. Another way AI is utilized in protecting military systems is through threat detection. AI algorithms can analyze vast amounts of data in a short period and identify potential threats that may go unnoticed by human analysts. This can help military systems stay one step ahead of cyber attackers and prevent any breaches or compromises. In today's digital age, where cyber threats are constantly evolving, the use of AI is crucial in maintaining a strong defense for a nation.

Threat Detection

AI-powered threat detection systems have become increasingly prevalent in the world of cyber security. These systems use advanced machine learning algorithms to analyze vast amounts of data from diverse sources, such as network traffic, logs, and system behaviour. Through the utilization of AI-powered threat detection systems, organizations can effectively pinpoint patterns associated with both recognized and unfamiliar threats, consequently facilitating the timely identification of potential cyber attacks. One of the major advantages of these systems is their capability to continuously learn and adapt. As new threats emerge, these systems can swiftly detect and analyze them, incorporating them into their collection of recognized threats. This not only enables early detection, but also allows for more effective prevention and mitigation of cyber attacks.

It is important to note these systems are not infallible. Constant monitoring and maintenance by experienced cyber security professionals is necessary to ensure the accuracy and effectiveness of these systems. Organizations must prioritize continuously updating and enhancing their threat detection systems to stay ahead in the constantly evolving cyber scene. In doing so, they can better protect their networks, data, and systems from potential attacks.

Organizations must prioritize the regular update and enhancement of their threat detection systems to keep up with the constantly evolving cyber threat landscape. This approach ensures the accuracy and effectiveness of these systems, enabling them to provide better protection for networks, data, and systems against potential attacks.

By utilizing AI for anomaly detection, organizations can observe behaviour and continuously monitor for deviations. This allows for the identification of suspicious activities that may indicate a cyber intrusion or compromise. One of the main advantages of using AI for anomaly detection is its ability to effectively detect irregularities in the behaviour of military systems. This is essential for organizations, as traditional methods of threat detection may struggle to keep up with the constantly evolving tactics of cyber attackers. With its continuous monitoring capabilities, AI systems swiftly detect potential threats and provide organizations with the necessary information to proactively address them, effectively mitigating the risk of cyber attacks. Furthermore, given the ever-increasing complexity and sophistication of cyber threats, having advanced detection systems in place, such as AI-based anomaly detection, becomes imperative to organizations. Not only does it provide real-time monitoring, but it also enables the analysis of vast amounts of data, empowering organizations to identify patterns and trends that may indicate a potential risk. This proactive approach to threat detection can help organizations stay one step ahead of cyber attackers and ensure the security of their systems and data.

Organizations are increasingly turning to AI-driven threat detection systems to combat the ever-growing threat of cyber attacks. These systems have the capability to analyze extensive amounts of historical data and utilize machine learning to identify patterns and potential threats. By staying one step ahead of cyber attackers, organizations can proactively protect themselves from potential breaches and ensure the security of their systems and data.

One of the key benefits of using AI in threat detection is its ability to continuously update and enhance itself. As cyber threats evolve and become more sophisticated, organizations need to be able to adapt and respond in real-time. By incorporating AI into their security measures, organizations can have a more dynamic and robust defence against cyber threats. This not only helps to prevent attacks, but also allows organizations to quickly respond and mitigate any potential damage. In addition to predicting and preventing attacks, AI-powered threat detection can also aid in incident response.

Cyber Threat Intelligence Integration

AI is helping the military stay on top of cyber security risks by integrating cyber threat intelligence feeds into their systems. This integration is critical in today's world, where cyber attacks have become more sophisticated and frequent. With AI constantly updating its knowledge about the latest cyber threats, military systems are better equipped to identify and respond to evolving risks. Using AI to manage cyber security risks also helps prevent potential attacks and minimizes the damage caused by cyber attacks.

By continuously monitoring and updating threat intelligence, AI-enabled systems are able to identify potential vulnerabilities and take proactive measures to prevent attacks. This not only helps protect sensitive military information, but also ensures the safety of personnel and operations. The seamless integration of AI and cyber threat intelligence also allows for more efficient and effective responses to cyber attacks. With AI constantly analyzing and updating data, military systems are able to quickly detect and respond to emerging threats. This not only helps minimize the damage caused by attacks, but also allows for faster recovery and restoration of systems. As technology continues to advance and cyber threats become more complex, AI will play a crucial role in ensuring the security and success of military operations.

AI's ability to automatically respond to and mitigate cyber threats is a crucial aspect of ensuring the security of military operations in today's rapidly advancing technology landscape. By utilizing AI, military organizations can quickly and effectively address and contain attacks, minimizing the potential damage and disruption to their systems. This not only helps protect sensitive information and resources, but also allows for a faster recovery and restoration process. In addition to its role in responding to threats,

AI also plays a key role in identifying and addressing emerging threats before they can cause harm.

By constantly learning and adapting to new threats, AI technology can stay one step ahead of potential attackers, providing an added layer of protection for military operations. This proactive approach to security is essential in today's ever-evolving cyber landscape, where traditional security measures may not be enough. As technology continues to evolve and cyber threats become increasingly sophisticated, the importance of AI in military operations will only continue to grow. By utilizing automated response mechanisms and constantly learning and adapting to new threats, AI is a crucial tool in ensuring the security and success of military operations. With its ability to detect, respond, and mitigate threats in real-time, AI is a vital component in safeguarding sensitive information and resources.

AI-driven behavioural analytics are a critical element in safeguarding sensitive information and resources within military operations. These advanced systems are capable of analyzing the behaviour of users, systems, and devices within military networks, detecting any unusual or suspicious activity. This allows security teams to quickly identify potential insider threats or unauthorized activities and take appropriate action. This level of real-time detection and response is crucial in maintaining the security and success of military operations.

Furthermore, AI's constant learning and adapting abilities make it an invaluable tool in the ever-evolving landscape of cyber threats. As new threats emerge, AI can quickly analyze and understand them, allowing for the development of effective defence strategies. This ensures that military networks and resources are continuously protected from potential attacks. With AI's ability to detect, respond, and mitigate threats in real-time, military operations can operate with confidence, knowing that their sensitive information and resources are secure. In addition to its security capabilities, AI also plays a crucial role in the success of military operations.

By automating response mechanisms, AI allows for faster and more efficient decision-making, freeing up human personnel to focus on other critical tasks. This not only improves the overall operational efficiency but also reduces the risk of human error. With AI as a vital component in ensuring the security and success of military operations, it is clear that this technology has become an essential and indispensable tool in modern warfare.

AI is not only used for detecting cyber threats, but it also plays a crucial role in analyzing network traffic patterns. This enables military operations to identify potential anomalies that could pose a security risk. By constantly monitoring communication patterns and data exhilaration attempts, AI acts as a proactive defence mechanism. It helps prevent potential cyber attacks and minimizes the risk of human error in identifying and responding to threats. Moreover, with the integration of AI in military operations, the overall efficiency of operations is significantly improved. AI can quickly analyze large amounts of data and provide insights that would have otherwise taken humans hours or even days to process. This not only saves time but also allows military personnel to focus on critical tasks that require human decision-making skills. With AI as a vital component, the security and success of military operations are enhanced, making it an indispensable tool in modern warfare.

AI technology has become increasingly important in modern warfare, with deep learning being a critical component. Through the use of deep neural networks, AI can quickly and accurately recognize complex and evolving threats that may otherwise take hours or even days for human personnel to process. AI's ability to process and analyze vast amounts of data quickly, coupled with its adaptability and accuracy, make it a valuable asset for military operations. With AI as a crucial component, the security and success of military operations are significantly enhanced, making it an essential tool for the protection of nations. However, with great power comes great responsibility, and the potential for adversarial attacks on AI systems is a constant threat.

To address this, there is a focus on developing AI defences against adversarial machine learning. Techniques such as robust model training and anomaly detection help fortify AI systems against manipulation attempts. This not only ensures the integrity and reliability of AI, but also mitigates the risk of adversaries exploiting AI for their own gain. As military operations become increasingly reliant on AI, it is crucial to continue investing in research and development of these defence mechanisms. One area where AI has made a significant impact is in Security Information and Event Management (SIEM). AI enhances SIEM solutions by automating the analysis of security events and logs. This accelerates the detection of security incidents, provides insights into potential threats, and facilitates a timely response by military cybersecurity teams. By leveraging AI, military organizations can stay ahead of potential threats and keep their critical systems and data safe from malicious attacks. As the battlefield continues to evolve, AI will undoubtedly play a crucial role in ensuring the security and success of military operations.

AI is essential in military cyber security teams as it can provide continuous monitoring and adaptation to changing cyber threats. This allows for regular updates and refinements of AI models, ensuring that critical military systems and data remain safe from malicious attacks. By leveraging AI, military organizations can stay ahead of potential threats and keep their operations secure. As the battlefield continues to evolve, AI's role becomes increasingly crucial in maintaining the security and success of military operations. With the use of AI, military cyber security teams can proactively identify and mitigate potential threats, reducing the risk of cyber attacks on critical systems.

The constant monitoring and adaptation provided by AI systems allow for quick and effective responses to emerging cyber threats, keeping military operations running smoothly and efficiently. In addition to its role in cyber security, AI also plays a significant role in enhancing military capabilities. With the use of AI-powered tools and technologies, military organizations can gather and analyze large amounts of data to make informed decisions and gain a tactical advantage on the battlefield.

Cyber Espionage

Preventing cyber espionage is a crucial step towards ensuring the safety and security of sensitive information. It is a multi-faceted and complex task that requires a comprehensive approach. This includes the implementation of technological measures, the formulation of effective policy frameworks, and maintaining constant vigilance. Cyber espionage is a serious threat that involves unauthorized access to sensitive information. It is often carried out by state-sponsored actors, criminal organizations, or other entities with malicious intent.

These actors have the goal of gathering intelligence and gaining a competitive advantage. As such, it is crucial to have a robust and proactive defence strategy in place to prevent cyber espionage. Technological measures such as firewalls, encryption, and intrusion detection systems are essential in protecting against cyber espionage. However, they are not enough on their own. Effective policy frameworks that outline security protocols and procedures must also be in place. Ongoing vigilance is also critical, as the threat landscape is constantly evolving. Regular security assessments and updates to defences are necessary to stay ahead of potential cyber espionage attempts. By implementing a comprehensive approach, organizations can better protect themselves against cyber espionage and safeguard sensitive information.

Organizations must prioritize maintaining strong cyber hygiene practices to effectively protect themselves against the ever-evolving landscape of cyber espionage. This includes regularly updating software and implementing a robust patch management system to address any known vulnerabilities. Additionally, utilizing strong and unique passwords is crucial in preventing cyber attacks that rely on weak or reused credentials. However, simply implementing these measures is not enough. Ongoing vigilance is a key to staying ahead of potential cyber espionage attempts. Regular security assessments and updates to defences are necessary to identify and address any new or emerging threats. This also involves staying informed about the latest tactics and techniques used by cyber criminals and adapting defences accordingly. By adopting a comprehensive approach to cyber security, organizations can enhance the protection of their sensitive information and reduce the threats of cyber espionage. This involves not only implementing robust cyber hygiene practices, but also investing in state-of-the-art security solutions and regularly assessing and updating their defences. With this proactive approach, organizations can better protect themselves against the ever-present threat of cyber espionage.

Implementing network segmentation is an effective way for organizations to further protect their sensitive information against cyber espionage. By dividing the network into smaller segments, it limits the ability for attackers to move laterally and access valuable data. This adds an extra layer of defence to the organization's cyber security strategy. In addition to network segmentation, deploying advanced endpoint security solutions is crucial in mitigating the risks of cyber espionage. These solutions include antivirus software, intrusion detection systems, and endpoint detection and response (EDR) tools.

These technologies work together to detect and prevent malware, which is a common tool used in cyber espionage attacks. Regularly updating and assessing these defenses is essential to stay ahead of evolving threats. Investing in these proactive measures may require significant resources, but it is a necessary step in protecting against the ever-present threat of cyber espionage.

Organizations must prioritize cyber security and continuously adapt and improve their defenses to stay one step ahead of attackers. Implementing robust cyber hygiene practices and leveraging cutting-edge security solutions are paramount for organizations to safeguard their invaluable information, ensuring the preservation of their esteemed reputation and financial standing.

In today's digital world, cyber espionage is an ever-present threat that organizations must constantly guard against. In the face of increasingly sophisticated cyber attacks, it is essential for organizations to make cyber security a top priority and constantly enhance their defences to outmanoeuvre attackers. To achieve this, organizations must implement strong cyber hygiene practices and utilize advanced security solutions. One way to safeguard sensitive information is by using encryption to protect data both in transit and at rest.

This security measure is critical as it guarantees that even if adversaries manage to gain unauthorized access to the data, they will be unable to comprehend it without the appropriate decryption keys. By utilizing encryption, organizations can greatly reduce the risk of their sensitive information falling into the wrong hands. The consequences of a successful cyber attack can be devastating for an organization, damaging their reputation and bottom line. Therefore, it is imperative for organizations to take proactive measures to protect their data and systems. By adopting robust cyber hygiene practices, leveraging advanced security solutions, and implementing encryption to safeguard sensitive data, organizations can effectively protect their information and combat the constant threat of cyber espionage.

Organizations should prioritize cyber security training for employees to raise awareness and strengthen their defence against cyber espionage. By educating employees on the tactics and techniques used by attackers, organizations can effectively empower their staff to readily identify and promptly counter potential threats. Regular training sessions can be instrumental in reinforcing the significance of robust cyber hygiene practices and the pivotal role that every individual plays in safeguarding sensitive data. In addition to training, organizations should also implement advanced security strategies to defend their defences against cyber espionage.

These solutions can include intrusion detection and prevention systems, next-generation firewalls, and security information and event management tools. By leveraging these technologies, organizations can proactively identify and respond to potential threats, significantly reducing the risk of successful cyber espionage attempts. By encrypting data both at rest and in transit, organizations can guarantee that even in the event of a security breach, the pilfered data will be rendered indecipherable and entirely useless to any potential attacker. This adds an extra layer of protection to sensitive information and can help mitigate the impacts of a successful cyber espionage attempt.

Collaborating with other organizations, industry groups, and government agencies through threat intelligence sharing initiatives is an excellent approach to achieve this goal. By sharing information about known threats and indicators of compromise, organizations can collectively defend against cyber espionage. This collaboration also enables organizations to identify patterns associated with sophisticated attacks using advanced threat detection systems. These systems utilize machine learning and artificial intelligence to identify and thwart emerging cyber threats, thus aiding in the prevention of successful attacks. Another important measure to protect sensitive information is to ensure the security of the supply chain. This includes thoroughly vetting suppliers, validating the integrity of software and hardware, and implementing secure procurement practices. By doing so, organizations can prevent the insertion of malicious components or software into their infrastructure. This is crucial, as cyberattackers often exploit vulnerabilities in the supply chain to gain access to an organization's systems and steal sensitive information. By investing in these security measures, organizations can safeguard their valuable assets and maintain the trust of their customers and stakeholders.

Collaborating with international partners, law enforcement agencies, and cybersecurity organizations to share information and coordinate efforts against cyber espionage campaigns. A collective approach is often necessary to address threats that span multiple jurisdictions. This includes working closely with other countries to gather intelligence and identify potential attackers. By sharing information and coordinating efforts, organizations can gain valuable insights into the tactics and techniques used by cybercriminals, allowing them to better protect their systems and data. Developing and enforce policies that govern the handling of sensitive information. Legal measures can provide a framework for prosecuting cyber espionage activities and holding perpetrators accountable. It is important to establish clear guidelines for how sensitive data should be stored, accessed, and shared within an organization. This not only helps to prevent data breaches, but also ensures that employees are aware of the proper protocols for handling sensitive information. In addition, having legal measures in place can serve as a deterrent for potential cyber espionage activities, as there are consequences for those who are caught engaging in such behavior. Implement continuous monitoring of networks and systems to detect and respond to cyber threats in real-time. A robust incident response plan helps organizations swiftly contain and mitigate the impact of a cyber espionage incident. By continuously monitoring their networks and systems, organizations can quickly identify any suspicious activity and take immediate action to stop it. This includes implementing advanced threat detection tools, as well as having skilled cybersecurity professionals who can respond to and mitigate potential threats. Additionally, having a well-defined incident response plan can help organizations minimize the damage caused by a cyber espionage attack and ensure a Swift recovery process.

Building Resilience

Organizations must prioritize building resilience against cyber attacks in order to safeguard their operations from potential security incidents. This involves taking proactive measures, implementing effective response strategies, and constantly improving their defences against cyber threats. By establishing a robust cyber resilience framework, organizations can significantly reduce the devastating impact of cyber attacks and guarantee uninterrupted operations, even in the midst of these imminent threats. One of the key aspects of cyber resilience is being prepared to withstand and adapt to cyber threats. This means having solid security protocols in place, such as firewalls, intrusion detection systems, and regular vulnerability assessments. Additionally, organizations must be ready to respond to any security incidents in a timely and effective manner. This requires the implementation of incident response plans, conducting frequent drills and simulated attacks, and having a dedicated team to manage cyber attacks. Continuously improving and evolving their cyber resilience strategies is also crucial for organizations. As cyber threats continue to evolve and become more sophisticated, organizations must stay ahead by implementing new technologies and strategies. This could involve investing in advanced security tools, conducting regular security training for employees, and staying updated on the latest cyber threats and trends. By continuously improving their cyber resilience, organizations can stay one step ahead of cybercriminals and safeguard their operations from potential attacks.

One fundamental aspect of enhancing cyber resilience is conducting frequent risk assessment and prioritizing cyber security risks. This step enables organizations to identify and understand the specific vulnerabilities and threats that their operations may face. By doing so, organizations can develop a risk management strategy that aligns with their objectives and includes appropriate measures to mitigate, transfer, or accept identified risks. This proactive approach ensures that organizations are well-prepared to handle potential cyber attacks. In addition to conducting risk assessments, organizations can also invest in advanced security tools to strengthen their cyber security defences.

Developing a comprehensive incident response plan is critical in protecting an organization's operations from potential cyber attacks. This plan should include a detailed outline of the steps to be taken in the event of a security breach. Clear definitions of communication protocols, roles and responsibilities, and predefined actions for containment, eradication, and recovery are essential to guarantee a seamless and efficient response. Investing in advanced security tools and conducting regular security training are important steps in strengthening your cyber security defences. However, it is equally vital to have a robust incident response plan in place. This plan plays a critical role in enhancing your organization's cyber resilience. This plan should minimize the impact and be updated to adapt to the ever-evolving cyber security scenery. By having a plan in place, organizations can minimize the impact of a cyber attack and quickly recover from any damages. As cyber threats evolve and become more sophisticated, it is essential for organizations to stay informed about the latest developments in the field. This includes staying up-to-date on emerging cyber threats and vulnerabilities, as well as understanding the tactics and techniques used by malicious actors. By staying informed, organizations can proactively identify and address potential vulnerabilities, ensuring their operations remain secure and resilient.

Regular training and awareness programs are essential in educating employees on cybersecurity best practices. By keeping them informed and vigilant, organizations can strengthen their first line of defense against common tactics used in cyberattacks, such as phishing and social engineering. Training can also empower employees to identify and report potential threats, allowing organizations to take proactive steps in addressing vulnerabilities. In addition to regular training, staying informed on the latest developments in the field is crucial for maintaining a strong security posture. This includes closely monitoring emerging cyber threats and vulnerabilities, as well as understanding the tactics and techniques used by malicious actors. By staying up-to-date, organizations can stay one step ahead and proactively identify potential risks before they become major security incidents. This also allows for more effective incident response and mitigation strategies, minimizing the impact of any potential attacks. In today's rapidly evolving digital landscape, staying on top of the latest cybersecurity developments is more important than ever. With new threats constantly emerging, organizations must be proactive in their approach and continuously educate and inform their employees. By doing so, organizations can ensure their operations remain secure and resilient in the face of potential cyberattacks.

Continuous monitoring is a critical component of a proactive cybersecurity strategy. By regularly tracking networks, systems, and user activities, organizations can quickly identify any anomalies and potential security incidents. With the ever-evolving threat landscape, real-time monitoring is essential for rapidly responding to emerging threats. This approach allows organizations to detect and mitigate risks before they escalate and cause significant damage. Additionally, organizations must continuously educate and inform their employees about cybersecuritybest practices. As the saying goes, "an organization is only as strong as its weakest link." Therefore, employees must be aware of the latest threats and how to handle potential attacks. Regular training and updates on cybersecurity developments can significantly improve an organization's security posture. It empowers employees to take an active role in safeguarding the organization's operations and assets. In conclusion, being up-to-date on the latest cybersecurity developments is crucial for organizations to maintain secure and resilient operations. This requires continuous monitoring of networks, systems, and user activities, coupled with educating and informing employees. By taking a proactive approach, organizations can detect and respond to threats quickly, minimizing the potential impact of cyberattacks. It also creates a culture of security awareness and responsibility within the organization, strengthening its overall security posture.

With the increasing prevalence of cyberattacks, organizations prioritize the security of their networks, systems, and user activities. This can be achieved through a combination of proactive measures and employee education. By regularly backing up critical data and regularly testing recovery processes, organizations can minimize the potential impact of a cyberattack. In the unfortunate event of an attack, having up-to-date backups ensures that systems and data can be restored quickly, reducing downtime and minimizing losses. In addition to these technical measures, organizations must also focus on creating a culture of security awareness and responsibility. By educating and informing employees about the importance of cybersecurity, organizations can empower their workforce to act as the first line of defense against potential threats. This not only strengthens the overall security posture of the organization, but also fosters a sense of accountability among employees. With a proactive approach to cybersecurity and a well-informed workforce, organizations can effectively detect and respond to threats, mitigating potential risks and protecting their critical assets.

A proactive approach to cybersecurity involves not only protecting against potential threats, but also implementing measures that limit the impact of an attack. By implementing network segmentation, organizations can isolate and contain the impact of a cyberattack, preventing it from spreading throughout the entire infrastructure. This not only strengthens the overall security posture of the organization, but also minimizes the potential damage that a cyberattack can cause. A well-informed workforce is a crucial aspect of implementing effective cybersecurity measures. By educating employees on potential threats and how to detect and respond to them, organizations can foster a sense of accountability among employees. This encourages employees to take an active role in protecting the organization's critical assets, making it more difficult for attackers to successfully breach the network. With a proactive approach to cybersecurity and a well-informed workforce, organizations can effectively mitigate potential risks and protect their critical assets from cyberattacks. Encryption is an essential tool for safeguarding sensitive data and is a crucial component of a comprehensive cybersecurity strategy. By utilizing encryption to protect data both in transit and at rest, organizations can ensure that their critical assets remain secure, even if they are intercepted or stolen by attackers. With encryption in place, organizations can rest assured that their sensitive information is protected from unauthorized access. In addition to encryption, organizations can also implement multifactor authentication to further enhance their cybersecurity efforts. By requiring employees to provide multiple forms of identification, such as a password and a biometric scan, organizations can significantly reduce the risk of unauthorized access to their critical assets. This approach also serves as an effective deterrent to potential attackers, as it significantly increases the difficulty of breaching the network. As technology continues to advance, organizations must remain vigilant in their efforts to protect their critical assets from cyberattacks. By taking a proactive approach to cybersecurity and ensuring that their workforce is well-informed, organizations can effectively mitigate potential risks and safeguard their sensitive information. With the right strategies in place, organizations can stay one step ahead of attackers and maintain the security of their critical assets.

Organizations must have a well-established patch management process to regularly update their software, operating systems, and applications. Timely patching is crucial for closing potential entry points for attackers and mitigating cyber risks. By ensuring that all systems and applications are up-to-date, organizations can strengthen their cybersecurity posture and protect sensitive information from being compromised. Furthermore, it is essential for organizations to provide ongoing cybersecurity training and education for their workforce. This will ensure that employees are well-informed about the latest security threats and how to identify and respond to them. With a knowledgeable and vigilant workforce, organizations can stay one step ahead of attackers and prevent potential cyberattacks. This proactive approach to cybersecurity can greatly reduce the risk of sensitive information being accessed or stolen by malicious actors. In addition to patch management and employee training, organizations must also have the right strategies in place to effectively respond to and recover from cyberattacks. This includes having a comprehensive incident response plan, regular backups of critical data, and a disaster recovery plan. By having these measures in place, organizations can minimize the impact of a cyberattack and maintain the security of their critical assets. With a proactive and multi-layered approach to cybersecurity, organizations can effectively mitigate potential risks and protect themselves from cyberattacks.

COMSEC

COMSEC is vital for the security of military communication. With cyber-warfare becoming more prevalent, it is essential to safeguard sensitive information exchanged within military networks and communication systems. The protection of this information is critical for the success of national defence. COMSEC is responsible for ensuring the confidentiality, integrity, and availability of sensitive data. It involves various measures and protocols to prevent unauthorized access, interception, or manipulation of information. One of the key considerations for ensuring military communication security is the use of encryption techniques. Encryption is the process of converting plain text into a code to prevent unauthorized access to sensitive information. This code can only be deciphered by authorized personnel with the correct decryption key.

Encryption helps to protect information from being intercepted and read by unauthorized parties, ensuring confidentiality. It also guarantees the integrity of the data. Any attempts to alter or modify the encrypted information will lead to the decryption process failing. This failure serves as a clear indication that the data has been compromised. Another essential aspect of military communication security is proper training and awareness. All military personnel must be trained on the importance of COMSEC and the protocols to follow to ensure its effectiveness. This training should also include the identification of potential threats and how to mitigate them. Furthermore, implementing regular security awareness campaigns can greatly enhance the significance of COMSEC and emphasize the vital role that each individual holds in its preservation. Proper training and awareness are crucial for maintaining military communication security, ensuring the protection of sensitive information and the success of national defence.

Encryption is a crucial aspect of COMSEC that entails transforming plaintext into cipher text, rendering it indecipherable without the appropriate decryption key. By implementing strong encryption algorithms, military communication can be better protected against potential breaches and unauthorized access. Regularly reviewing and updating the encryption methods we use is of utmost importance. This ensures that we constantly adhere to the latest security standards and effectively address any possible vulnerability. In addition to encryption, implementing robust key management practices is crucial to maintaining secure communication. This involves not only the creation and distribution of cryptographic keys but also their proper storage and destruction. Unauthorized access to these keys can compromise the entire communication system, making it vulnerable to interception and decryption. Therefore, it is essential to establish strict protocols for key management and regularly audit and update them to prevent any potential breaches.

Regular security awareness campaigns can also play a vital role in reinforcing the importance of COMSEC and educating individuals on their role in maintaining it. These campaigns can help to promote a culture of security and ensure that every member of the military understands the critical role they play in protecting sensitive information. By raising awareness and providing proper training, military communication security can be effectively maintained, ultimately contributing to the success of national defence.

Campaigns play a vital role in promoting a culture of security within the military. By raising awareness and providing proper training, every member of the military can understand the critical role they play in protecting sensitive information. This not only contributes to the success of national defence but also helps to ensure that military communication security is effectively maintained. With the constant advancement of technology, it is crucial that the military stays up-to-date with the latest security measures to protect against potential threats. One way to enhance the resilience of wireless communications is through the use of frequency hopping and spread spectrum techniques. These methods involve rapidly changing frequencies during transmission, making it challenging for adversaries to intercept or disrupt signals. This provides an added layer of protection against potential attacks and ensures that military communications remain secure.

Along with these techniques, it is essential to use secure and authenticated communication protocols to ensure the integrity and authenticity of messages. Implementing secure communication protocols is crucial in protecting against tampering, forgery, and man-in-the-middle attacks. These protocols provide an extra level of security by verifying the identity of the sender and ensuring that messages are not altered during transmission. By using these protocols, the military can have confidence in the security of their communications, allowing them to focus on their critical mission without worrying about potential breaches or attacks. In conclusion, with the implementation of campaigns, frequency hopping and spread spectrum techniques, and secure communication protocols, military communication security can be effectively maintained, contributing to the success of national defence.

Adhere to TEMPEST standards and employ secure voice and data transmission technologies to effectively secure military communications. TEMPEST standards focus on preventing unintentional electromagnetic emissions from electronic equipment, reducing the risk of eavesdropping. This ensures that sensitive information remains confidential and inaccessible to potential attackers. In addition, the use of secure voice and data transmission technologies, such as secure radios and encrypted data links, further enhances the security of military communications.

These technologies are specifically designed for military applications, making them highly resistant to interception and eavesdropping. This not only maintains the confidentiality of communications, but also allows military personnel to focus on their critical missions without having to worry about potential breaches or attacks. Overall, the implementation of TEMPEST standards and secure communication protocols significantly contributes to the success of national defense. By effectively maintaining communication security, military personnel are able to communicate and coordinate with each other without fear of sensitive information being compromised. This ultimately allows for more efficient and effective operations, ultimately leading to a stronger and more secure nation.

Effective authentication and access control measures are critical to safeguarding military communication systems. By implementing strong authentication mechanisms and enforcing access controls, only authorized personnel are able to access sensitive information, ensuring its confidentiality and integrity. This is especially important in the context of national defence, as any compromise of sensitive information could have devastating consequences. In addition to authentication and access control, physical security measures must also be taken to protect communication systems. This involves securing the physical infrastructure and components, such as communication equipment, data centres, and transmission facilities, from potential threats like unauthorized access, tampering, and sabotage.

By ensuring the physical security of these systems, the military can prevent any attempts to disrupt or compromise their communication networks. These measures significantly contribute to the success of national defense by creating a strong and secure communication network for military personnel to rely on. By effectively maintaining communication security, operations can run smoothly, allowing for efficient coordination and decision-making. This ultimately leads to a stronger and more secure nation, as the military is able to effectively protect and defend against potential threats.

The use of secure satellite communication allows for military personnel to effectively communicate, even in the most challenging operational environments. This is especially important in today's global landscape, where threats can arise from any corner of the world.

By utilizing satellite communication, the military is able to maintain a strong and secure network that can withstand potential attempts of interception or jamming. One of the key advantages of satellite communication is its flexibility and global coverage. This means that military personnel can rely on this system to communicate with each other, no matter where they are located in the world. This not only ensures reliable communication during operations, but also allows for efficient coordination and decision-making. This ultimately leads to a stronger and more secure nation, as the military is able to effectively protect and defend against potential threats with the help of this advanced communication system.

With the world becoming increasingly interconnected and dependent on advanced technology, it is crucial for the military to have reliable communication systems in place. These systems not only allow for efficient coordination and decision-making during operations, but also serve as a countermeasure against potential threats such as jamming and interference.

By implementing countermeasures, the military can detect and mitigate any attempts to disrupt communication, ensuring that it remains uninterrupted and reliable. To combat jamming and interference, the military utilizes advanced techniques and technologies. These include frequency-hopping techniques, which involve rapidly switching between different frequencies to avoid being targeted by jammers. Signal processing algorithms are also utilized to filter out any interference and ensure the integrity of the communication. Additionally, advanced antenna technologies are used to enhance the strength and reach of the signals, making them less susceptible to jamming and interference attempts. With these countermeasures in place, the military can maintain communication continuity and effectively protect and defend against potential threats.

In addition to ensuring the integrity and continuity of communication, the military also employs advanced encryption technologies to protect against potential cyber threats. These technologies scramble and secure the content of messages, making it nearly impossible for unauthorized parties to intercept or decipher sensitive information. This added layer of security further enhances the resilience and reliability of military communication systems. Furthermore, the use of advanced antenna technologies allows for greater range and strength of signals, making them less susceptible to jamming and interference attempts.

By continuously upgrading and improving these technologies, the military can stay ahead of potential adversaries and maintain a strong and secure communication infrastructure. This is crucial for successful operations and protection against potential threats. The military also employs strict network segmentation to further enhance the security of their communication systems. By dividing networks into smaller segments, any potential breaches or attacks are limited to a smaller portion of the overall network, minimizing the impact and reducing the chances of a complete system compromise. This approach also allows for easier detection and containment of threats, ensuring the overall security of military communication remains intact.

Continuous monitoring of communication networks is an essential part of modern military communication. By continuously checking for anomalies, unauthorized access, and potential security incidents, military forces can quickly detect and respond to any threats that may arise. This real-time monitoring is crucial in ensuring that any security breaches or attacks are quickly contained, minimizing the impact on the overall network and reducing the chances of a complete system compromise.

A continuous monitoring strategy also allows for easier detection and containment of threats. By breaking the network into smaller segments, any potential breaches or attacks are limited to a smaller portion of the overall network. This approach makes it easier to pinpoint the source of the threat and contain it before it can spread to other parts of the system. This proactive approach to security ensures that the overall security of military communication remains intact, protecting sensitive information and maintaining operational readiness. In addition to enabling rapid response to emerging threats, continuous monitoring also provides a more complete picture of the overall security of military communication. By constantly monitoring the network, military authorities can identify any weaknesses or vulnerabilities that may exist and take steps to address them before they can be exploited by malicious actors. This proactive approach not only minimizes the chances of a successful attack but also helps to prevent future threats, ensuring that military communication remains secure and reliable.

Provide ongoing training and resources to ensure military personnel are equipped to identify and mitigate potential vulnerabilities. This may include simulated attack scenarios, regular security briefings, and access control protocols. Regularly review and update security protocols and procedures to adapt to changing threats and technology advancements. This includes conducting risk assessments and implementing necessary changes to enhance security measures. Stay vigilant and encourage a culture of security awareness among all military personnel. This proactive approach not only minimizes the chances of a successful attack, but also builds a strong defense against future threats. By continuously evaluating and improving their security practices, the military can maintain secure and reliable communication networks.

Weapon system

Ensuring the protection of military hardware, software, and associated technologies against cyber threats, physical attacks, and unauthorized access is critical for weapon systems security. This is crucial for any nation to maintain its military power and deter any external threat. With the advancement of technology, modern weapon systems have become increasingly complex and sophisticated, posing a significant challenge to their security. It is not just about protecting physical assets, but also safeguarding sensitive information and preventing any compromise or manipulation. Military forces around the world have recognized the crucial importance of securing weapon systems and have implemented strict protocols and measures to ensure their safety.

This includes regular security audits, constant monitoring of network systems, and strict access control. The ever-evolving nature of cyber warfare has rendered it absolutely necessary for military forces to continuously enhance their security systems and maintain a proactive stance against potential threats. One of the key considerations for ensuring weapon systems security is to have a multi-layered approach. This means having various security measures in place to protect different aspects of the weapon system. This includes firewalls, encryption, intrusion detection systems, and physical security measures. It is also crucial to have a well-trained and vigilant workforce who can identify and respond to any security breaches. The primary objective of weapon systems security is to guarantee the safety and efficiency of military operations, and it demands unwavering dedication and effort to accomplish this.

In today's modern warfare, weapon systems are highly sophisticated and rely heavily on technology. This makes them vulnerable to cyber attacks, which can have devastating consequences on military operations. As such, it is essential to implement robust cyber security measures for embedded systems within weapon platforms. This includes securing the firmware, software, and communication protocols to prevent unauthorized access and exploitation. Alongside implementing technical measures, having a highly trained and alert workforce is essential in order to detect and respond effectively to any possible security breaches. T

his means providing regular training and updates on the latest cyber security threats and best practices. Without a knowledgeable and proactive workforce, even the most robust security measures may be ineffective. Ultimately, the goal of weapon systems security is to ensure the safety and effectiveness of military operations. By integrating tamper-resistant components and physical security measures into the design of weapon systems, we can significantly improve the security and effectiveness of our military operations. These measures function as an impenetrable shield against any unauthorized access or tampering, guaranteeing the constant security and optimal performance of weapon systems. Security is extremely important now because of the constant changing threats, particularly when it comes to possible physical attacks on our military systems. In addition to implementing these measures, it is crucial to also maintain a vigilant workforce.

With proper security protocols in place, we can effectively safeguard our military operations from potential threats. However, it is not just about protecting our systems and networks from external attacks. We must ensure the security of our supply chain to prevent any vulnerabilities or malicious code from being introduced during the manufacturing and assembly process.

By conducting regular vulnerability assessments and penetration testing, we can proactively identify and address potential weaknesses in our weapon systems. By doing so, we can stay one step ahead of potential adversaries and maintain the security of our operations.

These tests enable cover and counter vulnerabilities before they can be exploited by malicious individuals, securing the safety and efficiency of our military operations. In addition to regular testing, following secure software development practices is crucial when designing and building weapon system software.

By implementing these practices, can be ensured the integrity and reliability of critical systems that are essential for national security. By implementing secure coding standards, conducting regular code reviews, and performing security audits throughout the development lifecycle, we can significantly reduce the risk of introducing vulnerabilities into our systems. This not only protects operations in the present but also guarantees the long-term security and reliability of the weapon systems as technology continues to progress and evolve. With a strong focus on security throughout the development process, we can mitigate risks and confidently defend against emerging threats.

To safeguard weapon systems effectively, not only must robust authentication mechanisms and access controls be put in place, but it is also imperative to consistently update firmware and software. This is essential to ensure that the systems are equipped with the latest security patches and can effectively defend against evolving threats. Establishing a secure and controlled process for these updates, we can address any identified vulnerabilities and further enhance the overall security posture of our systems. This not only protects our operations in the present, but also ensures the long-term security and reliability of our weapon systems as technology continues to advance and evolve. Furthermore, a strong focus on security throughout the development process is crucial in mitigating risks and confidently defending against emerging threats. By incorporating security measures from the initial stages of development, we can proactively identify and address any potential vulnerabilities, rather than trying to fix them after a breach has occurred. This approach not only strengthens our current systems, but also sets a foundation for continued security and reliability as technology continues to evolve.

Conducting frequent red team exercises allows us to simulate real-world cyber threats and attacks on our weapon systems, helping us identify potential weaknesses and vulnerabilities that might be exploited by adversaries. This proactive approach allows us to address any potential vulnerability before they can be exploited, rather than trying to fix them after a breach has occurred. This not only strengthens our current systems, but also sets a foundation for continued security and reliability as technology continues to evolve. In addition to conducting red team exercises, we also utilize robust cryptographic algorithms to secure communication, data storage, and authentication processes within our weapon systems. Cryptographic security is critical for protecting sensitive information, ensuring that only authorized users have access to our systems. By implementing strong cryptographic measures, we can prevent unauthorized access and maintain the integrity of our data. Furthermore, we implement continuous monitoring and intrusion detection systems to detect any anomalous behaviour or potential security incidents in real-time. This allows for rapid identification of unauthorized activities, which is crucial for timely response and mitigation of potential threats. By continuously monitoring our systems, we can quickly identify and address any potential security issues, maintaining the security and reliability of our weapon systems.

By hardening the operating systems of embedded devices within weapon systems, we can reduce the potential attack surface and strengthen their resistance against exploitation. This could involve disabling unnecessary services and applying additional security configurations to bolster their defences. Taking these proactive measures will help to mitigate the risk of potential security incidents and protect against unauthorized activities. Furthermore, it is important to consider security throughout the entire lifecycle of weapon systems. This means incorporating security measures from the initial design phase, through development, testing, deployment, and even decommissioning.

To ensure the safety of our weapon systems, we adhere to international security standards and guidelines, which set the bar for the highest level of security. These standards enable us to maintain the security and reliability of our weapon systems, giving us the confidence to utilize them without the fear of external threats. With our compliance to recognized standards, we ensure interoperability and the adoption of best practices in security, making our weapon systems a formidable force. In addition to adhering to international security standards, we also provide specialized training for all personnel involved in the operation, maintenance, and development of our weapon systems. This ensures that our team is well-equipped to handle any potential security risks and effectively mitigate them. We also enhance awareness of cybersecurity risks and best practices among our team, empowering them to be proactive in identifying and addressing any potential threats. This training and awareness program plays a crucial role in maintaining the security and reliability of our weapon systems.

The integration of weapon systems within multi-domain operations is a complex process that requires careful consideration. We must fully understand the interconnectedness of cyber, space, land, air, and maritime domains in order to effectively address the holistic security challenges that arise. This integration allows for a more streamlined and effective approach to securing our weapon systems. Compliance with relevant legal and regulatory frameworks is crucial in ensuring the security of our weapon systems. By adhering to these standards, we can align our security practices with national and international regulations. This not only helps to mitigate risks, but also ensures that our weapon systems are consistently meeting the highest security standards. Securing weapon systems is an ongoing and ever-evolving challenge that requires a multi-faceted approach. We must constantly assess and adapt to new threats, while also adhering to established security best practices. By taking a proactive approach to addressing emerging threats, we can maintain the security and reliability of our weapon systems. This is why our training and awareness program is so crucial in empowering our team to be vigilant and proactive in identifying and addressing potential risks.

Information and Warfare

Information warfare is a form of warfare that revolves around the use of information, disinformation and psychological tactics. It takes place in the digital realm and is used to achieve strategic objectives. These objectives can include shaping perceptions, manipulating public opinion, and influencing decision-making processes. This type of warfare knows no boundaries and can be utilized by state actors, non-state entities, or even individuals, regardless of their country of origin.

One of the main purposes of information warfare and influence operations is to achieve political, military or economic goals. It is often used by state actors to gain an advantage over their adversaries. Non-state entities can also use it to further their own agenda or to disrupt the operations of their enemies. In some cases, individuals may also engage in these operations to achieve personal gain or to spread their ideology. As the digital realm continues to expand and evolve, information warfare and influence operations have become a major concern for national security.

Governments and organizations must be vigilant against these tactics and take measures to protect themselves and their citizens. This includes developing strategies to combat disinformation and propaganda, educating the public about the dangers of fake news, and strengthening cyber security measures to prevent cyber attacks. In conclusion, information warfare and influence operations are complex and ever-evolving tactics that have the potential to greatly impact political, military, and economic landscapes.

Information warfare is a multifaceted and constantly evolving tactic that can have significant impacts on political, military, and economic landscapes. One of the key objectives of information warfare is to gain a competitive advantage through the use of information. This can take many forms, such as disrupting communication channels, shaping public opinion, or sowing discord within a target group. One of the most concerning aspects of information warfare is the use of disinformation and propaganda. These tactics involve intentionally spreading false or misleading information to deceive, manipulate, or influence the perceptions of a target audience. This can be done through various mediums, including traditional media outlets, social media platforms, and even through direct communication with individuals.

Social media manipulation is another commonly used tactic in information warfare. With the widespread use of social media, influence operations often leverage these platforms to disseminate narratives, amplify certain viewpoints, and exploit algorithms to reach specific audiences. This can be achieved through the use of bots, trolls, and fake accounts, which can artificially amplify the impact of information and make it appear more credible. Additionally, information warfare may also involve cyber espionage, where state-sponsored actors seek to gather intelligence by infiltrating computer systems, networks, and databases.

Stolen information can then be used to gain a strategic advantage or influence decision-makers. This highlights the importance of strengthening cyber security measures to prevent cyber attacks and protect sensitive information from falling into the wrong hands. It is crucial to develop comprehensive strategies to combat disinformation and propaganda, educate the public about the dangers of fake news, and stay vigilant against evolving tactics of information warfare.

One of the biggest challenges in the fight against cyber attacks is attribution. It can be extremely difficult to identify the source of these attacks, as adversaries often use sophisticated techniques to conceal their identities. They may use proxies or false flags, making it nearly impossible to trace the attack back to its source. This lack of attribution can make it challenging for authorities to take action against those responsible, leaving sensitive information vulnerable to further attacks. Expansion In addition to cyber attacks, disinformation and propaganda have become increasingly prevalent in the digital age. These tactics, known as psychological operations, are used to manipulate and influence individuals or groups by targeting their beliefs, emotions, and behaviours.

Adversaries may use various forms of media and propaganda to spread false information and advance their own agenda. It is essential for governments and organizations to stay vigilant against these tactics and develop effective counter-disinformation strategies. Expansion To combat disinformation, it is crucial to educate the public about the dangers of fake news and promote media literacy. This includes encouraging fact-checking initiatives and teaching individuals how to recognize and resist manipulation. By equipping people with the knowledge and skills to identify and combat disinformation, we can reduce its impact and prevent it from spreading. It is also important for governments and organizations to work together to create comprehensive strategies to combat disinformation and protect sensitive information from falling into the wrong hands.

A key aspect of combating disinformation is through the establishment of international norms and agreements. These international efforts aim to create guidelines for state conduct in information warfare, such as the Tallinn Manual and discussions within the United Nations. These efforts are crucial in promoting responsible state behaviour and reducing the impact of disinformation. Furthermore, public-private collaboration is essential in countering information warfare. By working together, governments, private sector entities, and social media platforms can share intelligence, coordinate responses, and implement industry best practices. This collaboration can enhance resilience and prevent sensitive information from falling into the wrong hands. In order to effectively combat disinformation, it is vital for governments and organizations to work together in creating comprehensive strategies. These strategies should include measures to identify and combat disinformation, as well as protecting sensitive information. By having a united front, we can reduce the spread and impact of disinformation and promote responsible behaviour in the cyber world. This collaboration and cooperation are crucial in safeguarding our societies and protecting our information.

Security on Cyber Activities

Zero Trust Architecture (ZTA) framework

ZTA, for example, operates on the principle of "never trust, always verify," assuming that no user or device is inherently trustworthy, regardless of its location. This approach emphasizes continuous authentication and authorization, ensuring that access is granted only to those who have been properly verified and have the necessary permissions.

Integrating security into every phase of the software development lifecycle plays a critical role in strengthening the overall security posture. By embedding security considerations from the design phase onwards, organizations can significantly reduce the risk of vulnerabilities making their way into production systems. This proactive approach complements the shift away from solely relying on perimeter-based defence.

The transition from perimeter-based security to a more holistic approach is not a simple switch. It requires significant investment in new technologies, training, and processes. However, given the increasing sophistication and pervasiveness of modern cyber threats, it is a necessary investment. The failure to adapt will leave organizations vulnerable to the significant consequences of successful attacks, including financial losses, reputational damage, regulatory fines, and operational disruptions. The cost of inaction far outweighs the cost of transformation.

Data protection forms a cornerstone of ZTA. Data encryption, both at rest and in transit, is essential to protect sensitive information. Data loss prevention (DLP) tools monitor data movements to prevent unauthorized access or exfiltration. Furthermore, ZTA encourages the adoption of a least-privilege access model, limiting access to sensitive data to only those who absolutely require it. This reduces the potential impact of a data breach by limiting the amount of information that could be exposed. Regular data backups and disaster recovery planning are also integral components, ensuring business continuity in the event of a major incident.

The implementation of ZTA requires a significant investment in both technology and expertise. It demands a shift in organizational culture, requiring a greater emphasis on security awareness and best practices. It's essential for organizations to assess their current security posture, identify vulnerabilities, and establish a clear roadmap for migration towards a ZTA framework. This roadmap should incorporate various stages, starting with a pilot project focusing on a specific area of the network before gradually expanding across the entire infrastructure. A well-defined plan should also incorporate ongoing monitoring and continuous improvement measures to ensure the continued effectiveness of ZTA.

The benefits of ZTA, however, far outweigh the challenges. By shifting from a model based on implicit trust to one that demands constant verification, organizations can significantly reduce their risk profile. The granular control offered by micro-segmentation and robust IAM solutions minimizes the impact of successful attacks. Strong data protection measures reduce the risk of data breaches, and continuous monitoring improves the organization's ability to detect and respond to threats more rapidly. In essence, ZTA moves security from a reactive posture to a proactive one. This proactive approach offers superior resilience in the face of an increasingly sophisticated threat landscape.

Consider the example of a healthcare provider. Patient data is highly sensitive and subject to stringent regulatory requirements such as HIPAA. A traditional perimeter-based security model would assume that once a doctor logs onto the network, they have legitimate access to all patient data. However, a ZTA implementation would verify the doctor's identity at each access point. It would also restrict access based on the specific patient record the doctor needs to view, preventing unauthorized access even within the internal network. In case of a compromised account or a malicious insider, the damage would be limited to only those specific records, significantly reducing the impact on patient privacy and data integrity.

The retail sector presents another compelling case study. Retailers handle vast amounts of customer data, including credit card information and personal details. A breach can lead to significant financial losses and reputational damage. Implementing ZTA helps mitigate these risks by controlling access to sensitive customer data. ZTA can enforce strict authentication measures for employees accessing customer databases, reducing the chances of unauthorized access. Micro-segmentation further protects the data by limiting access to only authorized personnel and systems.

The financial services industry, with its stringent regulatory compliance requirements, heavily benefits from ZTA's granular control over access and data. Sensitive financial transactions require strong security measures. ZTA delivers this through multi-factor authentication, rigorous access control lists, and data encryption techniques that provide robust protection against unauthorized access, fraud, and data breaches.

Adopting ZTA requires a holistic approach, integrating technology, processes, and people. It necessitates a strong security culture within the organization, with employees trained and educated about the importance of security best practices and the implications of potential threats. It's not simply a matter of implementing new technologies; it's about establishing a new security paradigm that permeates every aspect of the organization. This includes employee training on security awareness, the establishment of clear security policies and procedures, and the deployment of robust incident response plans.

Similarly, Extended Detection and Response (XDR) offer a more comprehensive approach to threat detection and response. Instead of relying solely on perimeter-based defenses, XDR integrates data from various sources, including endpoints, networks, and cloud environments, to provide a holistic view of security posture. This allows security teams to detect threats more quickly and effectively, regardless of where they originate or how they enter the network.

Central to ZTA is the concept of continuous verification. This entails the ongoing validation of user and device identities and their access rights. This differs significantly from traditional security models that primarily focus on initial authentication. Continuous verification uses multiple factors to ensure ongoing authorization, monitoring user behavior, device posture, and location. This continuous monitoring involves techniques like multi-factor authentication (MFA), device posture assessment, anomaly detection, and behavioral analytics. For example, if a user attempts to access sensitive data from an unfamiliar location or device, the system can flag this activity and trigger additional verification steps. Similarly, unusual access patterns or data exfiltration attempts can be detected and prevented. This continuous verification ensures that even if a credential is compromised, the access is limited due to additional layers of security.

Data protection at rest and in transit is another integral pillar of ZTA. This involves implementing robust encryption techniques to protect data both when it is stored (at rest) and when it is being transmitted (in transit). Encryption ensures that even if data is intercepted, it remains unreadable to unauthorized parties. Data encryption at rest protects sensitive data stored on servers, databases, and other storage devices. Data encryption in transit protects data as it travels across the network, using protocols like TLS/SSL for secure communication. Organizations should implement end-to-end encryption wherever possible to ensure the confidentiality and integrity of sensitive data throughout its lifecycle.

The implementation of ZTA also necessitates a robust security information and event management (SIEM) system. A SIEM aggregates security logs from various sources across the network, enabling comprehensive monitoring and threat detection. This centralized view provides critical insights into network activity, identifying potential security incidents and providing evidence for forensic investigations. Furthermore, a SIEM can automate responses to security threats, initiating actions such as blocking malicious traffic or quarantining infected devices. In a ZTA environment, the SIEM is crucial for maintaining a comprehensive security posture and reacting to potential threats promptly. This centralized monitoring and response system enhances security agility and allows faster reaction times in case of incidents.

Transitioning to a ZTA involves a significant cultural and technological shift. Organizations must move from a mindset of implicit trust to one of continuous verification. This requires significant changes to network infrastructure, security policies, and employee training. The implementation is a phased approach, focusing on iterative improvements and prioritization of critical assets. The process involves a thorough assessment of existing infrastructure, identifying vulnerabilities and gaps in security, and establishing a detailed roadmap for implementation.

Many organizations start by focusing on high-value assets and sensitive data, implementing ZTA principles incrementally. This phased approach minimizes disruption and allows organizations to learn from each implementation step. The transition may involve integrating new tools and technologies, retraining staff, and refining existing security policies. Throughout the process, ongoing monitoring and analysis are crucial to ensure the effectiveness of the ZTA and identify areas for improvement.

The benefits of ZTA are undeniable in today's threat landscape. By eliminating implicit trust and continuously verifying every access request, ZTA significantly reduces the attack surface and limits the impact of security breaches. This proactive approach enhances security resilience and ensures that sensitive data remains protected. While the transition to ZTA requires considerable investment and effort, the enhanced security posture and reduced risk of data breaches ultimately outweigh the challenges. In an increasingly interconnected and complex world, the principles of Zero Trust are no longer a luxury but a necessity. The journey may be complex, but the destination—a more secure and resilient organization—is well worth the effort. Continuous adaptation and refinement are essential elements of a successful ZTA deployment, ensuring its ongoing relevance in the face of evolving threats and technological advancements. The implementation needs to be aligned with the business goals and security objectives of the organization, ensuring that the investment is strategically aligned with overall business priorities. Regular security assessments and penetration testing are also critical in evaluating the effectiveness of ZTA implementation and identifying potential weaknesses. This iterative approach ensures ongoing improvement and adaptation to the ever-changing cyber security scene.

Implementing Zero Trust in a hybrid cloud environment presents unique challenges and opportunities. The inherent complexity of managing resources across multiple platforms — on-premise data centres, private clouds, and public clouds—demands a nuanced approach to ZTA implementation. Unlike a purely on-premise or cloud-native environment, a hybrid cloud requires a unified security strategy that seamlessly integrates diverse security controls and technologies. This necessitates a robust identity and access management (IAM) system capable of authenticating and authorizing users and devices across all environments, irrespective of their location. Furthermore, the dynamic nature of cloud environments necessitates continuous monitoring and adaptation of security policies to accommodate changes in infrastructure and resource utilization.

One of the primary challenges in a hybrid cloud setting is maintaining a consistent security posture across disparate environments. On-premise infrastructure often relies on traditional security controls like firewalls and VPNs, while cloud-based resources utilize cloud-native security services such as virtual networks and security groups. Harmonizing these disparate security mechanisms is crucial for establishing a unified ZTA framework. This requires careful planning and integration of different security tools and technologies, ensuring consistent policy enforcement across all environments. For instance, consistent logging and monitoring across both on-premise and cloud platforms are critical, often demanding the integration of various SIEM systems and cloud security posture management (CSPM) tools. This unified visibility into security events is paramount for effective threat detection and response.

Another key challenge is the management of identities and access. In a hybrid cloud, users and devices might access resources from various locations and platforms. Therefore, a centralized IAM solution is necessary to manage user identities and enforce least privilege access across all environments. This solution should support various authentication methods, including multi-factor authentication (MFA), and should be integrated with both on-premise and cloud-based identity providers. The implementation must accommodate different authentication protocols and support seamless single sign-on (SSO) across different environments. This minimizes user friction while maintaining robust security. Federated identity solutions often play a vital role in enabling trust between different identity providers in a hybrid cloud setting.

Micro-segmentation plays a vital role in securing resources within a hybrid cloud environment under a ZTA framework. The isolation of sensitive data and applications within smaller, isolated segments limits the impact of a breach. This requires the implementation of micro-segmentation techniques across both on-premise and cloud infrastructure. In on-premise environments, this might involve VLANs and firewalls. In cloud environments, it leverages virtual networks, security groups, and network access control lists (ACLs). Tools that offer consistent micro-segmentation across hybrid environments, often using software-defined networking (SDN) technologies, are becoming increasingly vital. These tools allow administrators to define and manage micro-segmentation policies consistently, regardless of the underlying infrastructure. Careful consideration must be given to how network traffic flows between these segments, both within and across environments.

Data protection, both at rest and in transit, remains vital in a hybrid cloud environment. This requires robust encryption mechanisms for data stored on servers, databases, and other storage devices, whether on-premise or in the cloud. Similarly, data transmitted across the network must be protected using secure protocols like TLS/SSL or even more advanced encryption techniques. Key management in such a distributed environment is particularly critical, ensuring that encryption keys are properly managed and protected from unauthorized access. Consistent encryption policies must be applied across all platforms, and solutions for key rotation and lifecycle management must be in place to maintain a high level of security. The complexity grows further when considering encryption techniques for data stored in different cloud platforms, each with its specific data encryption services.

The role of a security information and event management (SIEM) system is magnified in a hybrid cloud setting. A centralized SIEM consolidates security logs from various sources, including on-premise servers, cloud platforms, and security tools. This provides a unified view of security events across the entire environment, enabling faster threat detection and response. Selecting a SIEM solution capable of ingesting and analyzing logs from diverse sources, including cloud-native logs, is crucial. This system should support real-time threat detection and automated responses, helping security teams to effectively manage and respond to security incidents quickly. The ability to integrate with cloud-based security tools, like CloudTrail and CloudWatch, is essential for obtaining a comprehensive view of cloud-based activity.

Continuous verification is a cornerstone of ZTA in any environment, but it's especially critical in hybrid cloud settings due to the increased complexity. This involves the ongoing validation of user and device identities and their access rights across all environments. This can involve combining various techniques such as MFA, device posture assessment, and behavioural analytics. However, integrating these technologies across disparate platforms can be complex. Solutions that provide a unified view of user and device posture across all environments, allowing for consistent policy enforcement, are critical for achieving effective continuous verification. The challenge lies in maintaining consistent monitoring capabilities while adapting to the dynamic nature of cloud environments.

The implementation of ZTA in a hybrid cloud environment necessitates a phased approach. Beginning with a thorough risk assessment identifying critical assets and high-value data is crucial. This is followed by prioritizing the implementation of ZTA principles on those assets. A phased approach minimizes disruption to ongoing operations while allowing the security team to gain experience and refine the implementation strategy. This iterative approach involves continuous monitoring and evaluation, allowing for adjustments and improvements based on real-world experience. This ensures ongoing optimization of the ZTA deployment, adapting to the changing threat landscape and evolving technological capabilities.

Tools and technologies play a critical role in enabling successful ZTA implementation in hybrid cloud environments. These include cloud access security brokers (CASBs), secure access service edges (SASEs), and cloud workload protection platforms (CWPPs). CASBs provide visibility and control over cloud application usage, helping to enforce least privilege access. SASEs offer secure access to cloud and on-premise resources, ensuring secure connectivity regardless of location. CWPPs protect workloads running in the cloud, offering security capabilities like vulnerability scanning and threat detection. Careful selection and integration of these technologies are vital for creating a unified and robust security posture. The choice should depend on the specific needs and infrastructure of the organization, considering factors like scalability, integration capabilities, and cost-effectiveness. Understanding the strengths and weaknesses of each tool and its compatibility with the existing infrastructure are vital considerations during the selection process.

Finally, successful ZTA implementation in a hybrid cloud setting demands a strong cultural shift within the organization. Security awareness training for employees is critical to foster a security-conscious culture. This training should emphasize the importance of ZTA principles, best practices, and the organization's security policies. Furthermore, establishing clear roles and responsibilities for security management across different teams is essential for effective collaboration and coordination. Regular security audits and penetration testing are vital to ensure the continued effectiveness of the implemented ZTA framework. This iterative approach enables the organization to identify weaknesses and adapt its security posture to mitigate emerging threats. The continuous refinement of ZTA implementation is essential for maintaining a robust and adaptable security framework in the face of ever-evolving threats.

Identity and Access Management (IAM) forms the base of any effective Zero Trust Architecture (ZTA). Without a robust and rigorously enforced IAM system, the core principle of "never trust, always verify" becomes significantly weakened. In a ZTA environment, every access request, regardless of its origin or destination, must be meticulously validated. This necessitates a sophisticated IAM system capable of handling a high volume of authentication and authorization requests while maintaining exceptional performance and scalability. The system must be able to identify and authenticate users and devices, determine their authorized access levels based on pre-defined policies, and continuously monitor their activities for any anomalies that might indicate compromised credentials or malicious behaviour.

The foundational element of any robust IAM system within a ZTA framework is strong authentication. This goes far beyond simple username and password combinations. Multi-factor authentication (MFA) is a non-negotiable requirement. MFA adds multiple layers of security, requiring users to provide more than one form of authentication before accessing resources. Common MFA methods include one-time passwords (OTPs) generated via authenticator apps, biometric authentication (fingerprint, facial recognition), hardware security keys (like Yubikeys), and push notifications. The selection of MFA methods should be tailored to the specific sensitivity of the data and the risk profile of the user. For highly sensitive systems, a combination of methods, such as a hardware security key and a biometric scan, might be necessary.

Beyond MFA, the IAM system must incorporate robust password management practices. This includes enforcing strong password policies that mandate complex passwords with a minimum length, a mixture of uppercase and lowercase letters, numbers, and symbols, and regular password changes. Password managers can assist in managing complex passwords securely. Furthermore, organizations should explore passwordless authentication options, which eliminate the reliance on passwords entirely and leverage methods like FIDO2 security keys for stronger, phishing-resistant authentication. These methods are intrinsically more secure as they eliminate the vulnerability of passwords being stolen through phishing or credential stuffing attacks.

Authorization, the second key component of IAM within a ZTA, determines what actions a verified user or device is permitted to perform. The principle of least privilege must be strictly adhered to, granting users only the necessary access rights to perform their jobs and nothing more. This minimizes the potential damage caused by a compromised account. Role-based access control (RBAC) and attribute-based access control (ABAC) are widely used to manage access permissions efficiently. RBAC assigns roles to users, each role associated with a specific set of permissions. ABAC provides more granular control by evaluating attributes of the user, the resource, and the context of the request to determine authorization.

The complexity of managing user access across multiple systems and applications can be alleviated through the use of a centralized identity provider (IdP). A centralized IdP enables single sign-on (SSO), allowing users to access multiple applications with a single set of credentials. This simplifies the user experience and reduces the risk of users reusing passwords across various applications. Federation services can extend this functionality across organizational boundaries, enabling seamless SSO across multiple organizations. This is particularly beneficial in scenarios involving mergers and acquisitions or collaborations where employees from different entities need access to shared resources. Careful consideration must be given to the selection of an appropriate IdP to ensure compatibility with existing systems and the ability to scale to meet future needs.

Continuous monitoring and auditing are critical aspects of IAM within a ZTA. The system must log all authentication and authorization attempts, including successful and failed logins, along with the associated timestamps, user details, and resource access information. This audit trail provides invaluable data for security analysis, enabling the identification of potential security breaches or suspicious activities. Regular audits of user access rights are equally crucial to ensure that permissions remain appropriate and that no unnecessary privileges are granted. The frequency of audits should depend on the criticality of the resources being accessed.

Identity governance and administration (IGA) play a vital role in maintaining the integrity and security of the IAM system. IGA encompasses processes for managing user lifecycle events, such as provisioning, de-provisioning, and modification of access rights. Automated provisioning and de-provisioning systems can streamline these processes, reducing manual errors and improving efficiency. This is especially critical in large organizations with a high turnover of employees. IGA also encompasses processes for identifying and resolving security vulnerabilities related to identity and access management, such as orphaned accounts or accounts with excessive privileges. Regular reviews of user access rights and the enforcement of strict access control policies are vital components of IGA.

Integration with other security tools and technologies is essential for a comprehensive ZTA strategy. The IAM system should be integrated with other security tools such as SIEM systems, XDR platforms, and CASBs to provide a holistic view of the security posture. This integration enables the correlation of security events from various sources, which enables the detection of sophisticated attacks and the timely response to security incidents. The IAM system should also be tightly integrated with other security measures to leverage data for contextual awareness, for instance, device posture assessment which can prevent access if a device does not meet security requirements.

IAM within ZTA is not a one-time project; rather, it is an ongoing process that requires continuous monitoring, adaptation, and refinement. The system must be regularly updated to address emerging threats and vulnerabilities, and security policies should be reviewed and adjusted as needed. Regular security audits and penetration testing of the IAM system are vital to ensure that it remains robust and secure. Maintaining a culture of security awareness and providing regular training to employees is paramount to ensuring the success of the IAM system. By focusing on the core principles of strong authentication, authorization, least privilege, continuous monitoring, and governance, organizations can build a robust and effective IAM system that truly supports the ZTA principles of never trust, always verify. This foundation of trust is crucial for mitigating emerging cyber threats and maintaining the integrity of organizational data and resources.

Data security and protection are vital in any organization, and the Zero Trust Architecture (ZTA) significantly enhances these capabilities. Unlike traditional perimeter-based security models that assume trust within the network, ZTA operates on the principle of "never trust, always verify." This fundamental shift in approach necessitates a robust and multifaceted strategy for protecting data, both in transit and at rest. This involves a layered approach incorporating encryption, granular access controls, and proactive data loss prevention (DLP) measures.

Encryption, a cornerstone of data security, takes centre stage within a ZTA environment. Data encryption transforms readable data into an unreadable format, rendering it useless to unauthorized individuals even if intercepted. This is crucial for protecting sensitive data both while it's being transmitted (data in transit) and while it's stored (data at rest). For data in transit, Secure Sockets Layer/ Transport Layer Security (SSL/TLS) protocols are essential. These protocols establish secure encrypted connections between communicating parties, ensuring that data exchanged between users, applications, and servers remains confidential. The implementation of HTTPS for all web traffic is a fundamental requirement within a ZTA framework. Beyond HTTPS, end-to-end encryption technologies can further bolster security, particularly for sensitive communications like email or messaging applications. End-to-end encryption ensures that only the intended recipient can decrypt and read the message, preventing unauthorized access even by the service provider.

Data at rest requires equally robust protection. This involves encrypting data stored on servers, databases, and storage devices. Various encryption methods are available, including disk encryption, database encryption, and file-level encryption. Disk encryption protects all data stored on a hard drive, while database encryption focuses on securing data within a database system. File-level encryption allows for granular control, enabling selective encryption of specific files or folders. The choice of encryption method depends on the specific requirements and sensitivity of the data. It's crucial to select strong encryption algorithms and to securely manage the encryption keys. Key management is a critical aspect of data security, as compromised keys can negate the effectiveness of encryption. Implementing a robust key management system, often involving hardware security modules (HSMs), is vital for safeguarding encryption keys and ensuring their availability.

Access controls are another vital component of data security within a ZTA. The principle of least privilege dictates that users should only be granted access to the data and resources absolutely necessary for their job functions. This minimizes the potential impact of a security breach, limiting the damage that a compromised account can inflict. Role-based access control (RBAC) and attribute-based access control (ABAC) provide effective mechanisms for enforcing granular access control policies. RBAC assigns users to predefined roles, each with a specific set of permissions. ABAC goes a step further by allowing for context-aware access control based on various attributes, such as user location, device posture, and time of day. This allows for highly granular and dynamic control over data access.

The transition from perimeter-based security models to a Zero Trust Architecture (ZTA) represents a fundamental shift in how organizations approach cyber security. Traditional security models, relying on a castle-and-moat approach, assumed implicit trust within the network perimeter. Once inside the network, users and devices were granted relatively unrestricted access to resources. This approach, however, is increasingly vulnerable in today's distributed and cloud-based environments. ZTA, in contrast, operates on the principle of "never trust, always verify." It eliminates the concept of an implicit trust boundary, instead verifying every access request regardless of its origin—internal or external.

This fundamental principle underpins the core tenets of ZTA, forming its architectural pillars. These pillars are not mutually exclusive; they work in concert to establish a robust and adaptive security posture. Let's examine these key elements in detail.

The first cornerstone is the principle of least privilege access. This dictates that users and devices should only be granted the minimum necessary access rights to perform their assigned tasks. This granular approach significantly limits the potential damage from a compromised account or device. Instead of broad network access, users are granted access only to specific applications, data, and resources required for their roles. This minimizes the attack surface and limits lateral movement within the network should a breach occur. For instance, a marketing employee might have access to marketing databases and applications but not to financial systems or sensitive customer data. This principle necessitates robust identity and access management (IAM) systems capable of managing fine-grained access controls and enforcing strict least privilege policies. Implementing effective Role-Based Access Control (RBAC) and Attribute-Based Access Control (ABAC) is crucial in achieving this level of granularity.

Building upon least privilege access is the concept of micro-segmentation. This involves dividing the network into smaller, isolated segments, each with its own security policies. This approach limits the impact of a security breach by confining it to a specific segment, preventing lateral movement to other parts of the network. Micro-segmentation can be implemented using various technologies, including virtual LANs (VLANs), software-defined networking (SDN), and network virtualization. Each segment can then have its own access control lists (ACLs), firewalls, and other security measures tailored to the specific needs and sensitivity of the data and applications within that segment.

Data Loss Prevention (DLP) is crucial to prevent sensitive data from leaving the organizational perimeter unintentionally or maliciously. DLP tools monitor data movement across various channels, including email, cloud storage, and external devices. These tools can identify sensitive data based on predefined rules and patterns, blocking or alerting on attempts to transfer or access that data without proper authorization. DLP solutions can be deployed at different points in the data flow, from the endpoint to the network gateway, providing comprehensive protection. For example, DLP tools integrated with email clients can prevent the transmission of sensitive data via email. Similarly, DLP tools can monitor cloud storage activity, preventing unauthorized uploads or downloads of sensitive data to cloud storage services.

Furthermore, organizations adopting ZTA should invest in robust security information and event management (SIEM) systems. SIEM systems collect and analyze security logs from various sources, providing a centralized view of security events. This enables detection of anomalous activity, including potential data breaches, and faster response times. Within a ZTA context, SIEM systems are even more critical, as the decentralized nature of the architecture requires effective centralized monitoring and correlation of security logs from diverse components. Data breaches are more easily detected and addressed by leveraging SIEM's capabilities for threat hunting, intrusion detection, and incident response.

The implementation of Data Discovery and Classification (DDC) significantly enhances data security in a ZTA environment. DDC involves identifying and categorizing sensitive data based on its nature and sensitivity. This is crucial for effective access control and DLP. By understanding the location and classification of sensitive data, organizations can implement appropriate security controls to protect it. This might involve more stringent access restrictions, advanced encryption, or regular audits to maintain compliance and prevent data breaches. DDC tools help automate this process, analyzing data repositories to identify and classify sensitive data automatically.

The secure handling of sensitive data requires a comprehensive approach, which often involves implementing strict data governance policies. Data governance frameworks dictate how data is handled, stored, and used throughout its lifecycle, emphasizing the importance of confidentiality, integrity, and availability. These policies define data classification schemes, access control rules, and data retention policies. Adherence to these policies is crucial for reducing the risk of data breaches and ensuring compliance with relevant regulations, like GDPR or HIPAA. Regular training for employees on data governance policies, security best practices, and the implications of data breaches is vital to maintaining a strong security culture.

Security Information and Event Management (SIEM) systems play a pivotal role in this ongoing vigilance. SIEMs act as central nervous systems, aggregating security logs from diverse sources across the entire organizational infrastructure. This includes endpoints, networks, cloud services, applications, and security devices. This consolidated view provides a comprehensive, real-time picture of the security landscape, allowing security analysts to identify patterns, detect anomalies, and respond to threats promptly. By correlating data from multiple sources, SIEMs can uncover subtle indicators of compromise (IOCs) that might otherwise go unnoticed. For instance, a SIEM might detect a series of seemingly innocuous events—a user accessing a sensitive file outside of normal working hours, followed by unusual network activity originating from that user's machine—and correlate them to indicate a potential insider threat or targeted attack.

The value of a SIEM extends beyond mere log aggregation. Advanced SIEMs employ sophisticated analytics, including machine learning and artificial intelligence (AI), to enhance threat detection capabilities. AI-powered algorithms can identify anomalies and deviations from established baselines, flagging potential threats for immediate investigation. These systems can analyze massive volumes of data far exceeding human capacity, identifying subtle patterns indicative of malicious activity. This proactive approach allows security teams to address threats before they can escalate into full-blown breaches. For example, an AI-driven SIEM might detect a surge in failed login attempts from a particular IP address, indicative of a brute-force attack, and automatically trigger an alert, potentially blocking the offending IP address before it can compromise user accounts.

Beyond SIEMs, organizations deploying ZTA should leverage a range of specialized monitoring tools. Endpoint Detection and Response (EDR) solutions provide deep visibility into endpoint activity, detecting and responding to threats on individual devices. Network traffic analysis tools monitor network communications, identifying malicious traffic patterns and data exfiltration attempts. Cloud security posture management (CSPM) tools continuously assess the security of cloud environments, identifying misconfigurations and vulnerabilities. Integrating these diverse tools with the SIEM provides a unified, holistic view of the security environment, enhancing the overall effectiveness of the ZTA framework.

Maintaining comprehensive audit trails is another critical component of effective ZTA monitoring. Audit trails provide a detailed record of all system activities, including user logins, file access, data modifications, and security configuration changes. This historical data is crucial for investigating security incidents, determining the root cause of breaches, and ensuring compliance with regulatory requirements. A well-maintained audit trail allows organizations to reconstruct the sequence of events leading up to a security incident, identifying the perpetrators, the affected systems, and the extent of the damage. This information is essential for effective incident response and mitigation, minimizing the impact of future attacks. The audit trail should be tamper-proof, and regular verification should take place to confirm its integrity.

Regular audits of security controls are equally important. These audits assess the effectiveness of the security measures in place, ensuring that they continue to meet the evolving threat landscape. This includes reviewing access controls, verifying the integrity of encryption, assessing the effectiveness of DLP mechanisms, and evaluating the security posture of cloud services. Penetration testing and vulnerability scanning are crucial aspects of these audits, simulating real-world attacks to identify vulnerabilities that could be exploited by malicious actors. Regular vulnerability scans should be conducted to identify and remediate known vulnerabilities in software and hardware components. Penetration testing goes beyond vulnerability scanning, simulating real-world attack scenarios to evaluate the effectiveness of security controls and identify potential weaknesses in the overall security architecture.

Compliance with relevant regulations and industry standards is another critical aspect of ZTA monitoring and auditing. Depending on the industry and geographic location, organizations may be subject to various regulations such as GDPR, HIPAA, PCI DSS, or others, all requiring specific security controls and audit practices. Regular compliance audits ensure that the organization's security practices align with these regulations, avoiding potential penalties and maintaining the trust of customers and stakeholders. Compliance audits often involve examining documentation, performing security assessments, and verifying the effectiveness of security controls. The documentation of these audits should be comprehensive and readily available for regulators or auditors.

The human element plays a central role in the effectiveness of ZTA monitoring and auditing. Security awareness training is vital to educating employees about security threats and best practices, minimizing the risk of human error. Regular training should cover topics such as phishing awareness, password security, social engineering tactics, and the importance of reporting suspicious activity. Employees should understand their role in maintaining a secure ZTA environment and how to report potential security incidents promptly and effectively. This proactive approach minimizes the risk of accidental breaches or unintentional disclosure of sensitive information.

Finally, the process of monitoring and auditing should not be static; it should be a continuous improvement cycle. Regular reviews of security logs, audit reports, and compliance assessments should identify areas for improvement and inform the evolution of security policies and practices. This iterative approach ensures that the ZTA framework constantly adapts to the changing threat landscape and remains effective in protecting organizational assets. The insights gained from monitoring and auditing should be used to refine security controls, enhance threat detection capabilities, and strengthen the overall security posture. This continuous feedback loop is essential for maintaining a truly secure and resilient ZTA environment. In conclusion, a robust monitoring and auditing strategy is not just a safeguard; it is the very foundation of a successful Zero Trust implementation, ensuring its enduring effectiveness in the face of ever-evolving cyber threats.

Extended Detection and Response

XDR (Extended Detection and Response) represents a significant evolution in security monitoring and incident response, building upon the principles of ZTA to provide a more holistic and proactive approach.

Traditional security information and event management (SIEM) systems have long been a cornerstone of security operations centres (SOCs). SIEMs collect and analyze security logs from various sources, aggregating data to provide a consolidated view of security events. However, SIEMs often struggle to correlate data effectively across different security domains. The sheer volume of data, the disparate formats of logs from different vendors, and the inherent complexity of modern IT infrastructures present challenges to SIEM's ability to provide timely and accurate threat detection. SIEM alerts often suffer from high false positive rates, overwhelming security analysts and making it difficult to prioritize and address real threats. Furthermore, SIEM's response capabilities are limited, often requiring manual intervention and investigation to contain and remediate incidents.

XDR addresses these limitations by taking a more integrated and proactive approach. Unlike SIEM, which primarily focuses on log aggregation and analysis, XDR leverages telemetry data from various sources to provide a unified view of the security landscape. This telemetry includes endpoint data (from devices like laptops, desktops, and servers), network data (from routers, firewalls, and switches), and cloud data (from cloud infrastructure and applications). By correlating this data across different security domains, XDR can identify patterns and anomalies indicative of malicious activity that would otherwise remain undetected by isolated security tools.

This integration of data sources offers several key advantages. For example, if an XDR solution detects malicious behaviour on an endpoint, it can correlate this event with network traffic and cloud activity to gain a comprehensive understanding of the attack. This comprehensive view allows security analysts to identify the full extent of the compromise, understand the attacker's methods, and take appropriate actions to contain and remediate the incident more effectively. The correlated data provides a richer context for incident investigation, enabling faster and more accurate threat detection.

The correlation capabilities of XDR are significantly more advanced than those of traditional SIEM systems. XDR employs advanced analytics and machine learning algorithms to identify subtle patterns and anomalies that would be missed by human analysts or simpler rule-based detection systems. These algorithms learn from vast datasets of known malicious activity, identifying subtle variations in behavior that might indicate a sophisticated attack. This proactive, AI-driven approach allows XDR to detect and respond to threats in real-time, reducing the dwell time of malicious actors within the organization's environment.

Furthermore, XDR's capabilities extend beyond detection. XDR platforms offer automated response capabilities, enabling security teams to automatically contain and remediate threats. This automation reduces the workload on security analysts, allowing them to focus on more complex incidents and strategic tasks. Automatic responses can include isolating infected endpoints, blocking malicious network connections, and removing malware from systems. These automated responses can significantly reduce the impact of successful attacks, minimizing damage and preventing further compromise.

The benefits of XDR extend beyond improved threat detection and response. XDR enhances incident investigation by providing a comprehensive timeline of events, making it easier to understand the attack's progression and identify the root cause. This enhanced investigation contributes to improved threat hunting and proactive security measures. By analyzing past incidents, security teams can identify vulnerabilities and improve their security posture to prevent similar attacks in the future.

Moreover, XDR offers improved security posture management by providing valuable insights into the organization's security health. XDR dashboards and reporting tools provide real-time visibility into the security landscape, allowing security teams to identify trends and patterns in malicious activity. This visibility empowers organizations to proactively address vulnerabilities and improve their security posture over time.

The implementation of XDR requires careful planning and consideration. Organizations need to assess their existing security infrastructure, identify the data sources that will be integrated into the XDR solution, and ensure that the XDR platform is compatible with their existing systems. Proper integration with existing security tools is crucial to avoid data silos and maximize the effectiveness of the XDR solution. A robust integration strategy ensures that XDR can seamlessly communicate and share information with other security tools, enhancing the overall security posture.

Furthermore, the successful implementation of XDR depends on skilled personnel. Security analysts need training and expertise to effectively use the XDR platform and interpret the data it provides. Training should focus on the platform's features and functionalities, as well as the interpretation of security alerts and the investigation of security incidents. This training ensures that the security team can maximize the platform's benefits and respond to threats effectively.

The cost of implementing XDR should also be considered. The initial investment in the XDR platform, as well as the ongoing costs of maintenance and support, must be factored into the budget. However, the long-term benefits of XDR, including reduced dwell time, improved incident response, and enhanced security posture, often outweigh the initial costs. A cost-benefit analysis should be conducted to determine the financial viability of XDR for a specific organization.

Choosing the right XDR solution is crucial. Organizations should evaluate different vendors and solutions based on their specific needs and requirements. Factors to consider include the platform's capabilities, scalability, integration with existing systems, and the vendor's support and reputation. A thorough evaluation process ensures that the chosen solution meets the organization's requirements and provides the desired level of security.

It's important to note that XDR is not a replacement for other security tools. It should be considered a complementary technology that enhances existing security measures. XDR works in conjunction with other security solutions, such as firewalls, intrusion detection systems, and endpoint detection and response (EDR) tools, to provide a layered security approach. This layered approach ensures that even if one layer of defence is breached, other layers are in place to detect and respond to threats.

The banking and finance sector operates within a uniquely challenging security landscape. The sheer volume of sensitive financial data handled daily, coupled with stringent regulatory requirements like GDPR, CCPA, and others depending on geographic location, and necessitates a robust and proactive security posture. Traditional security solutions often struggle to keep pace with the sophistication and velocity of modern cyber threats. This is where Extended Detection and Response (XDR) shines, offering a comprehensive and integrated approach to threat detection and response that addresses the specific needs of this sector.

One of the most significant applications of XDR in banking and finance is in fraud detection and prevention. Financial institutions are prime targets for various fraudulent activities, including phishing attacks, account takeover attempts, and payment card fraud. XDR's ability to correlate data from diverse sources – endpoints, networks, cloud environments, and security information and event management (SIEM) systems – provides a holistic view of user activities and network traffic. This allows security analysts to identify anomalous patterns and suspicious behavior indicative of fraudulent activity far more effectively than traditional methods. For instance, XDR can detect unusual login attempts from unfamiliar locations or devices, unusual transaction volumes or amounts, or suspicious communications with known malicious actors. By correlating these events across multiple data sources, XDR can paint a clearer picture of the attack, allowing for faster and more accurate detection. This speed is crucial; the faster fraud is detected, the less financial damage is done and the fewer customers are impacted.

The integration of threat intelligence feeds enhances XDR's fraud detection capabilities. By incorporating real-time information about emerging threats and malicious actors, XDR can proactively identify and respond to potential attacks before they cause significant damage. This proactive approach is essential in the ever-evolving landscape of financial cybercrime, where threat actors constantly adapt their tactics. The dynamic nature of these threats makes traditional signature-based detection methods inadequate; XDR's behavioural analysis capabilities are far better equipped to identify previously unseen attacks. This allows security teams to focus their resources on truly critical alerts, reducing alert fatigue and improving response times. The integration with threat intelligence also helps in identifying potential vulnerabilities within the bank's systems, allowing for proactive patching and mitigation strategies.

XDR's automated response capabilities further bolster its effectiveness in fraud prevention. Upon detecting suspicious activity, XDR can automatically initiate pre-defined response actions, such as blocking malicious IP addresses, quarantining infected endpoints, or suspending compromised accounts. This automated response significantly reduces the time it takes to contain a threat, limiting the potential impact of a successful attack. The automated responses are configurable and tailored to specific policies and risk profiles, ensuring that the response is proportionate to the threat level. This automated response capability minimizes human intervention, reducing the risk of human error and ensuring consistent, timely responses to threats. This is particularly crucial in high-pressure situations where manual intervention might be slow or inefficient.

Beyond fraud detection, XDR plays a critical role in ensuring regulatory compliance within the banking and finance sector. The industry is subject to an extensive array of regulations requiring meticulous record-keeping, thorough security audits, and robust incident response plans. XDR facilitates compliance by providing comprehensive audit trails of all security-related events, including threat detection, incident response, and remediation efforts. This detailed audit trail is vital for demonstrating regulatory compliance to auditors and regulators. The ability to easily retrieve and analyze this data speeds up compliance audits, reducing administrative overhead and associated costs. Furthermore, XDR's centralized data management capabilities streamline the process of generating reports required for compliance, reducing the risk of human error and ensuring data accuracy.

The implementation of XDR in banking and finance also helps address insider threats. These threats, stemming from malicious or negligent insiders, can be particularly damaging given the sensitive nature of financial data. XDR's ability to monitor user activities across various systems, coupled with its behavioural analysis capabilities, helps identify anomalous actions indicative of malicious or negligent behaviour. For example, an employee downloading large quantities of customer data or accessing systems outside their authorized access privileges could trigger an alert. This early detection and investigation capabilities significantly reduces the potential impact of insider threats. Detailed logs and access records, easily available through XDR, assist internal investigations, and can help build a strong case for disciplinary action or legal prosecution if necessary.

Another significant challenge faced by the banking and finance sector is the increasing complexity of their IT infrastructure. Many institutions operate hybrid cloud environments, with data and systems spread across on-premises, cloud, and edge locations. Traditional security tools often struggle to provide a unified view of this heterogeneous landscape, making it difficult to effectively detect and respond to threats. XDR excels in this scenario by integrating data from various sources, providing a consolidated view of the entire IT environment. This unified view enhances visibility into potential vulnerabilities and threats, allowing security teams to respond effectively, regardless of where the threat originates. The ability to manage security across this heterogeneous environment simplifies security management and reduces the overall complexity.

However, the implementation of XDR in the banking and finance sector is not without its challenges. The sheer volume of data generated by these institutions requires significant processing power and storage capacity. The selection of an XDR platform that can handle this volume of data without sacrificing performance is crucial. This requires careful planning and selection of an appropriately sized and scalable XDR solution. The cost of implementation and ongoing maintenance is also a significant factor. The selection of an XDR platform that aligns with the institution's budget and long-term security strategy is crucial. Proper planning and cost analysis are vital for a successful deployment.

Furthermore, integrating XDR with existing security tools and systems can be complex, requiring significant technical expertise and careful planning. Incompatibility between systems could lead to data silos and hinder the effectiveness of the XDR solution. This necessitates skilled personnel capable of managing the integration, maintenance, and operation of the XDR system. It also requires ongoing professional development to stay abreast of emerging threats and technologies.

Despite these challenges, the benefits of XDR in the banking and finance sector far outweigh the costs. Its ability to improve threat detection, accelerate incident response, and enhance regulatory compliance makes it an invaluable asset in protecting sensitive financial data and ensuring the stability of financial systems. By adopting a proactive security approach with XDR as a central component, financial institutions can significantly enhance their security posture and better protect themselves against the ever-evolving threats in the digital landscape. The strategic investment in XDR offers a demonstrable return on investment through reduced losses from fraud, improved operational efficiency, and enhanced regulatory compliance. The long-term benefits of a robust and resilient security posture far outweigh the initial investment in the implementation and ongoing management of an XDR system. Continuous monitoring, adaptation, and refinement are key to ensuring the ongoing effectiveness of the XDR deployment in this dynamic sector.

The healthcare sector faces a unique set of cyber security challenges. The industry's reliance on interconnected systems, coupled with the sensitive nature of patient data, makes it a prime target for cyber attacks. Patient data, including protected health information (PHI) under HIPAA in the US, and equivalent regulations globally, carries immense value on the dark web, leading to lucrative targets for cybercriminals. Ransom ware attacks, in particular, pose a significant threat, potentially disrupting critical operations and jeopardizing patient safety. Traditional security solutions often struggle to effectively address the multifaceted nature of these threats, highlighting the need for a more comprehensive and integrated approach. This is where Extended Detection and Response (XDR) offer a compelling solution.

XDR's ability to correlate data from various sources—endpoints, networks, cloud environments, and security information and event management (SIEM) systems—provides a holistic view of the healthcare IT infrastructure. This integrated approach is crucial in detecting and responding to sophisticated attacks that might otherwise go unnoticed by standalone security tools. For instance, an attacker might initially compromise an endpoint device, then laterally move through the network to access sensitive data stored in the cloud. Traditional solutions might only detect individual events, but XDR's unified view allows for the detection of this full attack chain, significantly enhancing the speed and effectiveness of threat detection.

In the context of ransom ware attacks, XDR's value becomes particularly evident. Ransom ware attacks often involve multiple stages, beginning with initial infiltration, followed by data exfiltration and encryption. XDR can detect anomalous activities associated with each of these phases. For example, unusual network traffic patterns, suspicious file access attempts and large-scale data transfers could all signal a ransom ware attack in progress. The correlation of these events across diverse data sources allows security analysts to identify the attack early, before data encryption occurs, drastically reducing the impact of the attack. This early detection is crucial, allowing for timely intervention and potentially preventing the widespread encryption of critical patient data.

Furthermore, XDR's capabilities extend beyond detection to automated response. Upon identifying a potential ransom ware attack, XDR can automatically initiate pre-defined actions, such as isolating infected endpoints from the network, blocking malicious IP addresses, or quarantining suspicious files. This automated response capability significantly reduces the time it takes to contain the threat, minimizing its impact and protecting critical systems. The automated responses can be customized to align with specific organizational policies and risk profiles, ensuring a proportional response based on the threat level. This automation is especially important in the healthcare sector, where rapid containment of a security incident is critical to maintaining operational continuity and patient safety.

The healthcare sector is heavily regulated, emphasizing the importance of data privacy and security compliance. Regulations such as HIPAA, GDPR, and others mandate stringent controls over the handling and protection of patient data. XDR significantly aids in meeting these compliance requirements. By providing comprehensive audit trails of all security-related events, XDR facilitates regulatory compliance audits. The ability to easily retrieve and analyze data concerning threat detection, incident response, and remediation efforts helps organizations demonstrate compliance to auditors and regulators. This reduces the time and effort spent on compliance activities and minimizes the risk of non-compliance penalties. The centralized data management capabilities of XDR further simplify the process of generating compliance reports, enhancing accuracy and reducing human error.

However, implementing XDR in the healthcare sector presents several challenges. The sector's heterogeneous IT infrastructure, often comprising a mix of legacy systems and modern technologies, can complicate integration with XDR solutions. Careful planning and integration strategies are essential to overcome this challenge.

Ensuring compatibility between XDR and existing security tools and systems requires expertise, and a phased approach is often recommended to mitigate disruption. The sheer volume of data generated within healthcare organizations, including electronic health records (EHRs), medical images, and various other forms of patient data, necessitates a robust and scalable XDR platform capable of processing and analyzing this information without impacting performance. This requires careful planning and the selection of a platform with sufficient capacity and processing power to meet the demands of the organization.

Another significant challenge is the availability of skilled cyber security professionals. The healthcare sector often faces a shortage of qualified personnel capable of managing and maintaining complex XDR systems. Investing in training and development is crucial to address this challenge, ensuring that staff possesses the necessary expertise to effectively manage the XDR solution. Ongoing professional development is essential to maintain knowledge of emerging threats and technologies, adapting the XDR strategy accordingly. This includes staying updated on the latest attack vectors and security best practices.

Moreover, the cost of implementing and maintaining an XDR system can be a significant barrier for some healthcare organizations. However, the return on investment (ROI) from XDR can be substantial, as it contributes to reduced financial losses from data breaches, ransom ware attacks, and regulatory non-compliance. The improved security posture, enhanced threat detection, and faster incident response offered by XDR can significantly lower the overall cost of security incidents, outweighing the initial investment. A thorough cost-benefit analysis should be conducted to evaluate the long-term benefits of XDR within the specific context of a healthcare organization.

Beyond ransom ware and data breaches, XDR plays a vital role in protecting against insider threats. Healthcare organizations are susceptible to malicious or negligent actions by insiders who have access to sensitive patient data. XDR's monitoring capabilities allow for detection of anomalous user behaviour that may indicate malicious intent. For example, unusual access patterns, excessive data downloads, or attempts to access unauthorized systems can be detected and flagged for investigation. This allows for early intervention and can help prevent significant data breaches or compliance violations. This monitoring is critical given the potential for significant harm from insider threats, which can be devastating to the reputation and operational stability of a healthcare organization.

Furthermore, XDR can facilitate improved collaboration between different security teams within a healthcare organization. The unified view of the security scenery provided by XDR fosters better communication and coordination between IT, security, and compliance teams. This collaborative approach enhances overall security posture by eliminating information silos and improving the efficiency of security operations. The centralized nature of XDR promotes a shared understanding of security events, leading to faster and more effective incident response.

The integration capabilities of XDR are a critical aspect of its effectiveness. The architecture must facilitate seamless data ingestion from disparate sources. This requires standardized data formats, APIs, and integration protocols to ensure interoperability. Many XDR vendors offer pre-built integrations with popular security tools and cloud platforms, simplifying the implementation process. However, custom integrations may be necessary in some cases to accommodate unique organizational requirements or legacy systems. Successful integration relies on careful planning and testing to ensure that data is correctly processed, correlated, and analyzed. Inconsistencies or errors in data integration can lead to false positives, missed alerts, and compromised threat detection accuracy. The selection of an XDR platform should therefore heavily consider its integration capabilities and compatibility with the existing security infrastructure. Organizations must assess the platform's ability to handle the volume and variety of data generated within their environment and the efficiency of its integration processes.

The core of XDR's effectiveness lies in its ability to analyze data from multiple sources, detect anomalies, and respond to threats in a timely and effective manner. This is typically achieved through sophisticated algorithms, often leveraging machine learning and artificial intelligence. These algorithms can identify subtle patterns and correlations that might be missed by human analysts, providing valuable insights into the behaviour of both legitimate and malicious actors within the organization's IT infrastructure. For instance, an XDR system might identify a previously unknown malware variant by correlating suspicious file behavior detected by EDR with unusual network connections observed by NDR. This combined information allows the security team to rapidly respond and contain the threat, minimizing potential damage.

Furthermore, the response capabilities of XDR are crucial. While detecting threats is essential, the ability to rapidly respond and contain them is equally vital. XDR platforms often include automated response capabilities, such as automatically quarantining infected endpoints, blocking malicious IP addresses, and isolating compromised systems. These automated responses can significantly reduce the time it takes to neutralize threats, mitigating the impact of security incidents. However, it is vital to carefully configure these automated responses to avoid unintended consequences. The balance between automated and manual response needs careful consideration, and a robust incident response plan should incorporate both capabilities.

The effectiveness of XDR also hinges on the quality and quantity of data it receives. The more comprehensive the data sources, the more accurate and insightful the threat detection and response capabilities will be. This highlights the importance of a well-defined data strategy for XDR implementation. Organizations need to identify and integrate relevant data sources across various domains, including endpoints, networks, clouds, applications, and security devices. Data normalization and enrichment are also critical steps to ensure consistency and accuracy. This process involves transforming data from diverse sources into a consistent format, standardizing data structures and terminology to avoid inconsistencies. Data enrichment involves adding context to the data to improve its analytical value, such as correlating IP addresses with geographic location or enriching malware samples with threat intelligence data. A well-defined data strategy is essential for maximizing the effectiveness of XDR, ensuring that the system receives the information needed to accurately detect and respond to threats.

Beyond the technical aspects, the successful implementation and management of XDR require a strong security operations team with the skills and expertise to operate and maintain the system. Security analysts need training to interpret the information provided by the XDR platform, investigate alerts, and take appropriate actions. This necessitates expertise in threat detection, incident response, and the intricacies of the XDR platform itself. The team needs to be able to configure and tune the system to optimize its performance and adapt to the evolving threat landscape. This involves setting appropriate alert thresholds, fine-tuning machine learning algorithms, and regularly reviewing and updating security policies. Organizations should invest in adequate training and ongoing professional development for their security team to ensure they possess the necessary expertise to leverage the full capabilities of the XDR system.

The integration of XDR with other security tools and technologies is critical to the success of the overall security posture. This includes integration with SIEM systems, threat intelligence platforms, vulnerability management systems, and incident response systems. Integration with SIEM systems provides a centralized view of security events, allowing for comprehensive analysis and correlation of data from multiple sources. Threat intelligence platforms provide valuable context and insights into known threats, helping to prioritize alerts and expedite incident response. Vulnerability management systems allow the identification and remediation of security weaknesses in systems and applications, minimizing the attack surface. Finally, integration with incident response systems facilitates efficient and effective handling of security incidents. A well-integrated security ecosystem enhances the overall effectiveness of the security operations and increases the resilience of the organization against cyber threats.

The implementation of XDR is not a one-time project but rather an ongoing process of continuous improvement. Regular review and refinement of the XDR platform's configuration, data sources, and alert thresholds are necessary to ensure its continued effectiveness. This requires close monitoring of system performance, review of alert volumes and accuracy, and feedback from security analysts regarding their experiences with the system. The system's performance should be regularly evaluated to identify any bottlenecks or areas for improvement. This ongoing process helps optimize the system for accuracy and efficiency and ensures it remains aligned with the organization's evolving security needs and the ever-changing threat landscape.

The cost of implementation and maintenance of an XDR solution should be carefully considered. This includes the cost of the software, hardware, professional services, and ongoing support. The long-term costs of staffing and training should also be factored in. The return on investment (ROI) of XDR is difficult to quantify definitively but is often measured by the reduction in the cost of security breaches, improved incident response times, and increased efficiency of security operations. A thorough cost-benefit analysis should be conducted before investing in an XDR solution, weighing the costs against the potential benefits to the organization.

In summary, XDR offers a powerful approach to threat detection and response, providing a more holistic and effective solution than traditional, siloed security tools. Its effectiveness hinges on its integration capabilities, its ability to analyze vast amounts of data from diverse sources, and its automated response features. However, successful implementation and management require careful planning, a skilled security operations team, and ongoing monitoring and refinement. The costs and benefits must be carefully considered before adopting an XDR solution. The ultimate goal is to enhance the organization's overall security posture, providing stronger protection against the increasingly sophisticated cyber threats that organizations face in today's digital landscape.

Deploying and managing an XDR system is a multifaceted undertaking that extends beyond the simple installation of software. It requires a strategic approach encompassing careful planning, meticulous execution, and ongoing refinement to ensure the system's effectiveness and alignment with the organization's evolving security needs. This process begins with a thorough assessment of the existing IT infrastructure and security landscape. This assessment should identify all relevant data sources—endpoints, networks, cloud environments, and security devices—that will feed into the XDR system. Understanding the volume and variety of data generated by these sources is crucial for selecting an XDR platform with sufficient capacity and processing power.

The choice of XDR vendor and platform is a critical decision, significantly impacting the deployment and management process. Organizations should carefully evaluate various vendors based on factors such as their reputation, experience, the capabilities of their platform, integration options, and the level of support they offer. This evaluation should involve detailed demonstrations, proof-of-concept testing, and thorough review of customer testimonials to ensure the selected platform meets the organization's specific requirements and seamlessly integrates with the existing security infrastructure. The vendor's ability to provide comprehensive training and ongoing support for the security team is also a critical factor.

Once the XDR platform is selected, the deployment process begins. This typically involves installing the necessary agents on endpoints, configuring network sensors, and integrating the XDR system with other security tools such as SIEM, threat intelligence platforms, and vulnerability management systems. This integration is crucial for ensuring a holistic view of the security landscape. The process of integrating the XDR system with existing security tools requires careful planning and execution. This includes defining data exchange protocols, mapping data fields, and establishing data flows to ensure seamless data transfer and correlation. Thorough testing is essential at each stage of the integration process to identify and resolve any issues before full deployment.

Scalability is a key consideration throughout the deployment and management lifecycle. The XDR system should be capable of handling the increasing volume and variety of data as the organization grows. This necessitates careful planning and selection of hardware and software resources capable of scaling to meet future demands. The system's architecture should be designed for scalability, allowing for easy addition of new data sources and agents as needed without impacting performance. Regular performance monitoring and capacity planning are essential to ensure the system remains responsive and effective over time.

Configuring the XDR system involves fine-tuning various parameters to optimize its performance and effectiveness. This includes setting alert thresholds, configuring automated response actions, and customizing reporting dashboards to meet specific organizational needs. Proper configuration is essential to reduce false positives and ensure that the system only alerts on genuine security threats. Regular review and adjustments to the configuration are necessary as the threat landscape evolves and new vulnerabilities emerge. The ability to fine-tune these settings is a crucial factor when selecting an XDR platform.

Ongoing maintenance is crucial to ensure the long-term effectiveness of the XDR system. This includes regularly updating the software, applying security patches, and monitoring system performance. The security operations team must actively monitor the system's alerts, investigate suspicious activities, and respond appropriately to security incidents. Regular review of the alert data is vital to identify trends, refine the system's configuration, and improve the accuracy of threat detection. This also ensures that the response protocols remain effective and aligned with the organization's incident response plan.

The security operations team plays a pivotal role in managing the XDR system. Their expertise in threat detection, incident response, and the intricacies of the XDR platform is essential for its effective operation. This team should receive appropriate training on the system's capabilities, its configuration, and the interpretation of its alerts. Ongoing professional development is essential to keep the team's skills up-to-date with the evolving threat landscape and the advancements in XDR technology. Regular training sessions, participation in industry conferences, and access to online resources can help ensure that the team possesses the necessary expertise to effectively manage the XDR system.

Data management is another crucial aspect of XDR system management. This involves ensuring the integrity, accuracy, and security of the data ingested by the system. Regular data backups should be performed to protect against data loss. Data retention policies should be established and adhered to, balancing the need for historical data analysis with the cost of storage and the potential for data breaches. Regular audits of data handling procedures are necessary to verify compliance with relevant regulations and to identify any security weaknesses.

The integration of the XDR system with other security tools and technologies extends beyond initial deployment. Ongoing management includes ensuring the smooth exchange of data and maintaining the compatibility between different systems. This requires close collaboration between the security operations team and the IT infrastructure team to address any integration-related issues that might arise. Regular testing and updates are necessary to maintain the seamless integration of the XDR system with other security tools, ensuring that the organization benefits from a comprehensive and coordinated security posture. The seamless flow of information between these systems is crucial for effective threat detection and response.

Regular reviews of the XDR system's performance and effectiveness are essential. These reviews should evaluate the system's ability to detect and respond to threats, the accuracy of its alerts, and the efficiency of its operations. The feedback from the security operations team is invaluable in identifying areas for improvement and fine-tuning the system's configuration. These reviews should also assess the system's compliance with organizational security policies and relevant regulations. The findings of these reviews should be used to inform continuous improvements to the system's configuration, data handling processes, and incident response procedures.

The cost of managing an XDR system is a significant consideration. This includes the costs associated with software licenses, hardware maintenance, staff training, and ongoing support from the vendor. Regular budgeting and cost analysis are essential to ensure that the organization can effectively manage the financial aspects of the XDR system. Regular cost-benefit analyses are necessary to ensure that the ongoing investment in the XDR system is justified by the improved security posture and reduced risk of cyber attacks. This necessitates monitoring key metrics such as incident response times, the number of security incidents, and the overall cost of addressing those incidents. The reduction in these costs should be weighed against the continued investment in the XDR system to ensure that the ROI remains positive.

DevSecOps

The evolution of cyber security necessitates a paradigm shift that extends beyond reactive measures and encompasses proactive security embedded within the software development process itself. This is where Security-Oriented DevOps, or DevSecOps, plays a crucial role. DevSecOps represents a fundamental change in how organizations approach software security, moving away from treating security as an afterthought to integrating it seamlessly into every stage of the software development lifecycle (SDLC). This shift-left approach, as it's commonly known, aims to identify and mitigate vulnerabilities early in the development process, significantly reducing the risk of deploying insecure applications.

Traditional software development methodologies often relegated security to a separate phase, typically near the end of the SDLC. This approach often referred to as "bolt-on security," proved inefficient and costly. Vulnerabilities discovered late in the process are expensive and time-consuming to fix, often requiring significant code rework and potentially delaying release schedules. Furthermore, late-stage security assessments might miss subtle vulnerabilities that could have been easily addressed earlier. The inherent complexity of modern software applications, coupled with the increasingly sophisticated nature of cyber threats, renders this traditional approach inadequate.

DevSecOps addresses these limitations by embedding security into every phase of the SDLC. This integrated approach ensures that security considerations are not just an afterthought but a fundamental aspect of the development process, from initial design and coding to testing, deployment, and ongoing maintenance. The goal is to build security into the application from the ground up, resulting in inherently more secure software. This proactive strategy offers significant advantages, including reduced vulnerability exposure, faster remediation times, and improved operational efficiency.

A key aspect of DevSecOps is automation. Automating security tasks, such as vulnerability scanning, penetration testing, and security code reviews, significantly streamlines the process and reduces the likelihood of human error. Automated security checks integrated into the continuous integration/continuous delivery (CI/CD) pipeline ensure that security is consistently enforced throughout the development process. This automation not only accelerates the development cycle but also enhances the consistency and reliability of security measures.

The implementation of DevSecOps often involves the use of specialized tools and technologies. Static Application Security Testing (SAST) tools analyze source code for potential vulnerabilities without actually executing the code, while Dynamic Application Security Testing (DAST) tools test the application during runtime to identify vulnerabilities in the application's behavior. Software Composition Analysis (SCA) tools are used to identify and assess the security risks associated with open-source components used in the application, ensuring that these components are free from known vulnerabilities. These tools provide automated checks for security flaws, reducing the burden on developers while enhancing the overall security of the application.

Another critical element of DevSecOps is the establishment of a security culture within the development team. Security should not be viewed as the sole responsibility of a dedicated security team; rather, it should be a shared responsibility across the entire development organization. Developers need to be empowered and trained to incorporate security best practices into their daily work. This requires a cultural shift within the organization, fostering collaboration and communication between development and security teams. Training programs, secure coding guidelines, and regular security awareness campaigns play a pivotal role in cultivating this security-conscious culture.

The benefits of DevSecOps are multifaceted. Firstly, it significantly reduces the number of vulnerabilities discovered in production environments. By identifying and addressing vulnerabilities early in the development process, DevSecOps minimizes the risk of security breaches and reduces the costs associated with remediating vulnerabilities after deployment. This proactive approach leads to more resilient and secure applications. Secondly, DevSecOps accelerates the software development lifecycle. The automation of security tasks and the integration of security into the CI/CD pipeline streamline the development process, reducing overall development time and accelerating time-to-market.

Thirdly, DevSecOps improves compliance with industry regulations and standards. Many industries, such as finance, healthcare, and government, are subject to stringent security regulations. DevSecOps helps organizations meet these regulatory requirements by embedding security into the development process from the outset. The automated security checks and consistent enforcement of security policies ensure compliance with relevant standards. Fourthly, DevSecOps enhances collaboration and communication between development and security teams. The integrated approach fosters a culture of shared responsibility, breaking down silos and improving overall security posture.

However, the implementation of DevSecOps is not without its challenges. Organizations need to invest in the necessary tools, technologies, and training to effectively implement DevSecOps. The initial investment in these areas can be significant, but the long-term benefits, such as reduced vulnerabilities and improved operational efficiency, often outweigh the costs. Organizations must also overcome the cultural resistance within the development team. A successful DevSecOps implementation requires a change in mindset, with developers embracing security as an integral part of their work. This requires effective communication, training, and ongoing support from leadership.

Furthermore, organizations need to establish a clear DevSecOps strategy that aligns with their overall security goals. This strategy should define the specific security practices, tools, and technologies that will be used, as well as the roles and responsibilities of different teams. A well-defined strategy provides a roadmap for implementation and ensures that the DevSecOps initiative is successful. Measuring the effectiveness of the DevSecOps initiative is crucial. Organizations need to track key metrics such as the number of vulnerabilities found, the time taken to remediate vulnerabilities, and the overall security posture of the applications. This data provides insights into the effectiveness of the DevSecOps program and allows organizations to make improvements over time.

The integration of DevSecOps into the software development workflow necessitates a paradigm shift in how security professionals interact with development teams. Instead of acting as gatekeepers, security personnel should become active participants and collaborators. This collaborative model fosters a culture where security is proactively addressed rather than being an afterthought. The shared responsibility model ensures that security is embedded into the design, development, and deployment of applications from inception. This approach not only improves the security posture but also significantly improves efficiency, eliminating the delays associated with addressing security issues at the end of the development cycle.

Understanding the capabilities of Extended Detection and Response (XDR) requires appreciating its multifaceted nature. Unlike traditional security solutions that operate in silos, XDR employs a unified approach, correlating data from various sources to provide a comprehensive view of the security landscape. This holistic perspective significantly enhances threat detection and response capabilities, allowing security teams to address threats more effectively and efficiently. The key lies in its ability to integrate data from endpoint detection and response (EDR), network detection and response (NDR), security information and event management (SIEM), cloud security posture management (CSPM), and other relevant security tools. This aggregation allows for the identification of patterns and connections that might otherwise remain hidden within isolated data streams. For example, a suspicious file downloaded onto an endpoint (EDR data) might only be flagged as suspicious by the EDR system itself. However, when correlated with unusual network activity (NDR data) and login attempts from an uncommon location (SIEM data integrated with authentication logs), the full picture of a potential targeted attack emerges – something a single solution could not deliver.

Shifting security left, a core tenet of DevSecOps, represents a fundamental paradigm shift in how organizations approach software security. Instead of treating security as an afterthought, tacked onto the end of the Software Development Life Cycle (SDLC), this approach embeds security considerations into every stage, from initial design and planning through deployment and maintenance. This proactive approach significantly reduces vulnerabilities, lowers the cost of remediation, and ultimately results in more secure and resilient applications.

The traditional approach to software security, often referred to as "shifting security right," involves performing security assessments and penetration testing only after the software is largely complete. This reactive method is inherently inefficient and expensive. Discovering vulnerabilities late in the development process necessitates costly rework, delays in release schedules, and potential reputational damage if the vulnerabilities are exploited in production. The longer a vulnerability remains undetected, the more extensive and costly the remediation process becomes. This is especially true for critical vulnerabilities that could expose sensitive data or disrupt critical business operations. For example, a flaw in authentication that allows unauthorized access could cost millions in remediation efforts after a successful attack compared to identifying and correcting it early in development.

By contrast, shifting security left emphasizes proactive security measures throughout the SDLC. This involves integrating security practices into each phase, ensuring that security is considered and addressed concurrently with development tasks, rather than as a separate process. This integration can take many forms, from incorporating security requirements into design specifications to automating security testing throughout the pipeline. This proactive approach leads to earlier identification and remediation of vulnerabilities, reducing overall development costs and improving the overall security posture of the software.

One key aspect of shifting security left is the introduction of security testing early in the development process. This might involve static application security testing (SAST) tools which analyze source code for potential vulnerabilities without actually executing the code. SAST tools can detect a wide range of flaws, including buffer overflows, SQL injection vulnerabilities, and cross-site scripting (XSS) vulnerabilities. These tools are incredibly useful in the early stages because they can pinpoint potential problems before the code is even compiled, minimizing the effort required for correction.

Dynamic application security testing (DAST) tools complement SAST by analyzing the running application for vulnerabilities. DAST tools actively probe the application for weaknesses by simulating attacks, effectively revealing security flaws in a deployed context. While SAST focuses on the code itself, DAST assesses the application's behavior and interaction with its environment, providing a more comprehensive picture of its security posture. Ideally, both SAST and DAST are integrated into the CI/CD pipeline, allowing for continuous security analysis throughout the development process.

Software Composition Analysis (SCA) tools play a decisive role in identifying and mitigating vulnerabilities associated with open-source and third-party components. Many modern applications rely heavily on pre-built libraries and frameworks, introducing potential security risks. SCA tools automatically scan codebases to detect the use of vulnerable components, providing developers with critical insights into potential vulnerabilities inherited from external dependencies. This allows developers to proactively address these security risks before deploying the application to production. Consider an instance where an outdated version of a widely used library is included; SCA can promptly alert the team, allowing for a swift upgrade to the most secure, updated version.

Integrating security awareness training into the development team's practices is another crucial element. Developers are not always security experts; security training enables them to better understand the implications of secure coding practices. This training can cover topics such as secure coding guidelines, common web vulnerabilities, and best practices for handling sensitive data. By equipping developers with the knowledge and skills to write secure code, organizations can significantly reduce the number of vulnerabilities introduced during development.

Implementing robust security automation is vital for efficient and effective security. This involves automating various security tasks throughout the pipeline, such as security scans, code analysis, and vulnerability remediation. Automation enhances efficiency, reduces manual effort, and ensures consistent security practices across all development projects. By automating these tasks, organizations can free up security engineers to focus on more complex and strategic issues. A well-integrated CI/CD pipeline can automatically trigger security scans upon each code commit, providing immediate feedback to developers and halting the process if critical vulnerabilities are detected.

Beyond tools and techniques, shifting security left requires a change in organizational culture. Security must be viewed as a shared responsibility, not solely the domain of a dedicated security team. This collaborative approach requires fostering a culture of security awareness and responsibility among all members of the development team, as well as across different departments involved in the software development process. Open communication channels, regular security training, and clear guidelines on security practices are crucial for building this collaborative culture. This is not just about technical processes; it's about fostering a mindset where security is prioritized and integrated into every aspect of the software development process.

The benefits of shifting security left are significant. Early identification and remediation of vulnerabilities reduces development costs, shortening the development cycle and avoiding delays. Furthermore, it lowers the risk of security breaches and reduces the impact of any potential incidents, protecting sensitive data and maintaining the organization's reputation. The increased security of applications contributes to greater customer trust and confidence. Improved code quality and reduced technical debt are often additional benefits.

Regular security assessments, continuous monitoring, and ongoing training are essential for maintaining a robust security posture. The ever-evolving threat landscape necessitates a dynamic approach, one that continually adapts and learns from past experiences. Continuous improvement of security practices, tools, and processes remains key to a successful implementation of

DevSecOps principles and the broader goal of "shifting security left." This proactive and iterative approach is crucial to successfully navigating the complex and ever-changing world of cybersecurity. Regularly reviewing and updating security processes is essential for effectiveness. This ongoing engagement guarantees sustained and robust security throughout the entire SDLC, and beyond, protecting organizational assets and ensuring the ongoing integrity of applications.

Building upon the foundational shift towards "shifting security left," the successful implementation of DevSecOps hinges critically on embedding secure coding practices into the very fabric of the software development lifecycle. This isn't merely about adding a security checklist at the end; it's about fundamentally changing how developers approach their work, integrating security considerations from the initial design phase through to deployment and beyond. This requires a multi-faceted approach encompassing robust training, the adoption of secure coding techniques, and the utilization of automated security tools.

One of the most fundamental secure coding practices is robust input validation. This seemingly simple step acts as the first line of defence against many common vulnerabilities. Failing to properly validate user inputs opens the door to a range of attacks, from SQL injection to cross-site scripting (XSS) and buffer overflows. Consider a web application that allows users to search for products using a text field. Without input validation, a malicious user could inject SQL code into the search query, potentially accessing or modifying sensitive data within the database. A properly validated input, however, would sanitize the user's input, preventing the injection of malicious code. This validation should encompass both the data type and the content itself, checking for unexpected characters or patterns that could be exploited. Different programming languages offer various tools and functions for input validation. For example, in Python, libraries like `bleach` can be used for sanitizing HTML and preventing XSS attacks, while regular expressions can be used to enforce data format requirements. In Java, using parameterized queries or prepared statements when interacting with databases effectively prevents SQL injection attacks. These techniques prevent malicious input from being interpreted as executable code.

Output encoding is another fundamental aspect of secure coding, closely related to input validation. While input validation focuses on sanitizing the data received from the user, output encoding focuses on ensuring that the data sent back to the user is rendered safely. Improper output encoding can lead to XSS vulnerabilities, allowing attackers to inject malicious JavaScript code into a web page and execute it in the user's browser. For instance, if a web application displays user-supplied data without properly encoding it, an attacker could inject JavaScript code into their profile name, which would then be executed by other users viewing their profile. Robust output encoding techniques, such as using HTML encoding, prevent this type of attack by converting special characters into their HTML entities, rendering them harmless. This simple measure can significantly reduce the risk of XSS attacks. The specific encoding method will vary depending on the context; for instance, encoding for HTML, JavaScript, XML, or URLs require different techniques. Consistent and context-aware encoding is paramount.

Preventing SQL injection is a critical aspect of database security. SQL injection attacks exploit vulnerabilities in how applications interact with databases. By injecting malicious SQL code into user inputs, attackers can manipulate database queries to gain unauthorized access to data or even modify database structures. To mitigate this risk, parameterized queries or prepared statements should be used instead of directly embedding user inputs into SQL queries. Prepared statements treat user-supplied data as parameters rather than executable code, preventing the injected code from being interpreted as part of the query. This technique significantly reduces the risk of SQL injection attacks, providing a robust safeguard against database compromise. In addition, regularly updating and patching the database management system is crucial to protect against known vulnerabilities. Staying informed on the latest security patches and implementing them promptly is a non-negotiable aspect of secure database management.

Cross-site scripting (XSS) vulnerabilities occur when an attacker injects malicious scripts into a website's output, which are then executed by the user's browser. These scripts can steal session cookies, redirect users to phishing websites, or even take control of the user's computer. Proper input validation and output encoding, as discussed earlier, are the primary defences against XSS attacks. However, additional security measures such as Content Security Policy (CSP) headers can further enhance protection. CSP headers allow web developers to define a white list of sources from which the browser is allowed to load resources, effectively blocking potentially malicious scripts from untrusted sources. Implementing a robust CSP policy can provide an extra layer of security against XSS attacks. Regular security audits and penetration testing are also essential in identifying and addressing potential XSS vulnerabilities before they can be exploited.

Beyond these specific vulnerabilities, secure coding practices extend to broader areas such as authentication and authorization. Authentication verifies the identity of a user, while authorization controls what actions the user is permitted to perform. Implementing strong authentication mechanisms, such as multi-factor authentication (MFA), is essential for preventing unauthorized access. Likewise, robust authorization controls ensure that users only have access to the resources and functionalities they are entitled to. This includes implementing the principle of least privilege, granting users only the minimum necessary permissions to perform their tasks. Regularly reviewing and updating access controls are crucial to maintain a secure system.

Secure coding practices also extend to the handling of sensitive data. This includes encrypting data both in transit and at rest, utilizing strong encryption algorithms and key management practices. Data masking and tokenization can protect sensitive information during development and testing by replacing sensitive data with non-sensitive substitutes. This protects data privacy and complies with regulations such as GDPR and CCPA. Data loss prevention (DLP) tools monitor and prevent sensitive data from leaving the organization's control. These tools integrate into the DevSecOps pipeline, scanning code and data for sensitive information and triggering alerts if unauthorized attempts to access or exfiltrate this data are detected.

The integration of secure coding practices into the software development process requires a significant investment in training and education. Developers need to be equipped with the necessary knowledge and skills to write secure code, understand common vulnerabilities, and apply appropriate security measures. This training should cover topics such as secure coding guidelines, common vulnerabilities (OWASP Top 10), secure design principles, and the use of security tools. Regular refresher training and awareness programs are necessary to keep developers up-to-date with the latest threats and best practices. This investment in training is essential to fostering a security-conscious culture within the development team. Furthermore, regular code reviews can identify security vulnerabilities that might have been missed during development. This peer review process ensures multiple sets of eyes scrutinize the code, catching potential issues before they reach production.

The transition from development and testing environments to a live production setting marks a critical juncture in the DevSecOps lifecycle. While rigorous security testing is paramount during earlier stages, the production environment demands a different approach – one focused on continuous monitoring, real-time threat detection, and rapid incident response. The stakes are significantly higher; a breach in production can directly impact customers, revenue, and reputation, potentially leading to severe financial and legal consequences. Therefore, a robust and proactive security posture in production is not merely desirable but absolutely essential.

One of the basis strategies for securing production environments is the implementation of a comprehensive Security Information and Event Management (SIEM) system. A SIEM aggregates security logs and events from various sources across the entire IT infrastructure – servers, networks, applications, cloud platforms, and endpoints. This centralized view provides a holistic understanding of the security landscape, allowing security analysts to identify patterns, detect anomalies, and respond swiftly to potential threats. Effective SIEM systems employ advanced analytics techniques, including machine learning and artificial intelligence, to sift through massive volumes of data and identify subtle indicators of compromise (IOCs) that might otherwise go unnoticed.

central to the success of a SIEM is the careful selection and configuration of its data sources. The system must be integrated with all relevant security tools and applications to ensure comprehensive data collection. This includes firewalls, intrusion detection systems (IDS), intrusion prevention systems (IPS), endpoint detection and response (EDR) solutions, and cloud security posture management (CSPM) tools. The data ingested by the SIEM should encompass a wide range of events, encompassing system logs, network traffic, application logs, and user activity. The more complete the data picture, the more effective the SIEM will be at detecting and responding to threats.

Furthermore, the SIEM should be configured to trigger alerts based on predefined rules and thresholds. These alerts should be tailored to the organization's specific security posture and risk profile. For example, alerts might be triggered by unusual login attempts, unauthorized access to sensitive data, or suspicious network activity. It's vital to avoid alert fatigue by meticulously crafting alert rules to minimize false positives. A deluge of irrelevant alerts can desensitize security personnel, leading to missed critical alerts. Careful calibration and regular review of alert rules are essential to maintain the effectiveness of the SIEM.

Beyond the SIEM, robust security monitoring involves employing a multifaceted approach that leverages various tools and techniques. Regular security assessments, including vulnerability scans and penetration testing, are crucial for identifying and remediating vulnerabilities in production systems. These assessments should be conducted on a regular schedule, with the frequency adjusted based on the criticality of the systems and the nature of the applications they support. Automated vulnerability scanning tools can significantly enhance the efficiency of these assessments, providing timely alerts about newly discovered vulnerabilities and allowing for prompt remediation.

Continuous integration and continuous delivery (CI/CD) pipelines, when properly implemented, provide a secure pathway for deploying code changes to production. However, this process itself must be monitored closely. Tracking and analyzing deployment logs, meticulously documenting all changes, and employing rollback mechanisms are crucial steps to ensure the security of the deployment process and allow rapid reversion if vulnerabilities are discovered post-deployment. Implementing canary deployments, which gradually roll out changes to a small subset of users before a full-scale release, can help identify and mitigate potential problems early on, minimizing the impact of any unforeseen security issues.

The concept of runtime application self-protection (RASP) deserves special attention in the production context. RASP agents reside within the applications themselves, monitoring their runtime behaviour and providing real-time insights into potential threats. Unlike traditional security solutions that primarily monitor external events, RASP agents can detect attacks occurring within the application's code, providing a far more granular level of protection. They can identify and block malicious code execution, prevent data breaches, and provide valuable insights into attack techniques. RASP complements other security measures, providing an additional layer of defense that can significantly improve the resilience of applications against sophisticated attacks.

Incident response is another critical aspect of production security monitoring. A well-defined incident response plan is essential for effectively handling security incidents, minimizing their impact, and ensuring a swift recovery. The plan should outline procedures for identifying, containing, eradicating, and recovering from security breaches. Regular drills and simulations are crucial to ensure that the incident response team is well-prepared to handle real-world scenarios. The effectiveness of the incident response process hinges on the organization's ability to quickly identify and isolate compromised systems, preventing further damage. A detailed post-incident analysis, documenting the causes of the incident, the actions taken, and the lessons learned, is essential for improving the organization's overall security posture and preventing similar incidents in the future.

Furthermore, the production environment necessitates robust logging and auditing capabilities. All security-relevant events should be meticulously logged and readily accessible for analysis. Logs should be centrally managed and secured, ensuring their integrity and availability. Compliance requirements often mandate the retention of logs for extended periods, necessitating a robust log management solution. The ability to easily search, filter, and analyze logs is crucial for incident investigation and security auditing. Regular log analysis can reveal potential security vulnerabilities and identify patterns of suspicious activity that might indicate an impending attack. This proactive approach helps prevent breaches before they can cause significant harm.

The security of the production environment is also closely tied to the security of the data itself. Data loss prevention (DLP) tools play a critical role in preventing sensitive data from leaving the organization's control. These tools monitor data flows, identifying and blocking attempts to transmit sensitive information outside the permitted channels. Data encryption, both in transit and at rest, is essential for protecting data from unauthorized access. Regular security audits of data access and usage patterns can identify and mitigate potential vulnerabilities related to data handling. Compliance with relevant data privacy regulations, such as GDPR and CCPA, is paramount and requires careful monitoring and enforcement of data security policies.

Automating Security Testing

The automation of security testing is crucial for efficiently implementing secure coding practices at scale. Static application security testing (SAST) tools analyze source code for vulnerabilities without executing it, while dynamic application security testing (DAST) tools test the running application. Software Composition Analysis (SCA) tools identify vulnerabilities in open-source and third-party components. Integrating these tools into the continuous integration/continuous delivery (CI/CD) pipeline ensures that security testing is performed automatically throughout the development lifecycle, providing immediate feedback to developers and preventing vulnerable code from reaching production. The automated nature of these tools ensures that security is not overlooked amidst the pressure of rapid development cycles. By seamlessly integrating security checks into the CI/CD process, organizations can significantly enhance their security posture without slowing down the development workflow. The cost savings associated with early identification and resolution of vulnerabilities far outweigh the initial investment in these tools and the training required to effectively utilize them.

Automating security testing within the CI/CD pipeline is no longer a luxury but a necessity for organizations serious about DevSecOps. The traditional approach of performing security testing as a separate, post-development phase is simply unsustainable in today's fast-paced development environments. The sheer volume of code changes, the rapid release cycles, and the ever-evolving threat landscape demand a more integrated and automated approach. This requires seamlessly integrating security tools into the CI/CD pipeline, ensuring that security checks are performed automatically at each stage of the software development lifecycle, from initial code commits to final deployment.

This automation dramatically accelerates the feedback loop, allowing developers to identify and address security vulnerabilities early in the development process. This "shift-left" approach reduces the cost and complexity of fixing vulnerabilities significantly. Addressing a vulnerability during the development phase is far less expensive and disruptive than discovering it after the software has been deployed to production. Delayed discovery often leads to costly remediation efforts, potential service disruptions, and reputational damage.

The core of automated security testing in CI/CD pipelines involves the use of several key tools and technologies: Static Application Security Testing (SAST), Dynamic Application Security Testing (DAST), and Software Composition Analysis (SCA). Let's examine each of these in detail.

SAST tools analyze the source code of an application without actually executing it. They employ sophisticated algorithms and pattern matching techniques to identify potential vulnerabilities within the code itself. These vulnerabilities can range from buffer overflows and SQL injection flaws to insecure coding practices and cross-site scripting (XSS) vulnerabilities. SAST tools provide developers with precise location information, enabling them to rapidly locate and address these issues directly within their IDE (Integrated Development Environment). Popular SAST tools include SonarQube, Checkmarx, and Coverity. The choice of tool often depends on the programming languages used within the organization and the specific types of vulnerabilities that need to be detected. Some SAST tools offer specialized plugins for particular programming languages or frameworks, providing greater accuracy and depth of analysis. The output from these tools is usually integrated into the CI/CD system's reporting mechanisms, providing a clear overview of security findings. False positives, a common concern with SAST tools, are often addressed through fine-tuning the tool's configuration and integrating context-aware rules based on the organization's coding standards and application architecture.

DAST tools, in contrast to SAST, test the running application rather than the source code. They simulate real-world attacks, probing the application for vulnerabilities such as cross-site scripting, SQL injection, and insecure authentication mechanisms. DAST tools provide a valuable complement to SAST, as they identify vulnerabilities that may not be apparent from static code analysis alone. These tools offer a runtime perspective, revealing vulnerabilities that emerge only during the execution of the application. Popular DAST tools include OWASP ZAP, Burp Suite, and Acunetix. Integrating DAST tools into the CI/CD pipeline typically involves running them at the end of the build process or before deployment. The results generated by DAST are analyzed for potential vulnerabilities and integrated into the pipeline's reporting system, alerting developers to runtime security flaws. The complexity and scale of DAST testing can necessitate sophisticated infrastructure and test environments that accurately reflect the production environment.

SCA tools, increasingly important in modern software development, analyze the composition of the application, identifying the use of open-source and third-party components. They then compare these components against known vulnerability databases, such as the National Vulnerability Database (NVD), to assess the risk associated with these dependencies. This is particularly critical in today's software development landscape, where a significant portion of applications are built using open-source libraries and frameworks. Vulnerabilities in these components can significantly impact the application's security. Popular SCA tools include Black Duck, Snyk, and WhiteSource. Integrating SCA into the CI/CD pipeline is crucial for identifying and mitigating risks associated with third-party components promptly. SCA tools are often integrated early in the development lifecycle, helping developers select secure and well-maintained components.

The effective integration of SAST, DAST, and SCA tools into the CI/CD pipeline requires careful planning and execution. This involves selecting the right tools, customizing them to the organization's specific needs, and integrating them seamlessly into the existing CI/CD workflows. Integration often involves custom scripting, leveraging the CI/CD system's APIs (Application Programming Interfaces) to trigger security scans at the appropriate points in the pipeline. It's crucial to avoid introducing bottlenecks and slowing down the development process, requiring careful consideration of the tools' processing time and resource requirements. The pipeline should be configured to halt the build process if critical security vulnerabilities are detected, preventing vulnerable code from being deployed. Automated alerts and notifications should be configured to inform relevant personnel promptly when security issues are identified.

Beyond these three core tools, additional technologies enhance the automated security testing within the CI/CD pipeline. Secret management tools, for instance, help secure API keys, passwords, and other sensitive information used during the build and deployment processes. These tools provide secure storage and access control for sensitive data, preventing exposure during testing and deployment. Security orchestration, automation, and response (SOAR) platforms provide a centralized platform for managing and coordinating security tools and processes, providing a unified view of the security posture across the entire CI/CD pipeline. These platforms often include features for automated remediation, incident response, and compliance reporting. The adoption of Infrastructure as Code (IaC) also enhances the security of the CI/CD pipeline itself, ensuring that the infrastructure used for building and deploying applications is configured securely and consistently.

The successful automation of security testing requires more than just the selection and integration of the right tools. It requires a cultural shift within the organization, empowering developers to take ownership of security and fostering a collaborative approach between development and security teams. This necessitates robust training and education programs that equip developers with the knowledge and skills needed to understand and address security vulnerabilities. Regular security awareness training and code review practices further enhance the effectiveness of automated testing, ensuring a holistic approach to securing applications.

The choice of specific tools and technologies will depend on several factors, including the organization's size, the type of applications being developed, the existing CI/CD infrastructure, and budget considerations. Regardless of the specific tools used, the underlying principle remains consistent: to seamlessly integrate security testing into the development workflow, enabling rapid feedback and continuous improvement. The value of automated security testing is not only in the identification and remediation of vulnerabilities but also in the continuous improvement of the development process, fostering a culture of security throughout the organization. The investment in automating security testing in the CI/CD pipeline represents a significant step towards achieving a robust and resilient DevSecOps program, resulting in more secure applications and reduced risk. This proactive approach provides significant long-term benefits, vastly outweighing the initial investment in terms of cost savings and reduced risk exposure. The ongoing monitoring and refinement of these processes are key to keeping pace with the ever-evolving landscape of cyber security threats.

Infrastructure as Code (IaC) represents a paradigm shift in how organizations manage and secure their cloud-based infrastructure. Departing from manual, often error-prone, processes, IaC leverages code to define and provision infrastructure components. This approach dramatically enhances security, consistency, and efficiency across the entire infrastructure lifecycle. Instead of relying on ad-hoc configurations and manual interventions, which are inherently susceptible to human error and inconsistencies, IaC promotes a repeatable, auditable, and scalable approach to infrastructure management. This translates directly into a significantly stronger security posture.

The core principle of IaC is to treat infrastructure as code, using descriptive languages like Terraform, Ansible, Chef, Puppet, or CloudFormation to define infrastructure components, their configurations, and relationships. These declarations are then processed by IaC tools to automatically provision and manage the infrastructure in a consistent and predictable manner. This automation eliminates the risk of manual misconfigurations, a frequent source of security vulnerabilities in cloud environments. By codifying infrastructure settings, organizations gain a level of control and predictability previously unattainable with manual methods. Changes to infrastructure are tracked through version control systems, such as Git, facilitating collaboration, auditing, and rollback capabilities, critical elements for maintaining a secure and robust environment.

One of the most significant benefits of IaC is its ability to enforce security policies consistently across all environments. Security best practices, such as the use of strong encryption, appropriate access controls, and regular patching, can be embedded directly into the IaC code. This ensures that every instance of a particular infrastructure component is provisioned with the same, pre-defined security configurations, eliminating the possibility of inconsistent security settings across different instances or environments. Moreover, IaC allows for the incorporation of security scanning and validation tools into the provisioning process. This means that security checks can be automatically performed before infrastructure is deployed, preventing the deployment of insecure configurations and reducing the likelihood of security breaches. This proactive approach is a cornerstone of a robust DevSecOps strategy, ensuring that security is built into the very fabric of the infrastructure.

IaC also streamlines the process of auditing and compliance reporting. The codified infrastructure provides a complete and readily-available record of all infrastructure components and their configurations. This eliminates the need for time-consuming manual audits, reducing the overhead associated with compliance initiatives and increasing the speed and accuracy of security assessments. The version control system's history offers an auditable trail of all changes made to the infrastructure, simplifying the identification of root causes in the event of a security incident. This granular level of traceability is invaluable for forensic analysis and compliance investigations.

The integration of IaC with CI/CD pipelines is a key enabler of a robust DevSecOps environment. IaC ensures that the underlying infrastructure is appropriately configured and secure before applications are deployed, eliminating infrastructure-related vulnerabilities as a potential attack vector. Moreover, the IaC scripts can be integrated into the CI/CD pipeline to automate the provisioning of test and staging environments. This not only simplifies the testing process but also ensures that these environments are configured identically to production, improving the accuracy and effectiveness of security testing. Automating the provisioning of these environments can drastically reduce the time and resources required for security testing, allowing for more frequent and thorough testing cycles.

However, the implementation of IaC is not without its challenges. The adoption of IaC requires a cultural shift within the organization, requiring IT staff to adopt a new way of working and develop new skills in IaC tools and scripting languages. Organizations will need to invest in training and development programs to equip their staff with the necessary expertise. Additionally, organizations need to establish robust governance and compliance processes for managing the IaC codebase, ensuring that changes are properly reviewed and approved before deployment. This involves implementing appropriate version control mechanisms, establishing clear change management procedures, and defining clear roles and responsibilities. Furthermore, the choice of IaC tool needs to be carefully evaluated based on the organization's specific needs, technological stack, and expertise. The complexity of some IaC tools may also require organizations to invest in specialized expertise to manage the IaC deployments and ensure optimal performance. It is crucial to choose tools that are well-integrated with existing infrastructure and align with the organization's long-term strategy.

The security implications of IaC extend beyond the straightforward automation of infrastructure provisioning. Secure coding practices must be followed when writing IaC scripts to prevent vulnerabilities from being introduced into the infrastructure itself. This includes securing secrets and credentials, carefully managing access control, and validating all inputs to prevent injection attacks. Furthermore, regular security audits of the IaC code itself are essential to identify and remediate any security vulnerabilities that may have been inadvertently introduced. The use of static code analysis tools specifically designed for IaC scripts can significantly enhance the security of IaC deployments by identifying potential security flaws before deployment. Regular penetration testing of the IaC-managed infrastructure is also essential to assess its resilience against real-world attacks. This testing can identify vulnerabilities that may not be apparent from code analysis alone, providing a valuable independent validation of the security of the deployed infrastructure.

One essential aspect often overlooked is the management of secrets within IaC. Hardcoding credentials directly into IaC scripts are a significant security risk, exposing sensitive information to unauthorized access. Instead, organizations should leverage dedicated secret management solutions that securely store and manage credentials. These solutions usually integrate with IaC tools, allowing for secure retrieval of credentials during provisioning without exposing them directly in the code. This ensures that even if the IaC code is compromised, the secrets remain protected. The use of a robust secret management solution is a critical element in securing IaC deployments. Moreover, organizations should adopt a least privilege principle when defining access control within IaC, ensuring that infrastructure components only have the necessary permissions to perform their designated tasks.

Bibliography

Andress, J. and Winterfeld, S., 2013. Cyber Warfare: Techniques, Tactics and Tools for Security Practitioners. Waltham: Syngress.

Bartlett, J., 2015. The dark net: inside the digital underworld. London: Melville House.

Bailey, M. and Oberheide, J. (2014) Malware and Mobile Security: Fundamentals, Principles and Practices. New York: McGraw-Hill.

Bayuk, J.L., Horowitz, B., Jansen, J., Moorthy, R., Phatak, D. and Sheikh, A., 2012. Cybersecurity policy guidebook. Hoboken: Wiley.

Buchanan, B. (2020) The hacker and the state: Cyber attacks and the new normal of geopolitics. Cambridge, MA: Harvard University Press.

Buczak, A.L. & Guven, E., 2021. Artificial Intelligence for Cybersecurity: Techniques, Applications, and Challenges. New York: Wiley.

Buyya, R. and Dastjerdi, A.V., 2016.Internet of Things: Principles and Paradigms.Morgan Kaufmann.

Buyya, R., Vecchiola, C. and Selvi, S.T., 2013. Mastering cloud computing: foundations and applications programming. Burlington, MA: Morgan Kaufmann.

Caldwell, T., 2017. Cybersecurity for Beginners. 2nd ed. San Francisco: Apress.

Castells, M., 2010. The Rise of the Network Society. 2nd ed. Oxford: Wiley-Blackwell.

Carr, J., 2011. Inside Cyber Warfare: Mapping the Cyber Underworld. 2nd ed. Sebastopol: O'Reilly Media

Chuvakin, A., Schmidt, C. and Zeltser, L. (2013) Logging and Log Management: The Authoritative Guide to Understanding the Concepts Surrounding Logging and Log Management. Waltham, MA: Syngress.

Chio, C. & Freeman, D., 2018. Machine Learning and Security: Protecting Systems with Data and Algorithms. Beijing: O'Reilly Media.

Clarke, R.A. and Knake, R.K., 2012. Cyber War: The Next Threat to National Security and What to Do About It. New York: HarperCollins.

Craig, A. and Valeriano, B., 2018. Cyber strategy: The evolving character of power and coercion. New York: Oxford University Press.

Damsgaard, J. and Scheepers, R., 2000. Managing the crises in intranet implementation: a stage model. Hershey, PA: Idea Group Publishing.

Dodge, M. & Kitchin, R., 2001. Mapping Cyberspace. London: Routledge.

Egele, M., Scholte, T., Kirda, E. and Kruegel, C. (2012) A Survey on Automated Dynamic Malware Analysis Techniques and Tools. Saarbrücken: VDM Verlag.

Erl, T., Mahmood, Z. and Puttini, R., 2013. Cloud computing: Concepts, technology & architecture. Upper Saddle River, NJ: Prentice Hall.

Goodfellow, I., Bengio, Y. and Courville, A., 2016.Deep Learning. Cambridge, MA: MIT Press.

Ghosh, R., 2020. AI and Cybersecurity: A Strategic Guide. New York: Apress.

Greenberg, A., 2019. Sandworm: A new era of cyberwar and the hunt for the Kremlin's most dangerous hackers. New York: Doubleday.

Greene, A., 2021. Zero Trust Networks: Building Secure Systems in Untrusted Networks. 2nd ed. Sebastopol, CA: O'Reilly Media.

Gubbi, J., Buyya, R., Marusic, S. and Palaniswami, M., 2013. Internet of Things (IoT): A Vision, Architectural Elements, and Future Directions. Elsevier.

Harley, D., Slade, R. and Gattiker, U. (2001) Viruses Revealed. New York: McGraw-Hill.

Hassani, H., Ghodsi, M. & Yeganegi, M.R., 2021. Artificial Intelligence in Cybersecurity. Cham: Springer.

Healey, J. (ed.) (2013) A fierce domain: Conflict in cyberspace, 1986 to 2012. Vienna, VA: Cyber Conflict Studies Association.

Hohpe, G. and Woolf, B., 2004. Enterprise integration patterns: designing, building, and deploying messaging solutions. Boston: Addison-Wesley.

Holler, J., Tsiatsis, V., Mulligan, C., Avesand, S. and Karnouskos, S., 2014.From Machine-to-Machine to the Internet of Things: Introduction to a New Age of Intelligence. Academic Press.

Hubbard, D. and Seiersen, R. (2016) How to Measure Anything in Cybersecurity Risk. Hoboken, NJ: Wiley.

Kello, L., 2017. The Virtual Weapon and International Order. New Haven: Yale University Press.

Kindervag, J., 2021. Zero Trust: Building a Resilient Cybersecurity Architecture. New York: Wiley.

Kumar, R., 2021. Artificial Intelligence and Cybersecurity: Advances and Innovations. Hershey, PA: IGI Global.

Lévy, P., 1998. Becoming Virtual: Reality in the Digital Age. New York: Plenum.

Lewis, F.L., Jagannathan, S. and Yesildirak, A., 1999. Neural network control of robot manipulators and nonlinear systems. London: Taylor & Francis.

Lewis, J.A. (2010) Cybersecurity and Cyberwarfare: Preliminary Assessment of National Doctrine and Organization. Geneva: UNIDIR.

Levy, M., 2009. Web 2.0 implications on knowledge management. Oxford: Chandos Publishing.

Lindsay, J.R. (2015) Restricting the use of cyber weapons: Limiting access, distribution, and destructiveness. London: Routledge.

Lindsay, J.R., Cheung, T.M. and Reveron, D.S. (2015) China and Cybersecurity: Espionage, Strategy, and Politics in the Digital Domain. Oxford: Oxford University Press.

Lovink, G., 2016. Dark fiber: Tracking critical internet culture. Cambridge, MA: MIT Press.

McAfee, A. and Brynjolfsson, E., 2017. Machine, Platform, Crowd: Harnessing Our Digital Future. New York: W. W. Norton & Company.

McGovern, G., Norton, C. and O'Dowd, R., 2001. The Web Content Style Guide: The Best Practice Guide to Writing for the Web. London: Financial Times Prentice Hall.

Minerva, R., Biru, A. and Rotondi, D., 2015.Towards a Definition of the Internet of Things (IoT).IEEE Internet Initiative.

Minoli, D., 2006. Enterprise architecture A to Z: frameworks, business process modeling, SOA, and infrastructure technology. Boca Raton: CRC Press.

Muniz, J. and Lakhani, M., 2019. Zero Trust Security: An Enterprise Guide. Indianapolis: Cisco Press.

Moustafa, N., 2022. Cyber Threat Intelligence: From Data to Intelligence. Cham: Springer.

Nguyen, N.G., 2022. AI-Powered Cybersecurity: Threat Detection and Response Using Machine Learning. Boca Raton: CRC Press.

Poster, M., 2006. Information Please: Culture and Politics in the Age of Digital Machines. Durham, NC: Duke University Press.

Rid, T. (2013) Cyber War Will Not Take Place. London: Hurst & Company.

Rid, T. (2020) Active measures: The secret history of disinformation and political warfare. New York: Farrar, Straus and Giroux.

Rittinghouse, J.W. and Ransome, J.F., 2017. Cloud computing: implementation, management, and security. 2nd ed. Boca Raton, FL: CRC Press.

Robertson, J., 2003. What's the intranet for? Sydney: Step Two Designs. Bandyopadhyay, D. and Sen, J., 2011.

Russell, S. and Norvig, P., 2021.Artificial Intelligence: A Modern Approach. 4th ed. Harlow: Pearson.

Singer, P.W. and Friedman, A., 2014. Cybersecurity and cyberwar: What everyone needs to know. New York: Oxford University Press.

Scarfone, K. (2022) Cybersecurity Threat Detection and Response: Using SIEM, SOAR, and XDR. Sebastopol, CA: O'Reilly Media.

Schneier, B. (2015) Data and Goliath: The Hidden Battles to Collect Your Data and Control Your World. New York: W.W. Norton & Company.

Stallings, W., 2019. Effective cybersecurity: A guide to using best practices and standards. Boston: Addison-Wesley.

Sullivan, C. (2023) Modern SOC: Building, Operating, and Managing Security Operations Centers. New York: Apress.

Weimann, G., 2016. Terrorism in cyberspace: The next generation. New York: Columbia University Press.

Ward, J. and Peppard, J., 2016. The strategic management of information systems: building a digital strategy. 4th ed. Chichester: Wiley.

White, N., 2007. Enterprise 2.0: collaborative technologies and the future of work. Cambridge: Harvard Business School Press.

Turban, E., Leidner, D., McLean, E. and Wetherbe, J., 2018. Information technology for management: on-demand strategies for performance, growth and sustainability. 11th ed. Hoboken, NJ: Wiley.

Turkle, S., 2011. Alone Together: Why We Expect More from Technology and Less from Each Other. New York: Basic Books.

Valeriano, B. and Maness, R.C. (2015) Cyber war versus cyber realities: Cyber conflict in the international system. Oxford: Oxford University Press.

Valeriano, B., Jensen, B. and Maness, R. (2018) Cyber Strategy: The Evolving Character of Power and Coercion. Oxford: Oxford University Press.

Zhang, Y. & Gupta, B.B., 2020. Machine Learning and Deep Learning Techniques for Cyber Security. Singapore: Springer.

Zegart, A.B. (2022) Spies, lies, and algorithms: The history and future of American intelligence. Princeton, NJ: Princeton University Press.

Zhou, Z.-H., 2021. Machine Learning. 2nd ed. Singapore: Springer.

About the Author

The Author is trained lawyer, President of an Educational Foundation,Representative of Brazilian institutions in Europe either involvedin military subjects (ADESG) either commercial and industrial- (the Federation of Chambers of Commerce and Industry ofSouth America). The Author also it is a researcher in geopolitics andnational defence. He is actually is involved in a number of professionalactivities of several areas like international partnerships havingin common development and cooperation. Author of several booksbooks, essays and articles concerning its activity and passed professionalexperience. He give universities lectures, conferences, and expertiseassessments.Read more at https://observare.autonoma.pt/investigador/artur-victoria/.

Read more at https://observare.autonoma.pt/investigador/artur-victoria/.

www.ingramcontent.com/pod-product-compliance
Lightning Source LLC
LaVergne TN
LVHW090307210926
848480LV00001B/158